SALES MANAGEMENT

F. O. BOACHIE-MENSAH
University of Cape Coast

*Our mission is to efficiently provide the world's finest, most comprehensive
book publishing service, enabling every author to experience success.
To find out how to publish your book, your way, and have it available
worldwide, visit us online at www.trafford.com*

Trafford rev. 07/07/2010

 www.trafford.com

North America & international
toll-free: 1 888 232 4444 (USA & Canada)
phone: 250 383 6864 ♦ fax: 812 355 4082

Dedication

This book is dedicated to Evelyn, Elizabeth and Stephen for their love and support.

Contents

List of Figures

List of Tables

List of Textboxes

Preface

The world of today is a dynamic and changing place. The rapid growth in technology, the globalisation of business, and increasing competition make sales and relationship skills more important than ever. Thus, sales organisations must deal with unprecedented change.

As a result of the growing economic and competitive pressures and sociocultural changes, companies are being forced to become more responsive to the customer—more market-oriented. The role of the sales force is expanding immensely. Today's salespeople are professionals who are as much marketing consultants as salespeople. This new calibre of salesperson is engaged in consultative relationships with the customer. The salesperson is expected not to just sell products but to solve customer problems. The focus is on building long-term relationships with customers.

As the nature of personal selling changes, so does the role of the sales manager. Sales managers of today are considered team leaders rather than bosses. They empower and collaborate with their salespeople rather than control and dominate them. Managers are required to manage multiple sales channels, such as telemarketing and electronic marketing, as well as field salespeople.

The sales manager who is familiar with these growing changes and best understands how the factors affect a salesperson's behaviour has an advantage in planning and directing that behaviour toward desired ends and in evaluating the results produced.

Sales Management is written to give business students the information they need to compete in the real world. The primary objective is to offer students a thorough, up-to-date, and integrated overview of the accumulated theory and research evidence relevant to sales management, plus the most recent practices and techniques employed by managers in the business world. The secondary objective is to emphasise the steps in managing the sales force through from recruitment, selection, and training to territory design, sales quotas, motivation, and control.

Sales Management is designed for use in a course on sales management at either the undergraduate or graduate level. It also provides a good source of reference for practising sales managers who want to improve their understanding of the subject. The text is made up of fourteen chapters.

Chapter one covers the nature and role of the professional sales manager. It also sets forth the basic responsibilities and the common characteristics of the sales manager.

Chapter two explains the nature and role of selling. It covers the responsibilities of salespeople and different types of personal selling situations. It also describes a systematic approach to personal selling.

Chapter three focuses on strategic sales planning and budgeting. It discusses the role of sales planning as it relates to marketing planning and total-company planning. It also looks at the purposes of the sales budget and the budgetary procedure.

Chapter four deals with organizing the sales force. The purpose of sales organisation and the major types of sales organisational structures are treated. Additional strategic organisational alternatives are presented.

Chapter five discusses the sales force recruiting process, the critical distinction between a job analysis and a job description, the sources of good candidates, and the basic qualifications needed for sales positions.

Chapter six describes the procedures and tools used to select the best applicants and explains what sales managers look for in application forms and interviews.

Chapter seven presents the many aspects of training a sales force. It covers the assignment of responsibility for sales training, training programme content, the methods for sales training, and the evaluation of training.

Chapter eight presents alternative approaches for assigning and managing sales territories to achieve sales objectives efficiently and effectively. It explains the procedures for setting up and revising sales territories and for scheduling and routing to optimise sales coverage and minimise wasted time.

Chapter nine addresses the different types of sales quotas, their purposes, and how they are developed, measured, and administered.

Chapter ten focuses on motivating the sales force. It describes the various theories of motivation and considers non-financial as well as financial rewards. It also discusses how the sales manager can use the motivational tools of sales contests and sales meetings effectively.

Chapter eleven is devoted to compensating the sales force. It deals with the importance, the purposes, and the basic objectives of an effective compensation plan. It also examines various compensation plans and how they need to be modified with changing market conditions.

Chapter twelve focuses on leading the sales force. It explains the nature of leadership and the distinction between leadership and management and the sources of leader power. Major leadership theories are described and evaluated. This chapter provides an analysis of the appropriate style of sales management leadership and the important activities of the sales manager, which direct the behaviour of the sales force.

Chapter thirteen deals with evaluating sales organization effectiveness. It relates sales volume, costs, and profitability analyses to various market segments, the procedures for which are explained. There is analysis of using contribution costs and full costs in allocating costs to market segments. Return on assets managed is presented.

Chapter fourteen examines the task of evaluating performance of the salespeople. It describes the techniques for setting performance standards for salespeople and objectively measuring actual performance.

Acknowledgments

The writing of a book like this is never the work of a single author or even a small group of authors; rather, there are many people and institutions whose contributions need to be acknowledged, and the author gratefully acknowledges his debt to those who contributed to the text.

I am grateful to the secretarial team of Mr. David Attah and Miss Cecilia Hayford for their efforts in word processing the work; to the authors and publishers whose works have been cited; to the reviewers and editors, who offered valuable critiques and thoughtful recommendations that have substantially improved the text; and to the publisher (Trafford Publishing) for a great job done. I owe all these people and institutions a great deal of intellectual debt, because they have contributed to make the book so successful.

Finally, special thanks go to my family members for their love and support.

F. O. Boachie-Mensah
April 2010

Chapter 1

The Nature and Role of Sales Management

Introduction

Sales management is one of the most important elements in the success of modern organisations. Getting things done through people has never been more challenging than it is today. This is especially true for sales managers, whose job is to generate more sales through salespeople. What makes this so difficult is that sales managers must continually adapt to a number of dramatic changes in their field. Customers have become exceptionally demanding. There has been rapid technological advancement, and globalisation has resulted in intense competition. Sales managers are expected to keep up with these trends and then provide the leadership required to guide the sales organisation to success.

This chapter covers the nature and role of the professional sales manager. It also sets forth the basic responsibilities and the common characteristics of the sales manager. Finally, it discusses the current trends affecting sales management and what is required of the sales managers of tomorrow.

The Meaning of Sales Management

The definition of "sales management" has changed dramatically over the years with different emphases. Currently, according to the American Marketing Association (2008):

> "Sales management is the planning, direction, and control of personal selling activities of a business unit, including recruiting, selecting, equipping, assigning,

routing, supervising, paying, and motivating as those tasks apply to the sales force."

Sales management involves three interrelated processes: (1) the formulation of a strategic sales programme; (2) the implementation of the sales programme; and (3) the evaluation and control of sales force performance. In formulating the strategic sales programme, sales management involves a number of activities including development of account management policies, demand forecasts, and quotas and budgets; sales organisation; sales planning; territory design; deployment; and routing. In implementing the sales programme, sales management activities include supervising, recruiting, selecting, training and motivating sales force. In addition, implementation requires the development of compensation systems and sales force incentive programmes. The evaluation and control of sales force performance involves the development of methods for monitoring and evaluating sales force performance. Sales management activities typically required for evaluation and control include behavioural analysis, cost analysis, and sales analysis.

Broadly speaking, the sales manager is in charge of personal selling activities, which involve face-to-face interactions with customers, and his/her primary responsibility is management of the personal sales force.

What Is a Sales Manager?

Nowadays, sales managers are professionals. They are being called upon to exercise, in a professional way, the key duties of all managers. They are expected to play a much more strategic role in the company. Sales managers, thus, plan, organise, lead, and control the personal selling activities of organisations. These are the prime responsibilities of sales managers, who are to ensure that the sales function makes the most effective contribution to the achievement of company's objectives and goals. In carrying out these responsibilities, sales managers perform the following activities (Anderson et al., 1992):

(1) Prepare sales plans and budgets.
(2) Set sales force goals and objectives.
(3) Estimate demand and forecasts sales.
(4) Determine the size and structure of the sales force organisation.
(5) Recruit, select, and train salespeople.
(6) Design sales territories, set sales quotas, and define performance standards.
(7) Compensate, motivate, and lead the sales force.
(8) Conduct sales volume, cost, and profit analyses.
(9) Evaluate sales force performance.
(10) Monitor the ethical and social conduct of the sales force.

Basic Responsibilities of Sales Managers

Basically, sales managers need to succeed in carrying out their roles within the broader framework of organisational objectives, marketing strategies, and target markets while continuously monitoring the macro environment and the company's stakeholders. A short general description of the functions of the sales manager is presented in the next section.

Sales Planning and Budgeting

Planning is the first of the jobs of the sales manager. This is so, because the plan gives the direction and strategy for all other sales management decisions and activities. Sales management planning tends to be tactical. Mostly sales planners are concerned with yearly or quarterly goals and objectives, departmental policies and procedures, and budgets. The critical element of the planning process is to determine organisational goals and objectives. Sales goals give the sales force broad, long-run direction and general purpose, while sales objectives make explicit what results are to be achieved within a specified time period. The departmental policies and procedures are the steps to be taken to effectively communicate to the organisation's target audience and to get them to have a beneficial sales experience. The management should write down the best practices and methods used to conduct sales within its business. This should include a text of how to answer the phone, talk to prospects, overcome sales obstacles, and handle frequently asked questions.

In view of the importance of funding to the implementation of a plan, there is the need for the preparation of a budget as part of the planning process. Simply put, a sales budget is a financial plan of expenditures required to attain the projected goals and objectives—that is, the assignment of monetary costs to the various parts of the plan, the purpose of which is to ensure that organisational resources are apportioned in the most efficient way over the period of the plan.

Estimating Demand and Forecasting Sales

Sales managers need to estimate market potential for the industry and sales potential for the company, before developing a final sales forecast on which to base all operational planning and budgeting for their sales forces.

Determining the Size and Structure of the Sales Organisation

Sales managers should determine the right number of salespeople to hire and the best way to structure the sales force. The number of salespeople and the structure of the sales force influence a lot of sales management decisions, which include sales forecasts, budgets, job descriptions, compensation methods, supervision, motivation, evaluation of sales force performance, and territory assignments.

Recruiting, Selecting, and Training Salespeople

Recruiting is the process of attracting qualified applicants for employment. It involves identifying sources of potential sales recruits, determining methods of reaching them, and finding strategies for attracting them to apply for a sales job.

Once applicants have been recruited, the sales manager should decide which applicants to select or reject.

Effective training and retraining of the salespeople has to focus on expanding their perspectives by blending sales and marketing concepts with sales training. Such broad-based training would help salespeople to recognise how their jobs mesh with the overall organisation and would prepare them for future responsibilities as sales and marketing managers.

Allocating Sales Force Efforts and Setting Sales Quotas

Effective allocation of sales force efforts must be preceded by designing sales territories. A sales territory refers to a market segment or group of present and potential customers who share some common characteristics relevant to purchasing behaviour. Sales quotas, on the other hand, are the motivational targets assigned to the sales force as a whole and to salespeople individually. After determining sales territories, the sales manager might design a formal pattern, or routing, for sales representatives to follow in calling on customers.

Compensating, Motivating, and Leading the Sales Force

Both financial and nonfinancial incentives should be included in decisions about sales force compensation. In addition to basic salary and commissions, financial compensation should include reimbursement of sales expenses and transportation. Nonfinancial incentives may comprise use of secretarial help, office space, a company car, life insurance, or a retirement plan.

Sales managers should constantly endeavour to keep the sales force highly motivated. Among other things, it is essential for the sales manager to understand the personal needs and aspirations of each salesperson. Managers must recognise that nearly all employees seek fulfilment beyond working conditions and financial rewards.

Closely linked to sales force motivation is leadership. Sales managers with leadership ability can inspire salespeople to achieve great success, make their work personally meaningful, and help them to achieve more than they ever thought they could.

Analyzing Sales Volume, Cost, and Profit

To attain improved profitability, sales managers need to analyze volume, cost, and profit relationships across product lines, territories, customers, salespeople, and sales and marketing functions. These analyses are to help identify unprofitable sales units so that sales managers can take appropriate corrective action to allocate sales force efforts better and improve profitability.

Measuring and Evaluating Sales Force Performance

Sales force performance needs to be measured and evaluated to decide commissions and bonuses for salespeople and sales managers and to make promotion decisions. Generally, however, the purpose of performance evaluation is to improve organisational profitability by improving sales force efforts.

Standards for the measurement of performance may include:

(i)   salesperson-to-salesperson comparisons,

(ii) current-to-past performance comparisons, and

(iii) actual-to-expected performance comparisons.

To effectively control and evaluate sales force performance:

(i)   standards of performance must be established;

(ii) actual performance must be compared to predetermined standards; and

(iii) appropriate corrective action must be taken to improve performance.

Monitoring the Marketing Environment

Sales managers, in addition to carrying all their basic roles, need to satisfy target customers within the constraints of an ever-changing marketing environment. A lot of companies are becoming both proactive and reactive in dealing with the stakeholders in both the micro- and macro-environment, which often bring about changes. Effective sales managers must be responsive to new market opportunities as well as to threats to existing markets.

Types of Sales Managers

Sales managers' responsibilities vary widely. Depending on the nature of the organisation, the sales manager's responsibilities and duties vary along a long continuum (Anderson et al. 1992). In some organisations, the sales manager may be little more than a supervisor of the sales force. Some organisations assign forecasting, planning, budgeting, and profit responsibilities to the sales manager. In others, the sales manager is the marketing manager in every way but position title. Depending on their hierarchical levels, sales managers may have several different position titles and responsibilities, as illustrated in Figure 1.1.

Figure 1.1 Sales Management Hierarchy with Corresponding Responsibilities

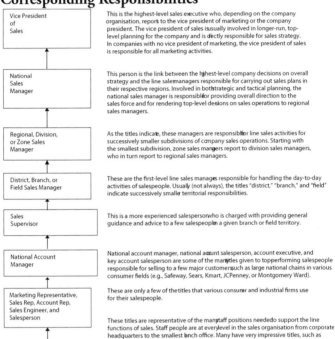

Vice President of Sales	This is the highest-level sales executive who, depending on the company organisation, reports to the vice president of marketing or the company president. The vice president of sales is usually involved in longer-run, top-level planning for the company and is directly responsible for sales strategy. In companies with no vice president of marketing, the vice president of sales is responsible for all marketing activities.
National Sales Manager	This person is the link between the highest-level company decisions on overall strategy and the line sales managers responsible for carrying out sales plans in their respective regions. Involved in both strategic and tactical planning, the national sales manager is responsible for providing overall direction to the sales force and for rendering top-level decisions on sales operations to regional sales managers.
Regional, Division, or Zone Sales Manager	As the titles indicate, these managers are responsible for line sales activities for successively smaller subdivisions of company sales operations. Starting with the smallest subdivision, zone sales managers report to division sales managers, who in turn report to regional sales managers.
District, Branch, or Field Sales Manager	These are the first-level line sales managers responsible for handling the day-to-day activities of salespeople. Usually (not always), the titles "district," "branch," and "field" indicate successively smaller territorial responsibilities.
Sales Supervisor	This is a more experienced salesperson who is charged with providing general guidance and advice to a few salespeople in a given branch or field territory.
National Account Manager	National account manager, national account salesperson, account executive, and key account salesperson are some of the many titles given to top-performing salespeople responsible for selling to a few major customers such as large national chains in various consumer fields (e.g., Safeway, Sears, Kmart, JCPenney, or Montgomery Ward).
Marketing Representative, Sales Rep, Account Rep, Sales Engineer, and Salesperson	These are only a few of the titles that various consumer and industrial firms use for their salespeople.
Assistant to Sales Manager, Sales Analyst, Sales Training Manager	These titles are representative of the many staff positions needed to support the line functions of sales. Staff people are at every level in the sales organisation from corporate headquarters to the smallest branch office. Many have very impressive titles, such as corporate vice president of sales or assistant national sales manager, yet have no line sales management authority. Usually, staff members in these positions assist in performing various related functions at different levels in the sales organisation (sales planning, sales promotion, sales recruiting, sales training, and sales analysis, for example).

Source: R. E. Anderson, J. F. Hair, Jr., and A. J. Bush, *Professional Sales Management* (New York: McGraw-Hill, 1992), 6. Reprinted by permission of McGraw-Hill.

Qualities of Effective Sales Managers

Sales managers lead the sales team. They should therefore possess certain qualities that will enable them to direct and guide the sales force in the accomplishment of organisational objectives. Four identified qualities (or abilities) common to effective sales managers are the following:

Ability to Define the Position's Exact Function and Duties in Relation to the Goals the Company Should Expect to Attain

Sales managers determine what is involved in their responsibilities. Whether or not they are provided with a job description, they draw up their own descriptions, consistent with the responsibilities assigned by senior management. Revisions are made whenever changes occur in the assigned responsibilities or in the company goals.

Ability to Select and Train Capable Subordinates and Willingness to Delegate Sufficient Authority to Enable Them to Carry Out Assigned Tasks with Minimal Supervision

An effective sales manager selects high-calibre subordinates and provides them with the authority to make decisions.

Ability to Utilise Time Efficiently

The time of sales managers is vital, and they plan it and use it carefully. They allocate working time to tasks yielding the greatest return. They arrive at an optimal division between office work and field division.

Ability to Exercise Skilled Leadership

Effective sales managers develop and improve their skills in dealing with people. They recognise the importance of skilled leadership in dealing with subordinates and with everyone else.

Integrating Sales and Marketing Management

So far, we have examined the nature and role of sales management. The issue now to be considered is the relationship between sales and marketing. Without thoroughly understanding the larger marketing framework within which the sales manager operates, few sales managers can appreciate the importance of integrating sales force planning efforts with overall marketing planning and strategies. It should be indicated that sales efforts influence, and are influenced by, decisions taken about the elements of a company's marketing efforts. It is important, therefore, that sales and marketing be fully integrated. The sales manager thus needs to understand and value the importance of integrating sales force planning and strategies. As Anderson et al. (1992) emphasise, sales management involves a specialised set of responsibilities and activities within the larger field of marketing management. In broad terms, the sales manager is really a marketing manager with the specific task of managing the sales force.

Marketing and sales are not the same, but neither are they in conflict with each other. According to Kurtz and Dodge (1991), marketing, which includes sales, is a long-range process dealing with creating an environment that produces a favourable buying decision on the part of the targeted customer; market share is the typical goal of marketing. Sales, on the other hand, deals with the execution of the marketing plan and is more short-range in nature; a purchase decision in favour of the salesperson is the goal of sales.

Marketing and sales strengthen each other. Marketing decisions that have the greatest impact on sales take into account these questions: (1) Which groups of consumers or market segments does the company want to serve?; (2) What is the makeup of the marketing mix?; and (3) What tasks are assigned to the sales force?

Most companies realise that it is not worthwhile to attempt to sell to every potential customer. A more practical approach is to pinpoint a group of consumers or a market segment whose needs or wants can be best served by the company's products. By targeting potential customers, the company focuses its marketing efforts where they can do the most good. Also, by concentrating on a limited number of customer types, the sales force benefits from specialisation that leads to improved selling performance through greater customer knowledge and attention—a crucial competitive factor in today's market.

Decisions made about the makeup of the marketing effort determine the emphasis placed on sales. Although most companies recognise the critical importance of sales at the point of customer contact, there is a wide variance in marketing mixes. The type of market served seems to have the greatest impact on the emphasis placed on personal selling or advertising. For instance, manufacturers of industrial products rely primarily on the efforts of salespeople and give little attention to advertising. Oftentimes the role of advertising is limited to securing sales leads.

Organisational Structure of a Sales-Orientated and a Marketing-Orientated Company

In many companies, the adoption of the marketing concept has been accompanied by changes in organisational structure, together with changes in the notion of what makes up the nature of selling. Examples of the possible organisational implications of adopting the marketing concept are illustrated in Figure 1.2 (a and b), which shows the organisational charts of sales-orientated and marketing-orientated companies.

As Jobber and Lancaster observe, perhaps the most significant difference between the pre– and post–marketing-orientated company is the fact that sales are later seen to be a part of the activity of the marketing function. Selling is only an aspect of the total marketing programme of a company, and this total effort should be coordinated by the marketing function.

Figure 1.3 shows an overview of the relationship between marketing strategy and management of personal selling (sales management), as suggested by Jobber and Lancaster (2000).

Figure 1.2 (a) Company organisational chart: sales-orientated company

Figure 1.2 (b) Company organisational chart: market-oriented company

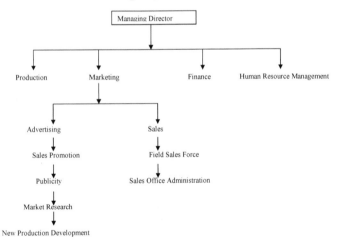

The Field Sales Force and Headquarters Marketing

Normally, an organisation's marketing team involves two basic groups, namely, the field sales force and the headquarters marketing team. The sales force personnel mostly work in their territories with their customers. But the headquarters marketing team supplies the support and service function that could assist sales managers in their jobs. This support includes the following:

1. **Advertising:** Coordination of product or service advertising, usually through an outside agency.
2. **Sales Promotion:** Development of brochures, catalogues, direct-mail pieces, and so on.
3. **Sales Aids:** Preparation of audiovisuals, flip charts, and other materials for sales presentations.
4. **Trade Shows:** Coordination of arrangements of participation in trade shows.
5. **Product Publicity:** Production and distribution of new releases to various media about products and services.
6. **Marketing Research:** Collection and interpretation of data concerning markets, products, customers, sales, and other factors.
7. **Marketing and Sales Planning:** Assistance in the preparation of marketing sales plans.
8. **Forecasting:** Preparation of sales forecasts and prediction of market trends.
9. **Product Planning and Development:** Help in planning and developing new or improved products.
10. **Market Development:** Support for entering new markets.
11. **Public Relations:** Help in explaining the actions of the sales force to the company's various stakeholders, which include employees, suppliers, the media, the shareholders, the financial community, government agencies, legislators, special interest groups, and the general public.

These support activities are either handled by in-house marketing staff or subcontracted to outside specialists such as advertising agencies, marketing research firms, consulting bodies, and public relations companies. Sales managers need to interact regularly with many of these headquarters marketing managers or outside firms, consulting bodies, and public relation companies.

Sales managers need specialists. Most sales managers and headquarters marketing services staffs would be able to do much better jobs if working together to their mutual benefit. By establishing friendly, cooperative relationships with the headquarters marketing managers, sales managers may obtain extra support and services to measurably improve sales force performance (Anderson et al. 1992).

Figure 1.3 Marketing Strategy and Management of Personal Selling

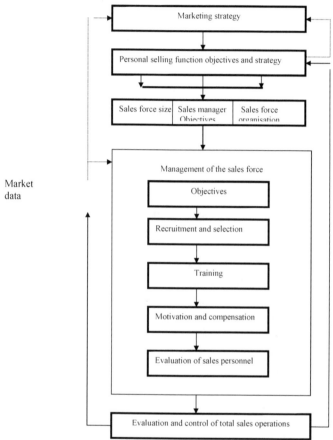

Source: D. Jobber and G. Lancaster, *Selling and Sales Management* (London: Prentice Hall, 2000), 26. Reprinted with permission of Prentice Hall.

Team Selling

As Anderson et al. (1992) observe, when complex product systems such as business services or computer installations are being sold, team selling is frequently employed, and the sales representative acts as the team coordinator in contacts with the buying organisation. Instead of having a lone salesperson contracting a single corporate purchasing agent, more and more companies are selling on many different levels by integrating their research, engineering production, marketing, and support management people with their customers. With this approach, the salesperson operates as an account coordinator or manager. Once established, the relationship between buyer and seller teams tends to be continuous and based on respect, performance, trust, and understanding. In most cases, important members of the sales team include:

- **Top Management.** More and more, top management is becoming a key part of the selling team, especially in the initial stages of contact with national accounts or during negotiations of major contracts. For example, in XYZ Systems Company's opening strategy, a top manager may write a letter that requests a meeting with the prospective customer's top operating officer. Rarely is XYZ Systems turned down at that level. At the first meeting, the regional sales manager, the local salesperson, and a systems engineer attend, along with the key manager to discuss how the system can benefit the client. If encouraging, this meeting is followed by a series of conferences and demonstrations that involve people throughout the prospect's organisation.
- **Technical Specialist.** These specialists work with sales representatives to provide technical advice and information sought by the customer before, during, and after the purchase. XYZ Systems Company assigns a technical specialist to work with each of its marketing representatives as part of a consultative team to anticipate and solve customer problems.
- **Customer Service Representatives**. These

representatives help in the installation, maintenance, and regular servicing of the products and systems that customers purchase.

In addition to forming sales teams, many organisations use two specialised categories of salespeople to round out their selling efforts or sometimes to substitute entirely for a direct sales force:

- **Inside salespeople** who sell from the office via telephone. They frequently respond to unsolicited inquiries from prospective customers, and they also generate leads for the direct sales force to follow up on. Telemarketing has become so popular that some companies are bringing all their salespeople back to headquarters (*Business Week* 1984).

- **Manufacturers' representatives**, or independent manufacturers' agents, who are paid a commission on the sales they generate. Employing reps is a relatively low-risk way to expand the sales force, because the cost-to-sales ratio is fixed.

Substitutability of Promotion Elements

Another reason for cooperation between the field sales force and headquarters marketing is the partial substitutability of the four promotional tools (advertising, personal selling, publicity, and sales promotion). Advertising is the most efficient tool in obtaining customer awareness of new products and services, whereas customer comprehension is influenced equally by advertising and personal selling. Closing the sale, however, can best be done by the salesperson. All types of promotion, especially advertising and follow-ups by the salespeople, can favourably enhance customer evaluation and satisfaction with products and services after purchase.

Top Management Support for Sales Managers

Sales managers know that the attitudes of top management are a powerful influence on how sales organisations function. Thus, it is in the best interest of sales managers to encourage top management to create the climate and profit orientation that will enable the sales organisation to function most efficiently and effectively. Top management can achieve this, as Anderson et al. (1992) suggest, by:

- developing and fostering a company-wide managerial orientation through up-to-date and meaningful job descriptions for all managers as well as their subordinates;
- establishing and maintaining open channels of communication with managers throughout the organisation, with special care taken to include the field sales force managers in headquarters' communications;
- including sales managers in training programmes with other functional managers in the organisation and encouraging special training seminars for sales managers at which they can discuss, with the guidance of a skilled moderator, their common problems; and
- providing sales managers with necessary tools and incentives for managing, including:
    1. managerial performance criteria, such as profit contribution, return on assets managed, development and maintenance of customers, sales force retention and development goals, sales-to-costs ratios, and market-share changes; and
    2. decision-oriented reports from headquarters, which allow analyses of customers, products, territories, salespeople, and functions in terms of cost and profit, instead of the traditional

accounting-oriented reports that summarise total organisation expenses.

Sales Management Trends

The turbulent business environment of today presents a variety of challenges. Sales organisations need to learn how to adapt to a continuously changing environment that revolves around customers with higher and higher expectations. Several dramatically changing trends—as identified by Taylor (1989) and Spiro et al. (2008)—make the sales manager's job complex, including:

- intense foreign competition,
- rising customer expectations,
- increasing buyer expertise,
- revolutionary developments in computer technology and communications,
- customer relationship management (CRM),
- sales force diversity,
- growing emphasis on controlling costs, and
- ethical behaviour and social responsibility

To adapt successfully to these dramatic trends, progressive sales organisations are significantly broadening the concept of sales management. There is an increased integration of marketing and sales functions. Field sales managers are gaining a better knowledge of headquarters marketing activities, and the headquarters marketing team is building a better understanding of selling and sales management. Each of the sales management trends is examined in the next section.

Intense Foreign Competition

The Ghanaian home market has become a very attractive market for foreign sellers, and the battle for domestic and world markets is expected to continue. Unless Ghana can develop and market innovative, top-quality, cost-effective products that match or exceed those of any competitor, its domestic market shares will be lost to foreign imports. The economic health of

Ghana will depend partially on how well salespeople and sales managers do their jobs as the country's sales industry faces intensifying competition from foreign products and services, particularly those from the developed economies.

Rising Customer Expectations

Customers are becoming more demanding. Even though customers of today may accept some product and service shortcomings, they will quickly switch to better products and services when they appear, as the success of foreign products in Ghana has demonstrated. Instead of putting so much sales and marketing effort into persuading prospects that superficially altered products are new and improved, organisations need to focus more attention on developing significant innovations in products and services and on ensuring in-depth customer satisfaction. Successful sales and marketing managers are becoming less defensive about their own company's offerings and trying to look at products and services from the perspective of their most critical customers.

Increasing Buyer Expertise

With budget and profit squeezes, buyers of all kinds are becoming increasingly skilful at obtaining value for their money. Many customers are beginning to treat more purchases like long-term investments. At the same time, organisations are developing more efficient purchasing processes and using buying committees, consisting of purchasing, engineering, and operations managers. The new purchasing processes require a new attitude on the part of the seller. The seller needs to place more emphasis on fostering long-term relationships of trust, respect, and understanding with buying organisations and less emphasis on persuasive selling techniques. Talented new types of professional salespeople are required to convey the new attitude in sales presentations to buying committees and to function as consultative account coordinators.

Revolutionary Developments in Computer Technology and Communications

There is an electronic revolution in computer technology and communications. The sales manager cannot afford to miss out on the revolutionary developments, because they offer great opportunities to win competitive advantages with customers. Among the important technological innovations for sales management, as summarised by Anderson et al. (1992), are:

1. **portable and desktop computers.** Instead of working with pages of numbers and computer printouts, sales managers of today can use a personal computer to call up charts, tables, and figures of various kinds to obtain an instant reading on the marketplace and sales force performance.

2. **videotape presentations and DVDs.** Sales presentations are being brought dramatically to life through the use of videotapes. For example, over two hundred salespeople at thirteen branch offices of XYZ Systems Company use videotapes to demonstrate the company's products, equipment, and furniture for educational, medical, and industrial laboratories. The videotape is especially valuable when the sales manager wants to communicate an identical message to all salespeople.

3. **videoconferencing.** To deal with the increasing annual cost of travel and employee downtime because of conferences, many organisations are turning to videoconferencing. For example, XYZ Systems Company introduced a new business machine to its numerous employees all at once via a videoconference that linked its various offices in Ghana and in South Africa.

4. **mobile communications equipment.** Mobile

telephones and electronic pagers (beepers) are making it possible for the sales manager to contact salespeople wherever they are, whether they are in a traffic jam or walking across a parking lot in a distant town. Mobile communications devices also enable salespeople to call ahead to customers to inform them about a possible delay, such as being stuck in traffic.

5. **electronic sales offices.** Word processors have already replaced electronic typewriters in many offices, and instead of keeping bulky files, some organisations are using high-speed laser copiers to convert incoming paper into retrievable electronic files. In electronic sales offices, sales managers can use their own desktop personal computers to call up a customer record for review, to edit the draft of a report, or to deliver a memorandum simultaneously to salespeople scattered all over the nation. s

Customer Relationship Management

As Turner (2008) submits, customer relationship management (CRM) is becoming mainstream technology for sales organisations. CRM refers to software solutions that help companies manage customer information. Salespeople input much of this information and then use it to expand their relationships with existing customers. The rapid expansion of this industry is led by companies such as Salesforce.com, Oracle, and Microsoft. In a recent survey in the United States of America, about one third of all organisations have already deployed CRM, and another third are in the process of implementing such a programme. This presents a challenge, however, because more than a third of those who have deployed CRM are not happy with the results. Problems often result because salespeople do not understand how to participate in the programme, nor do they see the benefits. As Spiro et al.

(2008) suggest, these issues can be avoided through proper training and effective leadership by the sales executives.

Sales Force Diversity

Over the past few decades, more and more women and minorities have successfully pursued careers in personal selling and are advancing into sales management positions. This is surprising, because sales was once dominated by men. Even though sexual discrimination still exists in the workplace, great progress has been made.

As Shapiro et al. (2008) observe, a controversial issue in this area involves the criteria used in hiring women into sales. Some industries, such as pharmaceutical sales, have been criticised for emphasizing physical attractiveness over professional qualifications. All sales organisations need to be careful that they do not perpetuate the negative stereotypes that have long been associated with the selling profession.

Growing Emphasis on Controlling Costs

Sales managers are emphasizing cost control as an important means of adapting to the new dramatically changing selling environment. With retail consideration and foreign ownership of major chains, today there is more power in fewer hands. Retailers can use this power to reduce their own costs by shifting more of their in-store labour burden to manufacturers. Thus, the relationship between the manufacturer's sales force and large retailers is very different from what used to be a few years ago. Salespeople of today will deal with a well-informed, powerful buyer. The solution for sales managers is to provide the sales force with better training in controlling costs and improving effectiveness in the new selling environment.

Ethical Behaviour and Social Responsibility

Ethical selling practices, just like all aspects of business, are critical. But there have been several instances in which salespeople have been involved in financial scandals. Prominent among the seemingly endless business ethics debacles are the Enron, WorldCom, and Arthur Anderson examples. In one aspect of the most famous case, Enron salespeople were accused of using wildly optimistic estimates for the forward price of commodities and other factors. This created the appearance that deals were profitable, when customers were actually losing money (Burr 2005).

Salespeople must realise that these activities are not only dishonest and unethical but illegal. Law enforcement authorities are becoming more and more aggressive in pursuing these cases, which includes taking legal action against specific salespeople. Sales managers have the challenge of first staying up-to-date on existing laws and then informing their salespeople through proper training.

Even without punishment from the authorities, the increasingly long-term nature of business relationships requires higher ethical standards than did earlier transactional selling approaches. It must be emphasised that long-term relationships and customer loyalty are impossible to maintain in an atmosphere of distrust brought on by unethical sales approaches. There is thus the need for highly ethical practices in selling and sales management. Sales organisations must endeavour to develop a formal code of ethical conduct to attempt to ingrain ethical behaviours in their organisational culture (Johnston and Marshall 2006).

Developing Sales Managers for the Future

To efficiently and effectively adapt to the sales management trends and to enable sales managers to help move their companies toward competitive excellence in the keenly competitive markets of the future, companies need to considerably broaden the concept of the sales manager's job. Organisations need to emphasise the selection and training of sales managers. Specifically, senior management needs to ensure that: (1) sales managers are selected on the basis of appropriate managerial criteria, (2) newly promoted sales managers are taught basic marketing concepts and strategies, (3) sales activities are fully integrated with overall marketing programmes, and (4) broad training is provided to develop talented salespeople into men and women who are capable of handling the job of sales management (Anderson et al. 1992).

Review Questions

1. How would you explain the concept of sales management?
2. What do you understand to be the main responsibilities of the sales manager?
3. How would you explain the relationship between sales management and marketing?
4. What criteria would you use to evaluate the performance of a sales manager?
5. Assume that you are a sales manager. What characteristics would you look for when promoting a salesperson to the position of district sales manager?

Chapter 2

The Nature and Role of Selling

Introduction

A sales organisation cannot be successful without a thorough understanding of the selling process. Consequently, the significance of the sales manager's knowledge of the personal selling process cannot be overemphasised. It will be difficult to manage a sales force intelligently without a good grasp of the selling process. Generally, good judgment favours the manager who is competent and knowledgeable about the field being administered. Thus, some exposure to selling seems warranted for students of sales management.

This chapter explains the nature and role of selling. It looks at the wide array of activities that salespeople perform, which are mostly those activities related to generating sales and satisfying customers. It thus covers the responsibilities of salespeople and different types of personal selling situations. It also describes a systematic approach to personal selling.

Selling Activities

Sales jobs involve a wide variety of activities. In view of the complexity of the purchasing process in many organisations, sales representatives spend a great proportion of their time collecting information about potential customers, planning, coordinating the activities of other functional departments, and servicing existing customers, in addition to making sales calls. It is difficult, though, to specify the full range of activities in which sales people engage, because they may vary greatly across companies and types of sales jobs (Churchill, Jr., et al. 2000).

Functions of Sales Representatives

Sales representatives are seen as persuasive leaders who sell the company's products and undertake distribution activities. Two major reasons for which a company needs sales representatives are:

(i) the realisation of the importance of the role of sales representatives; and

(ii) the main factors and motives of company existence coupled with prosperity.

The primary responsibility of a salesperson is to conclude a sale successfully. This is to ensure the prompt turnover of the company's products to the ultimate consumer by educating customers on the benefits that could be derived from the products. This task involves prospecting, planning the sales call, approaching the prospects, presenting the sales message, dealing with objections, and closing the sale. These skills are discussed later in detail in the section on the selling process.

Most salespeople also perform a number of secondary functions in order to generate sales successfully. These functions include:

- prospecting,
- maintaining customer records and information feedback,
- self-managing,
- handling complaints,
- providing service, and
- implementing sales and marketing strategies.

The details of each of these functions are discussed next.

Prospecting

Prospecting may be regarded as the searching for and calling upon customers who, up until then, have not purchased from the company. This activity is far more important in industrial selling than in retail selling. For example, a sales representative of office equipment may call upon many new potential customers, whereas a furniture salesperson is unlikely to search out new prospects—they come to him/her as a result of advertising and, perhaps, high street location (Jobber and Lancaster 2000).

Sources of Prospects

Some of the common sources of sales prospects are the following:

1. **existing customers.** A wealth of new prospects can be obtained simply by asking satisfied customers if they know of anyone who may have a need for the kinds of products or services being sold.

2. **trade directories. A** reliable trade directory such as the Yellow Pages and the Ghana Business Directory can be useful in identifying potential industrial buyers.

3. **inquiries.** These may arise as a natural consequence of conducting business. Satisfied customers may create inquiries through word-of-mouth from "warm" prospects. Many a company stimulates inquiries, however, through advertising, direct mail, and exhibitions. The next thing to do is to screen out those inquiries that are likely to result in a sale. A telephone call could be used to check on how serious the inquiry is and to arrange a personal visit should the inquiry prove to have potential. The process of checking leads to establish their potential is known as qualifying.

4. **the press.** This is also an important source of prospects. Advertisements and articles can give indications of potential new sources of business.

5. **cold canvassing.** This involves calling on every prospect who might have a need for the salesperson's product. A brand salesperson, for instance, may try

to call upon every house in a village. A variant of this method is "cool canvassing," in which only certain groups of people are canvassed—that is, those who are more likely to buy, since they possess some qualifying features; for example, only companies over a certain size may be judged viable prospects (Lee 1984).

Maintaining Customer Records and Information Feedback

All repeat call salespeople need to have a systematic approach to customer recordkeeping. Industrial salespeople would need to record the following:

1. name and address of company,
2. name and position of contact(s),
3. nature of business,
4. date and time of interview,
5. assessment of potential,
6. buyer needs, problems, and buying habits,
7. past sales with dates,
8. problems/opportunities encountered, and
9. future actions on the part of salesperson (and buyer).

Salespeople should be encouraged to send back to the head office information that is essential to the marketing of company products. Some of the kinds of information that may be vital to management are reports on goods, prices, shortages, competitive methods (such as test market activity by competition), and feedback on company achievement regarding product performance.

Self-Managing

The self-management aspect of a sales job is of unique importance, since a salesperson is often working alone with minimal personal supervision. A salesperson might have to organise his/her own call plan, which involves dividing territory into sections to be covered day by day and deciding the best route to follow between calls. The sales managers should be good time managers as well.

Handling Complaints

Dealing with complaints, effectively, would help an organisation to achieve the goal of creating customer satisfaction in order to generate profit. No matter how trivial the complaint might seem, the complaint needs to be treated with respect and the matter dealt with seriously. Basically, the ability of the salesperson to empathise with the customer and his/her problem and to react sympathetically can create considerable goodwill and help foster long-term relationships (Jobber and Lancaster 2000).

Providing Service

As Jobber and Lancaster observe, salespeople are in an excellent position to provide a consultancy service to their customers. Since they meet customers each year, salespeople become familiar with solutions to common problems. Thus an industrial salesperson may be able to advise customers on improving productivity or cutting costs.

Implementing Sales and Marketing Strategies

Salespeople are also entrusted with the responsibility of implementing sales and marketing strategies designed by management. Successful implementation can mean the difference between winning and losing new accounts. An effective method of gaining an account in the face of entrenched competition is the diversion. The aim of diversion is to distract a rival into concentrating its efforts on defending one account and therefore neglecting another (Jobber and Lancaster 2000).

Apart from the key functions listed above, we can also list some of the activities or roles of salespeople to, as follows:

1. create new customers,
2. build long-term relationships with customers,
3. provide solutions to customers' problems,

4. supply their company with market information, and
5. help customers use products after purchase.

Personal Selling Situations
Different Types of Sales Jobs

The diverse nature of the buying situation means that there are many different types of selling jobs. That is, selling varies according to the nature of the selling task. Consider the petty trader who moves from place to place selling his/her products. That job is different from that of a sales representative in a computer manufacturing company who is detailed to present computers to information and communication technology (ICT) executives of companies. Selling situations can be classified in several ways, and most sales jobs do not fall neatly into one category or another. General classifications of selling jobs are as follows:

1. response selling,
2. trade selling,
3. missionary selling,
4. technical selling, and
5. creative selling

The details of each of the types of selling jobs are presented next.

Response Selling

Response selling (or order taking) implies that the salesperson only reacts or responds to the customer's demands. In response selling, salespeople may perform one of three selling jobs.

(i) **Inside order-taking:** These salespeople "wait on committed customers." The typical inside order-taker is the retail sales assistant. The sales assistant's task is purely transactional—receiving payment and passing over the goods. Another form of inside order-taker is the sales clerk who stands behind the counter or waits to serve customers.

(ii) **Outside order-taking:** These salespeople visit the

customer, but their primary function is to respond to customer requests rather than to actively seek to persuade.

(iii) Delivering: These salespeople mainly engage in delivering the product. Typical examples are persons delivering milk, bread, newspapers, fuel oil, or soft drinks to the door. There is no attempt to persuade the household to increase the order size. Any changes are customer driven.

As Anderson et al. (1992) observe, salespeople in response selling situations may generate some sales by having a pleasant personality and by suggesting complementary products, but generally they create few sales. Usually, the main selling tasks are left to higher-level sales personnel in the organisation.

Trade Selling

In trade selling, which is similar to response selling, the salesperson operates as an order-taker, but he or she works in the field. A typical example is the soap salesperson calling on retailers.

The characteristics of trade selling, as summarised by Newton (1969), follow.

- The major aim is to build sales volume by providing customers with promotional assistance—that is, selling 'through'; for example, food, textiles, clothing, and wholesaling.
- Personal selling is subsidiary to nonpersonal activities.
- Reliance on low-pressure selling, with an emphasis on continuity and a thorough understanding of customer practice.

Trade selling consists largely of taking orders, expediting orders, restocking shelves, obtaining more shelf space, setting up displays, rotating stock, providing in-store demonstrations, and distributing samples to store customers.

Missionary Selling

Missionary selling tries to influence the "decider" instead of the purchaser or user of the product. The missionary salesperson only aims to build goodwill or to educate the actual or potential user and is not expected to take an order. A typical example of missionary selling is the pharmaceutical company's detail salesperson, who introduces and explains the products of drug manufacturers to medical doctors. Although physicians seldom buy or use the drugs themselves, they become the missionary salesperson's target market. Detail salespersons working at the physician level furnish valuable information regarding the capabilities and limitations of medications in an attempt to get the physician to prescribe the product. Missionary salespeople try to build goodwill, educate the deciders, and provide various services. Here the emphasis is on good coverage and presentation to make sure the deciders know of the product, its benefits, and its competitive advantages. Generally, missionary selling:

- builds sales volume by providing direct customers with personal selling assistance—that is, persuading ultimate users/consumers to buy from the company's immediate customers;
- is most typical of firms selling to distributors for resale; and
- is low pressure but requires energetic, articulate persons capable of making a large number of calls in order to cover all potential users—for example, medical representatives.

Technical Selling

Technical selling aims to solve the customer's problems through the advice of technically trained salespeople. The technical salesperson emphasises technical knowledge—for example, the engineering salesperson who is primarily a consultant to client companies. The technical support typically concerns use of complex products, system design, product characteristics, and installation procedures. Thus, these technical support salespeople may assist in design and specification processes, installation of equipment, training of the customer's employees, and follow-up service of a technical nature. Technical selling resembles professional consulting and is common in such industries as steel, chemicals, heavy machinery, and computers.

In summary, technical selling:

- increases sales to present customers through the provision of technical advice and assistance;
- requires an ability to identify, analyze, and solve customer problems and so places a premium on technical and product knowledge; and
- builds up buyer confidence and goodwill through the important factor of continuity.

Creative Selling

Creative selling calls for the salesperson to create demand among present and potential customers for tangible and intangible products and services. Examples of creative salespeople of tangibles are salespeople selling office supplies, automobiles, school textbooks, and real estate. Examples of creative salespeople of intangibles are salespeople selling insurance policies, advertising services, and educational courses.

Basically, creative sellers:

- secure new customers; and
- must be mature, experienced salespeople—due to the high level of rejection of new product propositions—who can take an objective view of failure and have a wider range of techniques to deal with buying objections.

As Anderson et al. (1992) identify, creative selling involves two distinct jobs: sales maintenance and sales development. The objective of sales maintenance is the creation of sales with present customers by maintaining and building on the good relationships already established. Sales development, however, concerns the creation of new customers and not just additional sales. When salespeople are expected to do both tasks, sales maintenance work usually drives out the more difficult sales development activities. Instead of calling on new prospects, where the expenditure of time may be unprofitable, most salespeople prefer to return to a known, friendly customer, where a profitable payoff is more likely.

The Uniqueness of Sales Jobs

Sales jobs bear certain features that differentiate them from other jobs in an organisation. Some of the common features that make sales jobs unique follow:

- The sales force is largely responsible for implementing a firm's marketing strategies. Moreover, it is the sales force that generates the revenues that are managed by the financial people and used by the production people.
- Sales people are typically the most visible representatives of a company to customers and to society in general. Many sales jobs require the sales person to socialise with customers who are frequently upper-level executives in their companies. Opinions of the firms and its products are formed on the basis of impressions made by salespeople in their work and in outside activities.
- The sales force operates with limited direct supervision. For success in selling, a salesperson must work hard physically and mentally, be creative and persistent, and show considerable initiative. This combination requires a high degree of self-motivation.
- By nature of the job, salespeople experience more rejections than acceptance—that is, more prospects choose not to buy. A salesperson who internalises rejection will quickly become discouraged.
- Sales jobs frequently involve considerable travelling

and time away from home. To reduce sales travel times, some firms redesign sales territories, route sales trips better, and rely more on telemarketing and electronic ordering. As noted by Etzel et al. (2000), salespeople deal with a seemingly endless variety of people and situations. These stresses, coupled with long hours and travelling, require mental toughness and physical stamina. Personal selling is hard work!

The Selling Process

Selling requires salespeople to develop an effective, systematic approach adaptable to the particular customer type and selling situation. There has been a suggestion of a number of conceptual schemes that outline various stages in the selling process and indicate the kinds of activities occurring at each stage. The essence of most of these schemes could be outlined by considering the selling process as consisting of seven major stages:

1. prospecting,
2. pre-approaching (planning the sales call),
3. approaching the prospect,
4. presenting the sales message,
5. dealing with objections,
6. closing the sale, and
7. following up on the sale (post-sales support).

Each of these stages is discussed in more detail next.

Prospecting

Sales representatives need to continually seek out or prospect for new customers. Prospecting is the first step in the selling process. A prospect is a qualified person or organisation that has the potential to buy the salesperson's product or service. As Futrell (1999) observes, prospecting is the lifeblood of sales, because it identifies potential customers. The two main reasons that a salesperson needs to look constantly for new prospects are: (1) to increase sales and (2) to replace customers who will be lost over time.

Basically, prospecting involves two related steps. It consists of identifying possible customers and then qualifying them—that is, determining whether they have the necessary potential to buy. Those are combined as a single step, because they are typically done at the same time. Some of the sources used by salespeople for prospecting include referrals, personal acquaintances, networking, and newspaper leads.

Pre-Approaching

After qualifying a prospect as a potential customer, the salesperson would need to plan how best to approach the prospect. In the pre-approach stage the sales representative needs to obtain strategic information about the prospective customer and ensure a favourable reception.

The pre-approach stage may involve finding out the past history of transactions, if any, by researching and finding out who the salesperson is dealing with and whether he/she has secured access to a decision maker, as well as finding out the habits, likes, dislikes, and aspirations of the prospects. Basically, the salesperson should endeavour to obtain all the information he/she can so that he/she can tailor his/her presentation to the individual customers.

Approaching the Prospect

Several methods can be effectively used to approach the prospect, depending upon the selling situation, which includes the introductory approach; the mutual acquaintance or reference approach; the customer benefit approach; the compliment or praise approach; the free gift or sample approach; the question approach; the product or ingredient approach; and the dramatic approach (Anderson et al. 1992). Each of these methods of approaching the prospect is highlighted below.

Introductory Approach

Many salespeople use a brief introductory approach followed by a second approach. Salespeople need to make sure their introduction is well-thought-out and smoothly executed, since they do not get a second chance to make a first impression. For example, they could say, "Hello, Mrs Asiamah. My name is Kwame Owusu, and I represent ABX Enterprise." In their introductions, salespeople should, among other things, identify themselves by name and by company.

Mutual Acquaintance or Reference Approach

Mentioning the names of several satisfied customers who are respected by the prospect could be quite a persuasive approach. As Anderson et al. (1992) suggest, testimonial letters from satisfied customers can be especially essential in selling products or services that involve high investment or social risk—for example, home computers.

Customer Benefit Approach

Apart from the fact that prospects seek to solve problems or obtain benefits through their purchases, they normally have one predominant buying motive, which sales representatives need to identify and appeal to. The following are examples of the customer benefit approach:

- "Independent research companies have judged our model 500 microcomputer to be the best value on the market for companies like yours."
- "Do you know that you can save 15 percent or more on transportation expenses by using our leasing plan?"

Compliment or Praise Approach

A sincerely delivered compliment can be a positive approach to a prospect and can set a pleasant atmosphere for the interview. An indirect compliment is often more effective than a direct one. Following are examples of complimentary approaches:

- "Congratulations on your recent promotion to assistant purchasing manager."
- "Your office is so attractively designed and your staff so pleasant that one of the highlights of my week is calling on you."

Free gift or Sample Approach

It is normal for door-to-door salespeople to deliver a cosmetic sample or free pen, which can help establish goodwill and gain entry to a prospect's home. The suggestion, though, is for salespeople to be mindful of the legal and ethical guidelines in using this approach.

Question Approach

Asking questions involves prospects in two-way communication early, since responses are required. Most salespeople avoid asking questions that prospects are likely to answer negatively.

Product or Ingredient Approach

Many a salesperson likes to carry a sample product or, at least, a graphic mock-up when first approaching prospects. This would allow prospects to see exactly what the salesperson is selling and permit smooth transitioning into the sales presentation or demonstration.

Dramatic Approach

In case other approaches fail, the sales representative could turn to a dramatic ploy. There are instances where vacuum cleaner salespeople have been known to scatter dirt around a room prior to demonstrating their product. In view of the fact that the prospect may resent such a blatant gimmick and become defensive, salespeople would do well to use this approach only when they are sure that the prospect would be receptive to it.

Presenting the Sales Message

The actual presentation starts with an attempt to attract the prospective buyer's attention, and then the salesperson should try to hold the customer's interest whilst building a desire for the product. Then the salesperson would try to close the sale.

A presentation involves using active selling skills. It is the step whereby the salesperson would tell the "product story" to the buyer, showing how the product would make or save money. The salesperson should describe the product features but concentrate on presenting customer benefits. Benefits should be analyzed at two levels: those benefits that can be obtained by purchase of a particular type of product, and those that can be obtained by purchasing that product from a particular supplier. For example, computer salespeople should consider the benefits of a personal computer compared to the benefits of a typewriter, as well as the benefits that his company's personal computers have over competitors' models.

Various communication tools can help the salesperson in the presentation by bringing into play more dramatically all the prospect's senses. Where possible, it is particularly effective to allow the prospect to participate in a demonstration of the product or service (Anderson et al. 1992). Some of the many tools available to salespeople include videotape players, video cameras, videodisc players, tape recorders, overhead projectors, slide projectors, portable compact computer terminals, and sophisticated PowerPoint systems with eye-catching graphical backgrounds. Some of the more traditional but effective visual aids that could be used by salespeople are product samples or models, flip charts, sales manuals, presentation boards, posters and tables, charts, graphs, and maps.

Basic Sales Presentation Strategies

As Anderson et al. suggest, in order to prepare an effective sales presentation to achieve precise objectives, salespeople must understand and consider alternative strategies, which are summarised in Table 2.1—stimulus response, formula, problem solution, need satisfaction, team selling, and depth selling.

Dealing with Objections

The prospect might have a variety of hidden or expressed objections to a purchase. Objections should be viewed as a positive sign of interest and involvement by the prospect. Objections highlight the issues that are important to the buyer.

In handling objections, the salesperson should use a positive approach, to turn the objections into reasons for buying. Jobber and Lancaster observe that an effective approach for dealing with objections involves two duties: the preparation of convincing answers and the development of a range of techniques for answering objections in a manner that permits the acceptance of the answers without loss of face on the part of the buyer.

Table 2.1 Basic Sales Presentation Strategies

Strategy	Method	Success Key
Stimulus Response	Walks the prospect through a series of leading questions (such as, "Wouldn't you like to earn more on your investments?).	Conditions the prospect to say yes selling process until the purchase decision.
Formula	Leads the prospect through the mental states of the buying process (attention, interest, desire, and action).	Leads the prospect to buy, one positive step at a time.
Problem Solution	Consults with the prospect to identify problems and alternative solutions.	Helps develop mutual trust while focusing on the prospect's reason for buying.
Need Satisfaction	Tries to find the prospect's dominant buying needs; this helps the prospect to clarify his or her real needs.	Focuses on buyer needs and helps the salesperson learn buyer motivations; generally ensures buyer satisfaction.
Team Selling	Uses the talents of several people to deal with the multiple concerns and influences of the buying team.	Increases the salesperson's effectiveness and saves time by putting key experts from the buying and selling teams together at the same time. Promotes teamwork and morale.

Depth Selling	Utilises a tailored mix of the above strategies	Maximises the impact of the sales presentation and increases the probability of sales success.

Methods and Strategies for Dealing with Objections

Various methods have been developed and tested to handle prospect objections successfully. Some of these are indirect denial, boomerang, counterbalance, denial, question, and failure-to-hear. Each of these is briefly explained as follows:

- **Indirect denial**: The salesperson should initially agree with the prospect and then gently take issue with the statement.
- **Boomerang**: The salesperson should turn the objection into a reason for buying but avoid making the prospect look ignorant for raising the objection.
- **Counterbalance:** The salesperson should counter an objection that cannot be denied by citing an even more important buying benefit.
- **Denial**: When the objection is invalid, the salesperson should tactfully but forthrightly deny the objection.
- **Question**: The salesperson should use questions to clarify objections and to "answer" objections indirectly.
- **Failure-to-hear**: Seemingly unimportant comments made under the prospect's breath should not be ignored by salespeople unless no response is the best alternative.

Closing the Sale

Closing refers to obtaining a final agreement to purchase. All the sales representative's efforts are wasted unless the client "signs on the dotted line"; yet that is where many a salesperson fails (Churchill, Jr., et al. 2000). Salespeople need to learn not only how to close but when to close.

Timing is very crucial to closing a sale. A general rule is to attempt to close the sale when the buyer displays heightened interest or clear intention to purchase the product. A salesperson should therefore look out for buying signals, which would indicate that the prospect is close to a decision and almost ready to put a signature on an order form and discuss the contractual arrangements.

A trial close may be used at various times in the sales presentation, depending upon the complexity and cost of the product. A trial close is simply a means of seeing whether the prospect is ready to buy and thus might be ready to close the sale.

Closing Techniques

There are a number of sales closing techniques that salespeople can use. Some of these are:

- **the choice close,** or offering alternative products to choose from;
- **the minor points close,** or obtaining decisions on minor points leading to gradual acceptance of the total product package;
- **the assumptive close**, or assuming the purchase decision is already made in order to compel the prospect to buy;
- **the stimulus response close,** or asking a sequence of leading questions to make it easier for the prospect to say yes when asked for the order;
- **the summary close**, or summarizing advantages and disadvantages before asking for the order; and
- **the standing-room-only (SRO) close,** or implying that the opportunity to buy is fleeting, because demand is great and few of the product are left.

Following up on the Sale (Post-Sales Support)

The final stage of the selling process is a series of follow-up services that can build customer goodwill and lay the foundation for many years of profitable business relations. This stage involves following up on sales. Promises that might have been made during the negotiations would have to be fulfilled. If the salesperson guarantees delivery by a set date, that would need to be upheld. Many buyers suffer from cognitive dissonance—that is, anxiety that they have not made the right choice—and the salesperson's follow-up call may help alleviate this dissonance by providing reassurance that the purchase was the right one. Additionally, following up on the sales to see if customers are satisfied with the product can encourage repeat business and improve the supplier's reputation for concern for its customers.

Review Questions

1. Compare the responsibilities of different sales positions, from responsive selling to creative selling.
2. What should be the responsibilities of the professional sales representative to the customer?
3. Why is personal selling an effective means of sales promotion? Is it always most important? Why or why not?
4. Why are many organisations seeking people with marketing experience for sales positions? Do you agree or disagree with this approach?
5. How does the salesperson determine whether a lead is a good prospect?

Chapter 3

Sales Planning and Budgeting

Introduction

A company should have workable plans so as to be able to get things done efficiently and effectively. Planning is the most crucial function that the sales manager does, because it creates the important framework for all other decision making. Planning requires that the sales manager anticipate the possible outcomes and future implications of his/her current decisions.

This chapter focuses on strategic sales planning and budgeting. It discusses the role of sales planning as it relates to marketing planning and total company planning. It also looks at the purposes of the sales budget and the budgetary procedure.

Benefits of Planning

Some the specific benefits that planning provides include the following:

1. **Budgeting improves morale** when the entire sales organisation actively participates in the process.
2. **Budgeting provides direction and focus** for organisational efforts.
3. **Budgeting improves the cooperation and coordination** of sales force efforts.
4. **Budgeting develops individual and collective standards** by which sales force performance can be measured and deviations identified in time to take corrective action.
5. **Budgeting increases the sales organisation's flexibility** in dealing with unexpected developments.

The Sales Management Planning Process

Planning as one sales management task is a continuous process. Planning allows sales managers to be proactive rather than merely reactive to the future. An outline of the planning process is submitted below.

Analysing the Situation

The planning process begins with an analysis of the current situation of the organisation. The manager needs to review the organisation's past performance and to judge its progress against that of the competition and its success in attaining objectives and goals. Some of the critical variables to study in the situational analysis should include:

1. **market characteristics**—number and types of potential buyers, their demographic and behavioural profiles, their attitudes and buying patterns, and their servicing;

2. **competition**—number and types of competitors, their strengths and weaknesses, their products, prices, brands, market shares, and characteristics, and the sales trends for each competitive brand;

3. **sales, cost, and profit data for current and recent years**—by product, market, territory, and time period;

4. **bundle of benefits offered**—as perceived by potential customers, products, brand names, prices, packages, and service;

5. **promotional mix**—advertising, personal selling, sales promotion, and publicity programmes; and

6. **distribution systems**—storage and transportation facilities, channels of distribution, and intensity of distribution.

Sales managers and all those involved in the planning process at any level should monitor internal and external events that might directly or indirectly influence their organisation. It would be of particular importance that the organisation's major strengths and weaknesses be matched against the existing opportunities and threats. For a company such as XYZ Systems Company, analysis of the relative strengths and weaknesses of an organisation might take the following form:

Strengths

- Our personal computers have the best reputation in the industry for ease of use.
- Our products are among the most innovative in the industry.
- We have strong advertising support for our brands.
- We are particularly strong in the high school and university markets.

Weaknesses

- Our prices are relatively high compared to those of competitive brands.
- Less software is available for our brands than for IBM-compatible machines.
- Our field sales force is small and inexperienced.
- Our products are not widely used in business organisations.

Setting Goals and Objectives

To ensure efficiency and effectiveness, all organisational units and personnel would need to understand overall company goals and objectives as well as individual goals and objectives. This enhances decision making by making it consistent and complimentary in pursuing the stated ends. For instance, the goals and objectives for the sales manager of the Eliza-Stevens Computer Company might include:

- **Goal** – Reduce sales force turnover to below the industry average by the end of the decade.
- **Objective** – Increase the number of new customer accounts by 15 percent next year.

Determining Market Potentials

The next step in the planning process, having specified the overall corporate goals and objectives, is the assessment of market potential—the maximum possible sales for an entire industry—and sales potential—the maximum possible sales for the company. Both of these are normally estimated for a specified period of time under the most favourable assumptions about the marketing environment and marketing expenditure.

Forecasting Sales

Analysis of market potential leads to the development of a more realistic sales forecast for the next quarter or year. A sales forecast predicts future sales for a prescribed period as an integral part of a marketing plan. The forecast is based on a set of assumptions about the marketing environment. It should be noted, though, that sales forecasting techniques could be very complex, making use of mathematical models and high-speed computers.

Selecting Strategies

This step involves determining the best way to achieve the organisational objectives set and the sales forecast developed. In general, strategic planning is the process of setting the overall corporate objectives, allocating total resources, and outlining broad courses of action. As Solomon (1978) emphasises, strategic decisions give the organisation a total plan of action to serve customers better, to take advantage of competitors' weaknesses, and to capitalise on the firm's strengths.

Growth Strategies

Figure 3.1 illustrates four types of growth strategies for sales management. In summary, the four types of growth strategies for sales management are:

(i) **market penetration.** Market penetration seeks to increase sales of current products in current markets by more intense marketing efforts.

(ii) **market development.** Market development tries to

open new markets for current products.

(iii) product development. Product development creates new or improved products for current markets.

(iv) diversification. Over the sales management level, other growth strategies may be: (1) to diversify by purchasing new businesses or product lines and (2) to obtain ownership or control over different levels of the channel of distribution.

Figure 3.1 Growth Strategies for Sales Management

	Current products	New products
Current markets	Market penetration	Product development
New markets	Market development	Diversification

Source: H. I. Ansoff, *Corporate Strategy* (New York: McGraw-Hill, 1965), 109. Reprinted with permission of McGraw-Hill.

The Business Portfolio Approach

Two main concepts relating to growth are the strategic business unit and the business portfolio matrix. Each of these concepts is explained next.

Strategic Business Units

Strategic business units (SBUs) are major business units within multiproduct companies that are treated as separate profit centres. SBUs are evaluated on the basis of their profit and growth potential just as if they were stand-alone companies. SBUs have a number of characteristics, including:

- a distinct mission,
- separate management,
- unique customer segments/their own competitors, and
- planning that is largely independent of other units in the company.

Many large manufacturing companies use the SBU concept. For instance, ABX Food Company may set up six SBUs: Soups, Beverages, Frozen Foods, Fresh Produce, Main Meals, and Grocery.

Business Portfolio Matrices

The most popular approach used by top managements in evaluating the strategic business units of the company is the business portfolio matrix. Three popular business portfolio matrices are:

- the growth-share matrix, which was developed by the Boston Consulting Group (BCG);
- the industry attractiveness/business strength matrix, which was developed jointly by General Electric and McKinsey and Company; and
- the life-cycle approach developed by Arthur Little, Inc.

For brevity, we discuss only the Boston Consulting Group matrix.

Boston Consulting Group Matrix

The most widely used of these three is the BCG'S growth-share matrix. It plots market share on the horizontal axis and market growth potential on the vertical axis. It allows all of a company's various businesses to be plotted in one of four quadrants labelled cash cows, stars, dogs, or question marks, as shown Figure 3.2.

- **Cash cows** are high-market share and low-market

growth products that should be milked for their continuing cash flow.

- **Stars** are high-market share and high-market growth products that deserve additional investment.

- **Dogs** are low-market share and low-market growth products that should probably be abandoned as quickly as possible.

- Question marks, or problem children, are low-market share and high-market growth products that require more cash investment than they are able to generate. Unless question marks can be converted to stars, these products should probably be dropped.

Figure 3.2 The BCG Growth-Share Matrix

		High	Low
G r o w t h R a t e	High	Stars	Question Marks
	Low	Cash Cows	Dogs

Relative market-share

Developing Detailed Activities

After deciding on the overall strategy, the next stage of the planning process is the incorporation of more detailed activities, or tactics, that focus on the implementation of the strategic plan. Tactical plans are the short-term actions undertaken to achieve implementation of the broader organisational strategy.

In the tactical plan, managers establish the objectives, the tactics, and the primary action plans that will be used by them and their sales force during the entire year. It is also in this section that managers will work with their sales representatives to create their territory plans and their key account plans.

Allocating Necessary Resources

Having tactical plans developed, the necessary resources would need to be allocated to carry out the plans.

Implementing the Plan

To ensure effective implementation of the plan, goals, objectives, strategies, and tactics must be well communicated throughout the organisation. Showing the tasks to be carried out in a specified time frame can ensure a timely implementation of the plan.

Controlling the Plan

It is important that a control device be built into the planning process. This will help management to control the operation of the plan. The control device must include a series of regular measurements that check progress toward specific objectives and indicate deviations in time to take corrective actions and get back on track.

Causes of Unsuccessful Planning

The common causes of unsuccessful planning result from the following:

1. a lack of commitment to planning, particularly among senior managers;
2. failure to see the scope of plans and the all-encompassing nature of the planning system;
3. failure to set meaningful, verifiable objectives likely to fit a future situation;
4. over-reliance on experience (it is not always true that what happened in the past is the best);
5. erroneous assumptions regarding the future marketing environment;
6. a hostile environment, for example, a period of change so rapid as to require constant planning adjustments without it ever being possible to achieve identifiable results;
7. poor and inflexible control techniques (planning

cannot be effective unless the people responsible for it know how well it is working); and

8. a lack of clear delegation, contributing to the failure of a planning system.

The Sales Budget

The sales budget is a plan for making profitable sales. It outlines who is going to sell how much of what during an operating period. Simply defined, a sales budget is a financial sales plan outlining how resources and selling efforts should be allocated to achieve the sales forecast. The sales budget, then, is a projection of what a given sales programme means in terms of sales volume, selling expenses, and net profit.

Purposes of the Sales Budget

Three main purposes served by the sales budget are planning, coordinating and controlling. Each of these is briefly discussed next.

Planning

For the sales department to attain its goals and objectives, the sales manager needs to outline key sales tasks and estimate their costs. Budgeting, therefore, is a type of profit planning in that it is an operational plan expressed in financial terms and drawn to provide a guide for action toward achieving the company's objectives. The sales planners show how the targeted sales volume can be reached, while keeping selling expenses at a level that permits attainment of the targeted profit.

Coordinating

The sales budget must be closely integrated with the budgets for other marketing functions so that the synergistic results of a coordinated marketing mix can be attained. The sales budget should give a reflection of a judicious allocation of resources and efforts designed to meet the goals and objectives for the sales department.

Controlling

Control is the key position in sales budgeting. The sales budget serves as a financial yardstick against which progress is measured. Any differences between actual results and budgeted figures are budget variances. Favourable variances give an indication of areas in which the sales manager might cut future budgets, whilst unfavourable variances show unanticipated costs that require analysis and corrective action. The sales budget itself then serves as an instrument for controlling sales volume, selling expenses, and net profits.

Preparation of the Annual Sales Budget

As Anderson et al. (1992) point out, budgeting offers the sales department important advantages by:

1. ensuring systematic approach to allocating resource;
2. developing the sales manager's sensitivity to profitable resource utilisation;
3. creating awareness of the necessity to coordinate selling efforts with other segments of the organisation;
4. establishing standards for measuring the performance of the sales organisation and its subdivisions; and
5. involving the entire organisation in the profit planning process, because each subdivision must submit a proposed budget.

Budgetary Procedure

Many an organisation has specified procedures, formats, worksheets, and timetables for developing the sales budget. The following are some of the various steps identified in systematic budget preparation.

Review and Analyse the Situation

Review and analyse the situation, beginning with the last period's variances. Where, when, and how much were deviations from planned performance, and who was responsible? Some common line items in each sales budget include the following:

- **Salaries** of salespeople, administrative support, sales supervisors, and managers.
- **Direct Selling Expenses** of travel, lodging, food, and entertainment;
- **Commissions and Bonuses**
- **Benefit packages**, which include social security, medical insurance, retirement contributions, and so on.
- **Office expenses** like mailing, telephone, office supplies, and miscellaneous costs.
- **Promotional materials**, such as selling aids, premiums, contest awards, product samples, price lists, and catalogues.
- **Advertising**

Communicate Sales Goals and Objectives

Communicate sales goals and objectives and their relative priorities to all management levels to ensure that managers are developing their budgets by using the same assumptions and general guidelines. To ensure their acceptance of responsibility for the budget and implementation of it, all supervisors and managers must be encouraged to contribute to its development.

Identify Specific Market Opportunities and Problems

Identify specific market opportunities and problems so that resources are budgeted in a way that enables salespeople and sales managers to exploit the opportunities and deal with the problems on a timely basis.

Develop a Preliminary Allocation of Resources and Selling Efforts

Develop a preliminary allocation of resources and selling efforts to particular activities, customers, products, and territories. Revisions can be made to this initial sales budget later.

Prepare a Budget Presentation to "Sell" the Sales Budget Proposal to Top Management

Each and every division of the organisation is often calling out for an increased allocation of funds. Top management receives more proposals than it is financially able to carry out simultaneously. Consequently, it is necessary to sell the sales budget to top management just as a salesperson makes a presentation to a prospect.

Implement the Budget and Provide Periodic Feedback

Implement the budget and provide periodic feedback to responsible subordinate managers and supervisors so that they have time to take corrective action on budget variances. It is the responsibility of the sales management to ensure that sales revenue and cost ratios remain within reasonable budget limits.

Review Questions

1. What assumptions might a sales manager make about the marketplace in preparing the annual plan?
2. How might you use one of the business portfolio approaches to analyse the telephony market for Ghana Telecom?
3. Discuss the relationship between sales planning and budgeting.
4. What do you expect to learn from a sales environment audit? When or how often do you think this type of audit should be conducted?
5. What important benefits does the sales department get from the use of objectives?

Chapter 4

Organizing the Sales Force

Introduction

In the management process, the manager must first establish his/her objectives and then plan the appropriate strategies and tactics to reach those objectives. To implement this planning, activities and people must be properly arranged and effectively coordinated. This is where the concept of organisation comes in. The fundamentals of organisation are essentially the same whether you are talking about organizing a sales force, a marketing department, a production department, or any group involved in a common effort.

Effective sales managers require sound organisation. They acknowledge that the sales organisation needs to achieve both qualitative and quantitative personal selling objectives. In essence, the firm has salespeople and sales managers who must engage in a variety of activities for the firm to perform successfully. A sales organisation structure must be developed to help salespeople and sales managers perform the required activities effectively and efficiently. This structure provides a framework for sales organisation operations by indicating what specific activities are performed by whom in the sales organisation. The sales organisation structure is the vehicle through which strategic plans are translated into selling operations in the marketplace.

This chapter deals with organizing the sales force. The purpose of sales organisation and the major types of sales organisational structures are treated. Additional strategic organisational alternatives are presented, including telemarketing.

The Purpose of Sales Organisation

The purpose of the marketing or sales organisation is to help attain the marketing and sales goals and objectives by:

1. **permitting the development of specialists**—reorganizing the sales department facilitates assignment of responsibility and delegation of authority. This generally depends on reshaping the structure so that it would be easier for specialists to develop.

2. **assuring that all necessary activities are performed**—as a sales organisation grows and specialisation increases, it becomes increasingly important that all necessary activities be performed. The effective sales manager should ensure that essential tasks are assigned to specific individuals.

3. **achieving coordination or balance**—good organisation achieves coordination or balance. Individuals vary in competence, potential, and effectiveness. By getting people to pull together as a team rather than as an assortment of individuals, the organisation accomplishes more collectively than its members could accomplish independently. Motivating individuals to work together toward common objectives is then essential to achieving coordination.

4. **establishing channels of communication**—the organisation structure must prevent a tendency toward communication problems. It must lead to easy channels of communication. Modern organisation theory suggests that sales departments should be divided into small, face-to-face, freely communicating groups.

5. **economizing of management time**—the important function of organisation is to reduce the time management needs for assessing market situations and taking action. Effective organisational structure requires flexibility and openness to change.

Setting Up a Sales Organisation

The five major steps involved in setting up a sales organisation are:

- define the objectives,
- determine the necessary activities,
- group activities into jobs or positions,
- assign personnel to positions, and
- provide coordination and control.

Define the Objectives

The first thing is to define the objectives for the sales department. The sales department's objectives, of course, must be derived from the long-term corporate objectives defined by top management. As Still et al. (1988) point out, three of the sales department's general objectives, all traceable to management's wish for the survival of the firm, may be summed up in three words: sales, profits, and growth.

Determine the Necessary Activities

Fundamental to sound organisational design is the recognition by management of the need to determine the necessary activities and their volume of performance. Determination of the performance must stem from a thorough examination of the sales department's qualitative and quantitative objectives.

Group Activities into Jobs or Positions

The activities identified as necessary—aimed at achieving certain objectives—are allocated to different positions. Classifying and grouping of activities makes sure that closely related tasks are assigned to the same position. Each position should contain a sufficient number of tasks as well as sufficient variation to provide for job challenge, interest, and involvement (Still et al., 1988).

Assign Personnel to Positions

The next step in the process is to assign personnel to the positions identified. The issue at stake is whether to recruit special individuals to fill the positions or to modify the positions to fit the capabilities of available personnel. Generally, what planners prefer whenever the situation permits is to have individuals grow into particular jobs rather than to have jobs grow up around individuals.

Provide Coordination and Control

Sales managers with line authority—that is, those who have others reporting to them—require a means to control their subordinates and to coordinate their efforts. They should not be made to carry so many detailed and undelegated responsibilities that they have little time for coordination. Nor should they have too many subordinates reporting directly to them.

Basic Types of Sales Organisations

An organisational structure is simply an arrangement of activities involving a group of people. The goal in designing an organisation is to divide and coordinate activities so the group can accomplish its common objectives better by acting as a group than by acting as individuals (Johnston and Marshall 2006). Designing a sales organisation's structure is difficult. Many different types of structures might be used, and many variations are possible within each basic type. If traditional practices are followed in designing the sales organisation, the resulting structure would take on characteristics of one or more of four basic types: line, line and staff, functional, and committee.

Line Sales Organisation

The line organisation is the simplest organisational structure and the one widely used in smaller firms and in firms with a smaller number of selling personnel. The chain of command runs from the top sales managers down through subordinates. All managers exercise line authority, and each subordinate is responsible only to one person on the next higher level. Thus, line sales managers have direct responsibility for a certain number of subordinates and report directly to management at the next highest level in the sales organisation. These managers are directly involved in the sales-generating activities of the firm and may perform any number of sales management activities.

Responsibility is definitely fixed, and those charged with it also make decisions and take action. The line of authority runs vertically through the structure, and all persons on any one organisational level are independent of all others on that line. An example of a simple line sales organisation is illustrated in Figure 4.1

The line sales organisation is typical in organisations where all sales personnel report directly to the senior sales manager. In these organisations, this manager tends to be overburdened with active supervision and has little time to plan or to work with other senior managers. Rarely, though, the line sales organisation is used where more than two levels of authority are present.

Line and Staff Sales Organisation

The line and staff sales organisation is common in large- and medium-size firms, which employ large numbers of sales personnel and sell diversified product lines over wide geographic areas. The line and staff structure creates more functional areas and provides the senior line sales manager with staff assistants to perform various specialised support activities. The assistant provides the line sales manager with specialised skills, which allows him or her to concentrate efforts on the sales force. Staff sales managers are, thus, not in the direct chain of command in the sales organisation structure. Instead, those in staff positions do not directly manage people, but they are responsible for certain functions (e.g., recruiting, selecting, and training) and are not directly involved in sales-generating activities. Staff sales management positions are more specialised than line sales management positions.

Although line sales managers have direct authority over others in carrying out operations of the organisation, staff sales managers do not have authority to issue orders or directives. Staff managers can only submit recommendations or assist the line managers.

Figure 4.1 Simple Line Sales Organisation

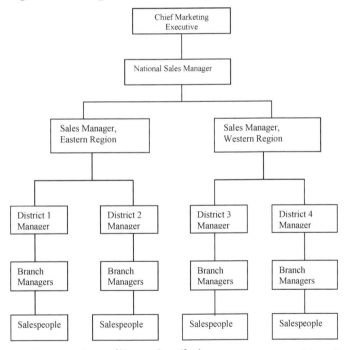

A comparison of line and staff sales management positions is presented in Figure 4.2. The regional and district sales managers all operate in line positions. The district sales managers directly manage the field sales force and report to a specific regional sales manager. The regional sales managers manage the district sales managers and report to the national sales manager. Two staff positions are represented in the figure. These training managers are located at both the national and regional levels and are responsible for sales training programmes at each level. The use of staff positions results in more specialisation of sales management activities. Staff managers specialise in certain sales management activities.

Figure 4.2 Line and Staff Sales Organisation

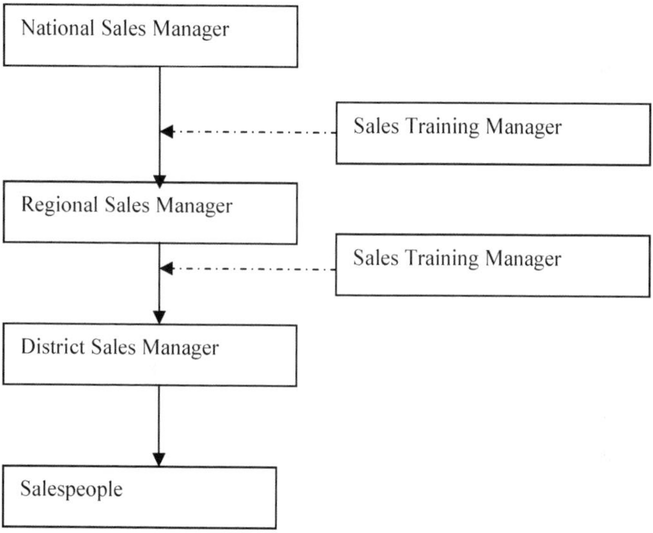

Functional Sales Organisation

In the functional organisation, the staff specialist is given line authority to control his or her function throughout the organisation, as illustrated in Figure 4.3. The sales manager directs the salespeople through the district managers; the director of sales training has authority over the salespeople for all training; and the manager of technical services exercises line authority over the sales force in providing technical services. In the functional structure, each manager is a highly qualified specialist whose job is to make sure that his or her function is accomplished. Thus in the functional sales organisation, salespeople receive instructions from several executives but on different aspects of their work.

Committee Sales Organisation

The committee is a method of organizing the executive group for planning and policy formulation whilst actual operations, including implementation of plans and policies, are left to individual executives. Thus, many companies have a sales committee— involving the general sales manager, the sales training manager, and others—that meets at regular times to draft training plans and formulate sales training policies. However, it is the sales training manager, if there is one, or the line and/or staff managers who are responsible for training in their own authority and take responsibility for the implementation of these plans and policies. Customer relations, merchandising, operations, and personnel may be some of the committees found in sales organisations.

Figure 4.3 Functional Sales Organisation

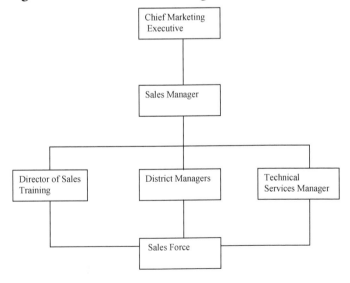

Field Organisation of the Sales Department

The field organisation involves all employees of the sales department who work away from the home office. The two main purposes of a field organisation are:

(i) to facilitate the selling task, and

(ii) to improve the chances that salespeople will achieve their goals.

Sales personnel rely on the field organisation for assistance and support. As Still et al. (1988) point out, the makeup of the field organisation is influenced by the organisational philosophy of management. Firms that believe in centralisation have complex supervising organisations; each salesperson is subjected to close supervision. Companies that consider decentralisation desirable, in contrast, would allow individuals in the field to operate more on their own.

Centralisation and Decentralisation in Sales Force Management

An important characteristic of the management structure within a sales organisation is its degree of centralisation— that is, the degree to which important decisions and tasks are performed at higher levels in the management hierarchy. A centralised structure is one in which authority and responsibility are placed at higher management levels. In the centralised sales organisation, almost all activities, including sales force management, are administered from a central head office. The central sales office has full responsibility for recruiting, selecting, training, compensating, supervising, motivating, controlling, and evaluating the sales force. Theoretically, field sales managers in the decentralised organisation handle all of these activities. A decentralised sales organisation is one in which there is decentralisation in management of various selling tasks and in performance of certain important personnel management activities.

It should be emphasised, though, that it is uncommon for sales force management to be characterised as fully centralised or fully decentralised. This is because management's appraisal of relative costs and effectiveness gives rise to some aspects being centralised and others decentralised.

Advantages of Centralised and Decentralised Sales Force Management

Centralisation in sales force management has certain advantages. Substantial economics are possible by centralizing certain functions. For instance, centralised sales force management enables smaller firms that have few salespeople and confine their operations to a small geographical area to keep the unit of sales high, the sales call frequency low, and the calibre of salespeople relatively high.

A decentralised sales force management is common in firms with large sales forces. Among the advantages of decentralised sales force management are (Still et al. 1988):

1. more intensive cultivation of the market and, consequently, a high sales volume to absorb the higher fixed costs;

2. more effective control, improved supervision, and increased sales productivity resulting from the addition of at least one intermediate level of sales managers and from reduction of geographical separation of managers and sales personnel;

3. improved customer service stemming from more effective control of sales personnel;

4. reduced need for and costs of territorial break-in times, since more salespeople are recruited from the areas to which they are assigned;

5. improved sales force morale, because of more frequent contact with the manager, reduction in travel time, and fewer nights away from home;

6. lower travel expenses as salespeople are dispatched from decentralised points, and fewer field trips by

home office sales managers are required; and

7. a built-in management development programme in which branch and district offices not only provide realistic training but serve as proving grounds for future high-level sales managers.

Types of Organisation within the Sales Department

All sales organisation efforts tend to centre around products, markets, and functions. These elements are blended together differently by separate companies. Sales departments have traditionally been organised through four criteria: (1) by geographic area, (2) by products, (3) by customers (or market channels), or (4) by function. A more recent innovation is some combination of these four. A brief description of each type of organisation follows.

Geographic Organisation

The geographic sales organisation is the simplest and most common method of organizing a company sales force. In this kind of organisation, each salesperson is typically assigned a geographic area and is responsible for all selling activities to all accounts within the assigned area. There is no attempt to specialise by product, market, or function. An example of a geographic sales organisation is illustrated in Figure 4.4. Again, note that this type of organisation provides no sales force specialisation, except by geographic area. Because of the lack of specialisation, there is no duplication effort. All geographic areas and accounts are served by only one salesperson.

The geographic sales organisation is most common with large firms with more selling operations. Some of the underlying reasons for geographic organisations are that:

(i) large numbers of customers vary by geographic location;

(ii) different selling problems are encountered in different areas;

(iii) certain products are more strongly demanded in some regions than in others;

(iv) more customers are added, and a wider area is cultivated; and

(v) increases in the size of the sales task take place.

Some examples of geographic organisations are hotel chains with regional divisions, magazine publishers with regional editions, and banks with out-of-city branches. Setting up geographic divisions is a way to trim the sales task down to manageable proportions.

Figure 4.4 Geographic Sales Organisation

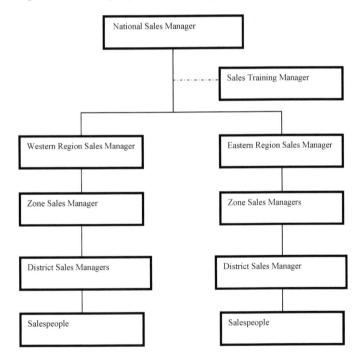

The advantages of the geographic organisation emanate from its decentralised structure, which enhances flexibility in adapting to the needs, problems, buying patterns, service requirements, and competitive conditions in the local markets. Some disadvantages include the increase in administrative expenses and the problems faced by top sales executives in coordinating several regional sales operations.

Product Sales Organisation

Another common type of organisation in large companies is based on the firm's product. Some companies have separate sales forces for each product or product category in their lines. Product sales organisation divides the sales tasks among subordinate line executives, each of whom directs sales operations for part of the product line. By using such divisions, more than one sales force may be required.

An example of a product sales organisation is illustrated in Figure 4.5. This organisation structure indicates two levels of product specialisation. There are two separate sales force. One sales force specialises in selling office equipment, and the other specialises in selling office supplies. Each of the specialised sales forces performs all selling activities for all types of accounts. The separate sales forces are each organised geographically. Thus, there will be duplication in the coverage of geographic area, with both office equipment and office supplies salespeople operating in the same areas. In some cases, the salespeople may call on the same accounts.

Figure 4.5 Product Sales Organisation

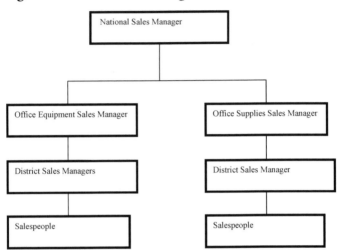

Organizing the sales force by product is applicable when companies' product lines become sufficiently complex, distinct, or diversified to demand increased individualised attention. Under this setup, products compete among themselves for profit, market share, and company resources.

Some advantages of product organisation of sales force include the increase of sales force knowledge of company products and provision of expertise in helping customers solve product related problems. Two disadvantages under this set up are the additional managerial expense and the possible irritation of customers who lose time because more than one salesperson from the same firm calls on them to present different products.

Customer (or Market) Sales Organisation

In customer (or market) sales organisation, salespeople are assigned specific types of customers and are required to satisfy all of the needs of those customers. Customer sales organisation is appropriate when nearly identical products are marketed to several types of customers and the problems of selling to each type are different. When the same, or similar, products are sold to a number of industries, they often find different applications in each industry. This is because the products are used for different purposes in each industry. Aircraft manufacturers, such Airbus or Boeing, have different marketing efforts for their government and commercial markets. Similarly, electricity companies separate their markets into residential and commercial accounts.

Figure 4.6 Customer Sales Organisation

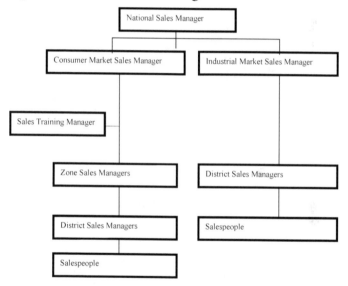

In the customer goods markets, companies pattern their sales organisations after the marketing channels (that is, channel of distribution). Because ultimate consumers may buy the product in different types of outlets, they frequently must be reached in different ways. The basic objective of market specialisation is to ensure that salespeople understand how customers use and purchase their products. Salespeople should then be able to direct their efforts to satisfy customer needs better.

The customer sales organisation shown in Figure 4.6 focuses on customer types. Separate sales forces have been organised for consumer and industrial markets. Salespeople perform all selling activities for all products but only for certain customers. This arrangement avoids confusion and duplication of sales effort in serving customers, because only one salesperson will ever call on a given customer. Several salespeople may, however, operate in the same geographic area.

Sales Organisation by Function

The sales organisation by function is structured by major selling functions, such as development of new accounts or maintenance of current customers. Different kinds of selling activities often require different abilities and skills on the part of the salesperson. Thus, it may be appropriate under certain circumstances for the firm to organise the sales force so different salespeople specialise in performing different selling functions. This structure offers specialisation and efficiency in performing selling activities, and it is generally best for companies that sell only a few or very similar products to comparatively few customer types (Anderson et al. 1992). One such sales organisation by function has one sales force specialise in prospecting for and developing new accounts while a second force maintains and services old customers.

Figure 4.7 illustrates a simple sales organisation by function. In this structure, an account development sales force performs sales-generating activities and an account maintenance sales force performs account-servicing activities.

Figure 4.7 Sales Organisation by Function

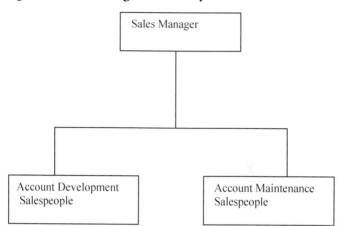

Combinations

Many companies organise on the basis of some combination of the four basic types of sales organisations. Figure 4.8 illustrates a sales force that is organised by functions, territories, products, and markets. Most companies develop some type of combination structure for the sales organisation to permit greater specialisation as they grow in size and complexity. The figure depicts a company with production, marketing, and engineering functional specialists; the firm sells consumer and industrial goods in both domestic and foreign markets. The consumer goods division sells three categories of products through three geographically organised sales force divisions. At ABX Business Machines, each sales staff is assigned a clearly defined industry group to serve. Salespeople are trained to sell systems of different but interrelated products and services in a consultative manner. Each of the company's sales groups can utilise the total support team of the company in analyzing, prescribing, developing, installing, and maintaining product systems for customers.

Figure 4.8 Combination Sales Organisation

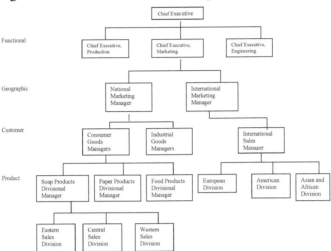

Telemarketing

One form of sales organisation by selling function that has gained great popularity in recent years is telemarketing, which involves the use of inside telephone salespeople and outside field salespeople to accomplish separate selling objectives. Telemarketing, or telephone selling, is a selling operation in which the telephone is used to contact potential customers and to solicit orders without any personal call upon customers' premises. Telemarketing has proven useful for carrying out selected selling activities (Herman 1987), including the following:

- prospecting for and qualifying potential new accounts, which can then be turned over to field salespeople for personal contact;
- servicing existing accounts quickly when unexpected problems arise, such as through the use of technical assistance hotlines;
- seeking repeat purchases from existing accounts that

cannot be covered efficiently in person, such as small or marginal customers and those in remote geographic locations; and

- gaining quicker communication of noteworthy developments like the introduction of new or improved products or special sales programmes.

Many companies, especially those dealing in relatively expensive products such as cars and home improvements, rely on their telemarketing sales force for their sales.

These companies support their telemarketing staffs with catalogues, brochures, participation in trade shows, and technical support staffs. Many other companies combine the efforts of their telemarketing staffs with those of their outside sales force in an effort to make their total sales organisation more efficient and more productive. Telemarketing is normally conducted from call centres in which trained operators accept and send thousands of calls a day.

Functions of the Telemarketing Staff

There are four functions that the telemarketing staff can serve: sales support, order taking, customer service, and account management. We briefly explain each of these activities next.

Sales Support

The telemarketing staff may be employed to prospect for new accounts. Some leads may be received through toll-free telephone numbers; others may come in the form of written enquiries. The telemarketer qualifies these prospects, sets up appointments for the outside sales representative, and sometimes warms up the outside sales prospect for the field salesperson to close.

The telemarketer saves time that the field salesperson would often be wasting in trying to find and qualify prospects. The telemarketing personnel can follow up on five to ten prospects in the time it would take the field person to drive from one prospect to another.

Order Taking

The telemarketing salesperson can handle existing customers, who are just recording or who are difficult to reach in person. The field salesperson benefits by being able to concentrate on closing new accounts and handling large existing accounts that require a personal contact.

Customer Service

Many a telemarketing salesperson is employed to deal with customer complaints, assist customers with technical information, conduct customer surveys, and maintain strong customer relations. These tasks are essential for producing information about the customer of the company and are able to play a big role in the development of new products. They also assure the customer that the company still cares after the sale has been made, thus increasing goodwill and improving the company's image.

Account Management

The telemarketing personnel are used for the account management function. In carrying out this function, the telemarketer is responsible for all customer contact for a certain group of accounts, which involves orders, billing, credit, complaints, and product information. The telemarketers, by handling a specific group of accounts, are able to establish a rapport with the customer, which enhances their ability to satisfy the needs of the customer. Account management will be discussed further in a later part of the chapter.

Guidelines for Telemarketing

The following is an eight-step guide to telemarketing, which has been published by the Bell Telephone System of America:

(1) Identify yourself and your company.

(2) Establish rapport; this should come naturally since you have already researched your potential clients and their business.

(3) Make an interesting comment (e.g., to do with a special offer).

(4) Deliver your sales message; emphasise benefits over features.

(5) Overcome objections; be skilled at objection-handling techniques.

(6) Close the sale; when appropriate, do not be afraid to ask for the order or fulfil another objective (e.g. Can I send you a sample?).

(7) Action agreement; arrange for a sales call or the next telephone call.

(8) Express your thanks.

Organizing to Service Major Customers

Companies have realised the need to pay special attention to their major customers. Thus, many organisations are developing new organisational approaches to deliver the customer service necessary to attract and maintain large and important customers. Companies refer to these major customers with different terms, such as "key accounts" or "national accounts." The loss of such customers would substantially affect a company's sales and profits. The importance of major accounts is increasing as large multinational companies seek to coordinate their purchasing across subsidiaries operating in many different countries.

Major Accounts Management

To provide the kinds of service demanded by such major customers, many organisations adopt a selling philosophy of major account management. This stresses the dual goals of making sales and developing long-term relationships with major customers (Churchill et al. 2000). Two types of major account organisations are of particular importance. National account management (NAM) focuses on meeting the needs of specific accounts with multiple locations throughout a large region or entire country. For example, the distribution company KwikSource has formal national account management programmes for major accounts that have many locations nationwide. Major accounts from the printing, publishing, retail, grocery, manufacturing, and food processing industries are provided special services, pricing, and delivery schedules. These major accounts have a single contact point within KwikSource and the same contract for all of their locations.

Global account management (GAM), by contrast, serves the needs of major customers with locations around the world. Typically, a global account manager will be located at the customer's headquarters. This manager directs the activities of account representatives in that customer's other locations worldwide. Often, a global account management team is assigned to each customer. This team might consist of product specialists, applications specialists, sales support specialists, and others.

Identifying Major Accounts

Although major account programmes differ considerably across firms, all firms must determine how to identify their own major accounts and how to organise for effective coverage for them. Not all large accounts do qualify as major accounts. As illustrated in Figure 4.9, a major account should be of sufficient size and complexity to warrant special attention from the sales organisation. As Futrell (1999) suggests, an account can be considered complex if it meets the following criteria:

- its purchasing function is centralised;
- top management heavily influences its purchasing decisions;
- it has multi-site purchasing influences;
- its purchasing process is complex and diffuse;
- it requires special price concessions;
- it requires special services; and
- it purchases customised products.

Figure 4.9 Identifying Major Accounts

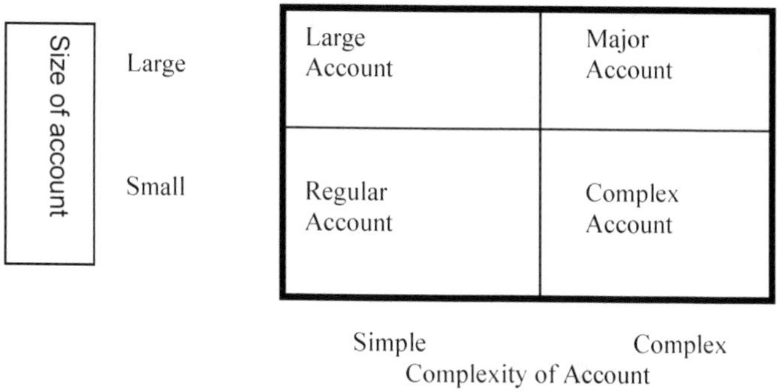

		Simple	Complex
Size of account	Large	Large Account	Major Account
	Small	Regular Account	Complex Account

Complexity of Account

Alternative Organisational Approaches for Dealing with Major Accounts

Many organisations adopt special organisational arrangements for the major account management function. These arrangements include:

1. **assigning major accounts to sales executives.** The use of sales or marketing executives to call on the organisation's major accounts is a common practice, especially among smaller firms that do not have the resources to support a separate division or sales force. It is also common when the organisation has relatively few major accounts to be serviced. These sales executives are responsible for coordinating all activities with each assigned account. This major account responsibility is typically in addition to the executives' normal management activities.

2. **creating a separate major account division.** Some firms create a separate corporate division for dealing with major accounts. For example, some garment companies have separate divisions for making and selling private label clothing to large general merchandise chains. This approach allows for close integration of manufacturing, logistics, marketing,

and sales activities.

3. **creating a separate major accounts sales force.** It is also common for organisations to create a separate major accounts sales force. This approach is a type of market specialisation in which salespeople specialise by type of account based on size and complexity. Each salesperson is typically assigned one or more major accounts and is responsible for coordinating all seller activities to serve the assigned accounts. There are different ways to organise such separate sales forces. For example, as in a case cited by Churchill et al. (2000), the national account sales operation was treated as a separate functional area on a par with the firm's marketing and sales department and reported directly to the general manager.

Criteria for Constructing a Sound Sales Organisation

The following are suggested criteria for constructing a sound sales organisation:

- **A market-oriented approach**: The customer should be recognised as the organisation's reason for existence, and the organisation should be designed to serve the customer's needs best.
- **An approach designed around sales actives**: An organisation should be designed to accomplish major sales activities, such as planning, sales development, and customer service.
- **Defined areas of authority and responsibility**: Individual responsibility should be clearly communicated in writing and sufficient authority should be allocated to accomplish the work assigned.
- **A reasonable span of control**: Further to handling administrative responsibilities, sales managers must be able to control the sales force adequately through

frequent direct contact.

- **Flexibility**: Flexibility can be enhanced by ensuring that a trained replacement is ready to move into any single position and by utilizing staff specialists to release the sales manager from routine paperwork.
- **Coordination and balance**: Sales managers should not allow any unit or individual to exercise excessive influence on operations.

Quality of the Sales Organisation

To ensure the overall quality of the sales organisation, which affects the effectiveness of the organisation in general, the sales manager needs to consider the following practical guidelines (Anderson et al. 1992):

1. **Be sure that authority equals responsibility.** It would be difficult for salespeople to perform effectively without the authority to make necessary decisions.
2. **Put salespeople where they fit best.** Consider geography and personality types and compare for inside and outside positions in the sales force or national and local accounts.
3. **Be willing to delegate.** The task of the sales manager is to accomplish stated objectives through the efforts of the sales force.
4. **Be more than just an efficiency expert.** Qualitative considerations should not be ignored. Even while focusing on quantitative issues, the manager must consider the human element.
5. **Hold sales force personnel accountable for what they do**. This is the basic means of maintaining control.
6. **Be flexible**. An organisational structure that worked yesterday may not be the best one for today. The sales force organisation must be open to new ideas.

7. **Know what needs to be done**. Organisation of the sales force should be directed toward the accomplishment of sales goals.

8. **Organise the sales force to avoid unequal distribution of workloads**. Inequality of work for full-time salespeople results in dissatisfaction and reduced output.

As Anderson et al. emphasise, following these steps should result in an effective and efficient sales force. A well-considered and carefully designed sales organisation would be a useful aid to sales personnel, their customers, and the firm. But the critical part of any sales organisation is the quality of its people.

Review Questions

1. Explain the conflict between the need to centralise and the need to decentralise sales responsibilities.

2. Compare and contrast the workload and incremental productivity approaches for determining the optimal size of a sales force.

3. Describe how you might set up a line and staff organisation to run a marketing department.

4. What types of specialists might a sales manager effectively use? What organisation design would you suggest for their effective utilisation?

5. Explain the need to centralise and the need to decentralise sales responsibilities.

Chapter 5

Recruiting the Sales Force

Introduction

Recruiting and selecting the sales force is an important part of implementing the personal selling strategy. It is one of the most essential responsibilities of the sales manager because, for most customers and prospects, the salespeople are the company. The firm's sales success is certainly influenced by what the salespeople say, how they handle themselves, and how they react in face-to-face interactions with customers.

The sections of this chapter discuss the meaning and importance of recruitment and selection and the specific methods and procedures that managers might use at each stage of the recruitment and selection process. The recruitment process is complex, and the selection of the right candidate is a function of many different criteria. Companies use a variety of tools to help them identify the right candidates.

This chapter discusses the sales force recruiting process, the critical distinction between a job analysis and a job description, the basic qualifications needed for sales positions and the sources of good candidates.

What Is Recruitment?

According to Anderson et al. (1992), recruitment is the process of finding potential job applicants, telling them about the company, and getting them to apply. Recruiting efforts should find applicants who will potentially be good employees. Assuming that the job analysis has been done, the sales job descriptions written, and the list of job specifications prepared, there are three main steps in recruiting and selecting a sales force. Step one is to evaluate the sources from which salespeople with good potential are obtainable. Step two is to tap the identified recruiting sources and build a supply of prospective salespeople. Step three is to select those who have the highest probability of success. Selection is discussed in Chapter six.

The Purposes and Importance of Recruitment

Recruiting and selecting the sales force is an important part of implementing personal selling strategy. Recruitment of salespeople is a continuous activity, since the company always searches for the right people for the right job.

The general purpose of recruitment is to provide a pool of potentially qualified job candidates to select from. More specifically, the purposes of recruitment, as summarised by Futrell (1998), are to:

- determine the present and future staffing needs of the sales force in conjunction with the human resource plan;
- increase the pool of job applicants with minimal cost;
- help increase the success rate of the selection process by reducing the number of unqualified or overqualified job applicants;
- boost the probability that job applicants, once recruited and selected, will stay with the organisation for a reasonable period of time;
- start identifying and preparing potential job applicants who will be appropriate candidates;
- evaluate the effectiveness of various techniques of and locations for recruiting job applicants;
- meet the organisation's responsibility for affirmative action programmes and other legal and social obligations regarding the composition of its sales force; and

- increase sales force performance.

Responsibility for Recruitment

The recruitment function may be performed by the human resource manager and/or the sales manager. The system could be centralised, in which case the initial promotion, contacting, and screening is often implemented by a human resource department. At that point, the process primarily involves screening out the obviously unqualified candidates. Once the candidates pass this screen, they are typically interviewed by at least two members of the sales management. When recruiting is decentralised, it is usually implemented by either the sales manager or a person assigned to that function within the local office. But again, as on a centralised basis, the basic hiring decision is made by the sales manager once the candidate has passed through the initial screening process.

According to Patty (1979), a company will typically use a centralised system when recruiting for:

- highly technical positions,
- a position for which extensive centralised training is given, and
- sales positions that are considered the first stepping stones on the way to top management.

The Recruitment Process

In general, the steps in the recruitment process are:

- conduct a job analysis,
- prepare a job description,
- identify the sales job qualifications,
- attract a pool of sales recruits, and
- select the best recruits.

Many firms would go through each of these steps, even though existing firms should have completed the first three steps. Each of these steps is explained next. It should be emphasised that the final step (selection) will not be discussed until the next chapter.

F. O. Boachie-Mensah

Conduct a Job Analysis

Research relating salespeople's personal characteristics to sales aptitude and job performance suggests that there is no single set of traits and abilities that sales managers can use as criteria in deciding what kind of recruits to hire. Different sales jobs require different skill sets, and this suggests that people with different personality traits and abilities should be hired to fill them.

As indicated earlier, most companies, particularly larger ones, have written job descriptions for sales force positions. Unfortunately, those job descriptions are often out of date and do not accurately reflect the current scope and content of the positions. The responsibilities of a given sales job change as the customers, the firm's account management policies, the competition, and other environmental factors change. But firms often do not conduct new analyses or prepare updated descriptions to reflect those changes. Firms also create new sales positions, and the tasks to be accomplished by people in these jobs may not be spelled out.

Consequently, a critical first step in the hiring process is for management to make sure the job to be filled has been analysed recently and that the findings have been written out in great detail. Without such a detailed and up-to-date description, the sales manager will have more difficulty deciding what kind of person is needed. In addition, prospective recruits will not really know for what position they are applying.

Conducting a job analysis helps to identify the duties, requirements, responsibilities and conditions involved in the sales job to be filled. A conventional job analysis should include these steps:

(i) **Analyse the environment in which the salesperson is to work**. For example, what is the nature of the competition faced by the salesperson in this job? What is the nature of customers to be contacted, and what kinds of problems do they have?

86

(ii) Determine the duties and responsibilities that are expected of the salesperson. In this respect, information should be acquired from a) salespeople, (b) customers, and (c) the sales manager and other marketing managers—e.g., the distribution manager and the advertising manager.

(iii) Spend time making calls with several salespeople, observing and recording the various tasks of the job as they are actually performed.

Prepare a Job Description

A job description is the ultimate result of a formal job analysis. A job description is used in recruiting, selecting, training, compensating, and evaluating the sales force and, in view of that, the description should be done in writing so that it can be referred to regularly.

The written job description allows both prospective job applicants and current salespeople to know precisely what the duties and responsibilities of the sales position are and on what basis the new salesperson will be evaluated.

Content of the Job Description

As Johnston and Marshall (2006) suggest, good descriptions of sales jobs typically cover the following dimensions and requirements:

1. The nature of product(s) or service(s) to be sold.
2. The types of customers to be called on, including the policies concerning the frequency with which calls are to be made and the types of personnel within customer organisations who should be contacted (e.g., buyers, purchasing agents, and plant supervisors).
3. The specific tasks and responsibilities to be carried out—including planning tasks, research and information collecting activities, specific selling tasks, other promotional duties, customer servicing

activities, and clerical and reporting duties.

4. The relationships between the job occupant and other positions within the organisation. To whom does the job occupant report? What are the salesperson's responsibilities to the immediate superior? How and under what circumstances does the salesperson interact with members of other department, such as production or engineering?

5. The mental and physical demands of the job—including the amount of technical knowledge the salesperson should have concerning the company's products, other necessary skills, and the amount of travel involved.

6. The environmental pressures and constraints that might influence performance of the job—such as market trends, the strengths and weaknesses of the competition, the company's reputation among customers, and resource and supply problems.

An example of a job description that addresses most of these dimensions is presented in Table 5.1

Identify the Sales Job Qualifications

The duties and responsibilities set out in the job description should be converted into a set of qualifications that a sales recruit would need to have in order to perform the sales job satisfactorily. The job description should include such specific qualifications as education and experience. But many companies also attempt to identify personality traits that are perceived to make better salespeople, like self-confidence, assertiveness, and affableness.

Job qualifications should specifically spell out the characteristics and abilities a person must possess in order to carry out the requirements of the sales positions.

Attract a Pool of Sales Recruits

The next important stage in the recruitment process is attracting a pool of applicants for the sales position to be filled. Large firms with a sales force have a continuous need to identify, locate, and attract potentially effective salespeople. The candidates recruited become the reserve pool of sales staff from which new salespeople will be chosen.

Table 5.1 Job Description

JOB TITLE SALES REPRESENTATIVE – BUSINESS DIVISION (BD)	JOB CODE
ESTABLISHMENT – DEPARTMENT MARKETING BD SALES	DATE

Function

Promotes and consummates the sale of office systems and related equipment, paper, accessories, and other supplies within an assigned geographic territory, for the Business Division (BD).

Major Activities

A. Establishes and maintains close liaisons between the company and customers within an assigned geographic territory for the ultimate purpose of selling BD products.

B. Establishes and maintains a working rapport with customers by providing expertise in the analysis of systems problems and the application of BD products and services to the solution of these problems.

C. Provides service to customers by recommending changes in operating procedures, assisting them in planning for office systems applications, recommending equipment purchases and supervising their installations, suggesting methods of quality control, and checking to determine that equipment and systems function properly.

D. Provides accurate and timely information on office products and demonstrates to customers the benefits derived from utilizing these products in his or her business. Keeps customers and prospects updated on new products and office systems.

E. Assists customers in achieving the high-quality capabilities of the company's office products.

F. Prepares a variety of reports and correspondence including data reports on activities, expenses, market acceptance of office products, product problems, market needs, etc.

G. Studies customers' systems needs and formulates written proposals to satisfy these with the general philosophies established by BD. Outlines systems recommendations incorporating products in customer proposals; cites advantages and operating cost reductions resulting from the proposed system.

H. Maintains a thorough familiarity of the products of other manufacturers to deal with questions posed by customers and prospects in daily activities.

I. Participates in and/or originates customer seminars and education programmes by instructing customers and their personnel in the capabilities of office systems and the proper application and operation of BD products. Provides information and assistance at trade shows and exhibits to interested persons.

J. Keeps abreast of the new developments and trends in office equipment and systems to be capable of understanding customer needs and to be better prepared to provide workable solutions to customer systems requirements.

K. Handles product complaints and makes recommendations to the marketing centre regarding goodwill replacements of products.

L. Advises district, and/or regional, and/or BD management of any information pertinent to BD activities gathered as a result of observations made in the field. Reports include new systems applications, activities of other manufacturers, equipment modifications and improvements, customer needs, etc.

M. Follows up on all sales leads as quickly as possible. Makes new calls on potential customers to stimulate interest in BD products.

N. Plans activities in a manner that provides for adequate territory coverage. Allocates time on the basis of maximum potential yield and/or priorities established by the district sales manager.

Scope of the Position
A. Accountability

1. Reports to the district sales manager of the marketing centre to which he/she is assigned. May direct the activities of less experienced sales representatives assigned to assist on a project basis or for training and development purposes.

2. Is responsible for reviewing unusual, complex, and/ or sensitive problems, proposals, or controversial matters with supervision before taking any action. Manages the assigned territory with considerable independence.

3. Is responsible for having a thorough knowledge of all BD products and services and capable of effectively analyzing, from a systems viewpoint, customers' problems and needs to develop new business by demonstrating the capabilities of BD products to satisfy these needs.

4. Is capable of independently meeting expected sales goals for all categories of products in the assigned territories.

5. Is responsible for submitting knowledgeable reports on emerging trends in the marketplace, on market needs, and on ideas for new products that demonstrate a thorough understanding of the company's position in the marketplace and the direction it must pursue to maintain and improve its position.

6. Shows increasing expertise and professionalism in customer contracts, diagnosis of customers' needs, analysis of systems, and preparation and presentation of proposals for new systems based on sound economic evaluations.

7. Is expected to exhibit maturity and competence in running the assigned territory with a minimum of direction. Has demonstrated the ability to develop large accounts, multiple sales, etc.

B. Innovation

1. Has a thorough understanding of the capabilities of other manufacturers' products and effectively uses this information to serve customers' needs.

2. Demonstrates originality and creativity in solving systems problems and meeting the needs of the market.

3. Is responsible for consistently aiding customers by disseminating information on new methods, systems, and techniques that are applicable to their operations.

Job Knowledge		
A. College degree or the equivalent in applicable training and experience.		

Job Knowledge
  A. College degree or the equivalent in applicable training and experience.
  B. Completion of the basic BD training programme.
  C. A thorough knowledge of all billing, credit, and distribution procedures, paperwork, and policies and capability to resolve complex problems in these areas with a minimum of confusion, frustration, and inconvenience for all parties concerned.
  D. This level of activity is generally achieved with four years' selling experience, or the equivalent, with the assigned products where the individual is subjected to all types of problems and challenges covering the entire product line.

WRITTEN BY		APPROVED DATE

Source: G. A. Churchill, Jr., N. M. Ford, O. C. Walker, Jr., M. W. Johnston and J. F. Tanner, *Sales Force Management* (Boston: Irwin, 2000), 359–360. Reprinted with permission of Irwin.

Sources of Sales Force Recruits

Sales managers can go to a number of places to find recruits or leads concerning potential recruits. Internal sources consist of other people already employed in other departments within the firm, whereas external sources include people in other firms (who are often identified and referred by current members of the sales force), educational institutions, advertisements, and employment agencies.

Each source is likely to produce candidates with somewhat different backgrounds and characteristics. Therefore, while most firms seek recruits from more than one source, a company's recruiting efforts should be concentrated on sources that are most likely to produce the kinds of people needed. Research suggests that firms use different sources for finding recruits, depending on the type of sales job they are trying to fill. When the job involves missionary or trade selling, firms rely most heavily on a variety of external sources, such as advertisements, employment agencies, and educational institutions. When the job involves technical selling and requires substantial product knowledge and industry experience, firms focus more heavily on employees in other departments within the company and on personal referrals of people working for other firms in the industry. The relative advantages and limitations of each of these sources of new recruits are discussed in more depth in the following sections.

The sales manager needs to evaluate each potential source to decide which ones will offer the best recruits for the sales position to be filled.

Factors to Consider in Evaluating Recruiting Sources
The recruiting effort varies significantly from company to company. Some of the factors management should consider when deciding which recruiting sources to use are:

(i) **the nature of the product.** A highly technical product requires an experienced, knowledgeable person. The company might look at persons in its own production department or at experienced persons from other firms.

(ii) **the nature of the market.** Experienced salespeople might be needed to deal with well-informed purchasing agents or with high-level executives.

(iii) **the policy on promoting from within.** If this policy is the rule, recruiters would know where to look first.

(iv) **sales training provided by the firm.** A firm that has its own sales training programme can recruit inexperienced salespeople. But when a salesperson needs to be productive quickly, it might be necessary for the firm to look for experienced recruits.

(v) **the personnel needs of the firm.** If the firm is looking for career salespeople, then colleges and universities are not good sources of recruits, because many graduates want to be managers.

(vi) the sources of successful recruits in the past. Past sources of successful recruits can be used again, as long as there have been no changes in the sales position.

(vii) legal considerations. In deciding on the sources of recruits, a firm should consider civil rights, laws, and other regulations.

Internal Sources of Recruits

Sources of the sales force recruits within the company include the following:

Company Salespeople

Present salespeople's recommendations may constitute an excellent source. Salespeople have wide circles of acquaintances, since they frequently meet new people and have many friends with similar interests. Many of their contacts have potential as salespeople. Salespeople are a particularly valuable source of recommendations when jobs must be filled in remote territories.

Company Executives

Recommendations of the sales manager and other company executives are an important source. Sales managers' personal contacts may yield high-calibre people because of their understanding of the needed qualifications.

Internal Transfers

Other departments and the non-selling section of the sales department are additional internal sources. Employees desiring transfers are already familiar with company policies, and the human resource department has significant detailed information about them.

Advantages of Recruiting Current Company Employees

Recruiting current employees for the sales force has distinct advantages, including the following:

1. Existing company salespeople have established

performance records, and they are more of a known quantity than outsiders.

2. Recruits from inside the firm usually require less orientation and training, because they are already familiar with the company's products, policies, and operations

3. Recruiting from within can boost the morale of employees as they become aware that opportunities for advancement are available outside of their own departments or divisions.

External Sources of Recruits

There are a number of commonly used external sources of sales recruits. These sources include the following:

Direct Unsolicited Applications

Almost all companies receive unsolicited walk-in and write-in applications for sales positions. Some sales managers favour immediate hiring of applicants who take the initiative in seeking sales jobs, the reasoning being that it indicates selling aggressiveness. But others reject all direct applications, because they believe the percentage of qualified applicants from this source is low.

Employment Agencies

Employment agencies are among the best and the worst sources. Most of the time, the situation depends on the relationship between the agency and the sales manager. Employment agencies are sometimes used to find recruits, usually for more routine sales jobs such as retail sales. However, executive search firms specialise in finding applicants for more demanding sales jobs. Some sales managers have had unsatisfactory experiences with employment agencies. They claim that agencies are sometimes overzealous in attempting to earn their fees, and they tend to send applicants who do not meet the job qualifications. Others argue, however, that when a firm has problems with an employment agency, it is often the fault of the company for not understanding the agency's role and not providing sufficient information about the kinds of recruits it is seeking. When a firm carefully selects an agency with a good reputation, establishes a long-term, good working relationship, and provides a clear statement of the job's objectives as well as detailed descriptions of job qualifications, the agency can perform a valuable service. It locates and screens job applicants and reduces the amount of time and effort the company's sales managers must devote to recruiting.

Salespeople Making Calls on the Company

The purchasing director is in contact with salespeople from other companies and is in a position to evaluate their on-the-job performances. The purchasing director meets top-calibre salespeople for whom jobs with the company would be attractive both financially and in other respects.

Employees of Customers

Customers of a company may recommend employees in their organisations who have reached the maximum potential of their existing jobs. Sometimes a customer's employees have the kinds of knowledge that make them attractive as prospective salespeople. For instance, department store employees can make good salespeople for the wholesalers or manufacturers that supply the store, because they are familiar with the product and the procedures of store buyers. A customer's employees should be recruited only with the prior approval of the customer.

Sales Forces of Non-competing Companies

Salespeople for non-competing companies are usually attractive recruiting prospects. Such people have selling experience, and for those who have worked for companies in related industries, there is the attraction of knowing something about the product line.

Sales Forces of Competing Companies

Salespeople recruited from competitors' sales forces are trained, have experienced selling similar products to similar markets, and should be ready to sell almost immediately. Such personnel may require only minimal training. However, competing salespeople are costly sources, since premium pay must generally be offered to entice salespeople to leave their present positions. Some sales managers, as a matter of policy, refrain from hiring competitors' salespeople, because the practice is perceived as unethical.

Educational Institutions

Polytechnic school, vocational school, technical institute, college, and university placement officers are a common source of recruits for firms that require salespeople with sound mental abilities or technical backgrounds. Most educational institutions, in fact, allocate resources to career management departments that will enhance the development of careers for their graduates. Educational institutions are a particularly effective source when the sales job is viewed as a first step toward a career in management. College graduates are often more socially poised than people of the same age without college training, and good grades are at least some evidence that the person can think logically, budget time efficiently, and communicate reasonably well. Large companies are often successful in recruiting from universities and polytechnic schools, but small companies tend to be more successful in recruiting from small educational institutions or from other sources.

Advertisements

A less selective means of attracting job applicants is to advertise the available position. When a technically qualified or experienced person is needed, an advertisement might be placed in an industry trade or technical journal. More commonly, advertisements are placed in the personnel or marketplace sections of local newspapers to attract applicants for relatively less demanding sales jobs that do not require special qualifications. A well-written ad can be very effective for attracting applicants.

As suggested, however, this is not necessarily a good thing. When a firm's advertisements attract large numbers of applicants who are unqualified or only marginally interested, the firm must engage in costly screening to identify legitimate candidates. If a firm does use newspaper ads in recruiting, it must decide how much information about the job it should include in the ads. Many sales managers argue that open ads, which disclose the firm's name, the product to be sold, the compensation, and the specific job duties, generate a more select pool of high-quality applicants, lower selection costs, and decreased turnover rates than ads without such information. Open ads also avoid any ethical questions concerning possible deception. However, for less attractive, high-turnover sales jobs—such as telemarketing selling—some sales managers prefer blind ads, which carry only minimal information, sometimes only a phone number. These maximise the number of applicants and give the manager an opportunity to explain the attractive features of the job in a personal meeting with the applicant. In Ghana, national newspapers such as the *Daily Graphic*, *Ghanaian Times*, the *Mirror*, and various trade journals are used in recruiting both for low-level sales positions and for top-calibre sales and sales management positions.

The Internet

Increasingly, many companies are using Internet recruiting sites to fill sales positions. Companies post jobs and request that candidates submit their applications over the Internet. The applications are then reviewed, and an appropriate action is taken. In many cases, younger candidates are as comfortable submitting applications over the Internet as they are filling them out on paper. In addition, by targeting the Internet application to specific Internet job postings, the company can direct the information to the right people very efficiently.

F. O. Boachie-Mensah

Review Questions

1. What are the major steps involved in the recruiting process?

2. Why should sales managers conduct job analyses before recruiting salespeople?

3. Prepare a list of the qualifications you feel are necessary to fill a sales job.

4. Explain the factors that sales managers should consider when deciding which recruitment source to use.

5. What are the most frequently used sources of salespeople? Should a firm use only one or a few of these potential recruit sources?

Chapter 6

Selecting the Sales Force

Introduction

In chapter five, we discussed the process by which sales managers determine the number and type of salespeople needed and how to recruit applicants. The recruiting process provides the sales manager with a pool of applicants from which to choose.

The selection process involves choosing the applicants who best meet the qualifications and have the greatest aptitude for the job. There are numerous tools, techniques, and procedures that can be used in the selection process. Organisations normally use the major tools of initial screening interviews, application forms, in-depth interviews, reference checks, and physical examinations in selecting the salespeople. These tools are described in detail in this chapter.

This chapter describes the procedures and tools used to select the best applicants and explains what sales managers look for in application forms and interviews.

The Selection Process

The recruiting process provides the sales executive with a pool of candidates from which to choose. The selection process involves choosing the candidates who best meet the qualifications and have the greatest aptitude for the job. There are a number of tools, techniques, and procedures that can be used in the selection process. Companies generally use initial screening interviews, formal applications, in-depth interviews, reference and credit checks, physical examinations, and tests as selection tools. Each of these tools is examined next.

Initial Screening Interviews

The initial screening interview is used for the purpose of eliminating obviously unqualified candidates, thus saving the time of interviewers and applicants. The applicant is provided information about the company and general details about selling positions in it. A number of companies also ask applicants to complete interview application forms, which obtain information about the applicant's basic qualifications, education, experience, health, and so forth. The application form should not be long, and the applicant should be able to complete it in a few minutes. The purpose of the interview application form is to enable management to determine whether the applicant meets predetermined minimum qualifications.

Formal Applications

Although professional salespeople often have curriculum vitae to submit to prospective employers, many personnel experts believe a standard company application form makes it easier to assess applicants. A well-designed application form helps ensure that the same information is obtained in the same form from all candidates. The formal application form serves as a central record for all pertinent information collected during the selection process. A formal application form is filled out after a preliminary interview indicates that a candidate has potential as a company salesperson. The completed formal application amounts to a standardised written interview, since most of the information that it contains could be obtained through personal interviews.

Information requested on the application form usually includes name, address, position applied for, physical condition, educational background, work experience, membership in organisations, previous positions, reasons for leaving the applicant's last job, outside interests and activities, and personal references. Other important questions on the form relate directly to the sales position for which the application is made. Application forms will vary from company to company. On all forms, however, it is illegal to include any questions that are not related to the job.

In-Depth Interviews

The interview is the most used selection tool, and in some companies, it comprises the entire selection system. The personal interview is used to help decide if a person is right for the job. It can bring out personal characteristics that other selection devices are not able to reveal. In addition to probing into the applicant's history, personal interviews enable managers to gain insight into the applicant's mental abilities and personality. An interview provides a manager with the opportunity to assess a candidate's communication skills, intelligence, sociability, aggressiveness, empathy, ambition, and other traits related to the qualifications necessary for the job. The interview also serves as a two-way communication channel, meaning both the company and the applicant can ask questions and learn about each other.

The interviewer reviews the completed application form before the interview and refrains from asking questions that have already been answered. Looking over the completed application form indicates areas that require further questioning. An example of the interview form that addresses most of the areas of inquiry is presented in Table 6.1.

Types of Interviews

Interviews differ, depending on the number of questions that are prepared in advance and the extent to which the interview guides the conversation. Three main types are:

1. **the structured interview**, in which the interviewer asks each candidate the same set of questions. Structured interviews are useful for initial screening but are not useful for probing for in-depth information;

2. **the unstructured interview**, or the informal and

undirected interview—the goal of an unstructured interviewing approach is to get the candidate to talk freely on a variety of topics; and

3. **the semi structured interview**, in which the interviewer has a pre-planned list of major questions but allows time for interaction and discussion—this is a flexible approach and can be designed to meet the needs of different candidates as well as different interviews.

Reference and Credit Checks

If an applicant passes the personal interview, a reference check is often the next step. References provide information on the applicant not available from other sources. References are normally checked while the application form is processed and before the final interview takes place.

The best way to obtain information from references is by personal contact. This is because a majority of people are more frank orally than in writing. A telephone call may substitute for personal contact, when a reference is located at a distance. In an attempt to offset a tendency for references to be biased in favour of an applicant, many companies try to talk with persons not listed as references but who know the applicant. For references to be a useful selection device, the sales manager would need to be resourceful and pursue leads that are not directly given. People who are often excellent sources for candid appraisals include present or former employers, former customers, reputable citizens, mutual acquaintances, and teachers.

Table 6.1 Applicant Interview Form

Business Division

Applicant Interview Form

Applicant name: .... Date ....

Interview with: Time:

		Rating:
1.		5 --- Excellent
2.		4 --- Above Average
3.		3 --- Average
4.		2 --- Fair
		1 --- Poor

Directions: Check the square that most correctly reflects characteristics applicable to candidate. An outstanding candidate would score from 95 to 100.

	1	2	3	4	5
General appearance					
1. Neatness, dress					
2. Business image					
Impressions					
3. Positive mannerisms					
4. Speech, expressions					
5. Outgoing personality					
6. Positive attitude					
Potential sales ability					
7. Persuasively communicates					
8. Is Aggressive					
9. Sells and manages large accounts					
10. Makes executive calls					
11. Organizes and manages a territory					
12. Works with others					
13. Has had successful prior experience					
14. Has potential for career growth					
Maturity					
15. General intelligence, common sense					
16. Self-confidence					
17. Self-motivation, ambition					
18. Composure, stability					
19. Adaptability					
20. Sense of ethics					

General comments: ....

Overall rating (total score): ....

Would you recommend this candidate for the position? ....

Why or why not? ....

Source: M. W. Johnston and G. W. Marshall, *Sales Force Management* (Boston: McGraw-Hill, 2006), 285. Reprinted with permission of McGraw-Hill.

A number of firms run credit checks on applicants for sales positions. Credit files are compiled by local credit bureaus, and special reports are provided by such organisations. If a heavy burden of personal debt is found, it may indicate financial worries interfering with productivity or a motivating factor serving to spur productivity; to determine which requires further investigation.

Physical Examinations

Most firms require physical examinations, since good health is important to a salesperson's success. Many sales jobs require a degree of physical activity and stamina. Consequently, even though physical examinations are relatively expensive compared with other selection tools, many sales managers see them as valuable aids for evaluating candidates (Johnston and Marshall 2006). Because of the relative high cost, the physical examination is generally not given until a recruit has passed most of the steps in the selection process.

Psychological Tests

Psychological tests are aimed at measuring an applicant's mental abilities and personality traits. Psychological tests are the most controversial device made use of in the selection process. But research indicates that test profile data can be useful to management in the process of selecting and classifying sales applicants who are likely to be high performers.

Types of Psychological Tests

Seven basic psychological tests used in the selection process of sales personnel are explained next.

Intelligence (General Mental Ability) Tests

Intelligence tests are useful for determining whether an applicant has sufficient mental ability to perform a job successfully. Intelligence tests measure raw intelligence and trainability. Recent research has indicated that a salesperson's cognitive ability or intelligence is the best indicator of future job performance (Kern 1988). General intelligence tests are designed to measure an applicant's overall mental abilities by examining how well the applicant comprehends, reasons, and learns.

The Wonderlic Personnel Test (WPT; www.wonderlic.com) is one common general intelligence test. It is popular because it is short; it consists of fifty items and requires only about twelve minutes to complete. The WPT can be administered and scored with pencil and paper, on a personal computer, or on the Internet. When the Internet is used for the administration of the WPT, test results are emailed to the organisation. Finally, it is available in more than fifteen languages, including Chinese and Russian (Johnston and Marshall 2006). When the job to be filled requires special competence in one or a few areas of mental ability, a specialised intelligence test might be used to evaluate candidates. Tests are available for measuring such things as speed of learning, number facility, memory, logical reasoning, and verbal ability.

Knowledge Tests

Knowledge tests are designed to measure what the applicant knows about a certain product, service, market, and so forth.

Sales Aptitude Tests

Sales aptitude tests measure a person's innate or acquired social skills and selling know-how as well as tact and diplomacy. Sales aptitude tests are designed to determine whether an applicant has an interest in, or the ability to perform, certain tasks and activities. For example, the Strong Interest Inventory (www.cpp-db.com) asks respondents to indicate whether they like or dislike a variety of situations and activities. This can determine whether the applicant's interests are similar to those of people who are successful in a variety of different occupations, including sales. Other tests measure skills or abilities, such as mechanical or mathematical aptitude, that might be related to success in particular selling jobs (Johnston and Marshall 2006).

One problem with at least some aptitude tests is that instead of measuring a person's innate abilities, they measure current level of skill at certain tasks. At least some skills necessary for successful selling can be taught, or improved, through a well-designed training programme. Therefore, rejecting applicants because they currently do not have the necessary skills can mean losing people who could be trained to be successful salespeople.

Vocational Interest Tests

Vocational interest tests measure the applicant's vocational interest, the assumption being that a person is going to be more effective and stable if he or she has a strong interest in selling.

Personality Tests

Personality tests try to measure the behavioural traits believed necessary for selling, such as assertiveness, initiative, extroversion, emotional adjustment, self-confidence, and perseverance. For example, the Edwards Personal Preference Schedule measures twenty-four traits, including sociability, aggressiveness, and independence. Such tests, however, contain many questions, require substantial time to complete, and gather information about some traits that may be irrelevant for evaluating future salespeople. Consequently, more limited personality tests have been developed in recent years that concentrate on only a few traits that are thought to be directly relevant to a person's future success in sales. These are often designed and administered by individual testing services. For example, Walden Testing (www.waldentesting.com) has specific tests to assess an individual's selling skills (Johnston and Marshall 2006).

Polygraph Tests

The polygraph test, or the lie detector test, measures blood pressure, respiration, heartbeat, and skin response as indicators of personal honesty. Because of questions raised about its validity, the use of polygraph testing is restricted in most situations by legal authorities, except in very few situations, such as those involving national security.

Attitude and Lifestyle Tests

The main purpose for attitude and lifestyle tests is to assess honesty and spot drug abusers.

Guidelines for the Appropriate Use of Selection Tests

Historically, the use of selection tests has been controversial. Over the years, several concerns have been raised under legal and social pressure related to the lack of validity and possible discriminatory nature of some testing procedures. Nevertheless, selection tests have changed, and perhaps managers have learned more about how to use them as a legitimate part of the selection process.

The following are suggestions to improve the usefulness to sales managers of psychological tests as selection tools, as summarised by (Johnston and Marshall 2006):

1. Test scores should be considered as a single input in the selection decision. Managers should not rely on them to do the work of other parts of the selection process, such as interviewing and checking references. Candidates should not be eliminated solely on the basis of test scores.

2. Applicants should be tested on only those abilities and traits that management, on the basis of a thorough job analysis, has determined to be relevant for the specific job. Broad tests that evaluate a large number of traits not relevant to a specific job are probably inappropriate.

3. When possible, tests with built-in internal consistency checks should be used. Then the person who analyzes the test results can determine whether the applicant responded honestly or was faking some answers. Many recently designed tests ask similar questions with slightly different wording several times throughout the test. If respondents are

> answering honestly, they should always give the same response to similar questions.

4. A firm should conduct empirical studies to ensure that the tests are valid for predicting an applicant's future performance in the job. This kind of hard evidence of test validity is particularly important in view of the government's equal employment opportunity requirements.

As the Johnston and Marshall emphasise, tests can be useful selection tools if these suggestions are followed. In particular, tests can identify areas worthy of further investigation, if they are administered and interpreted before a final round of interviewing.

Making the Selection

After the completion of all other steps in the selection process, the firm must make a decision about whether or not to hire each applicant. The firm must review everything known about a particular applicant. The goals and ambitions of the applicant must be matched against present and future opportunities, challenges, and other types of rewards that are offered by the job and the firm.

A decision to hire is followed by a formal offer; the terms should be written for the protection of both the recruit and the firm. Most firms require that all new recruits sign contracts containing all important, job-related information. As Sahu and Raut (2003) point out, such an agreement contains a number of terms and conditions such as duties, authorities, sales territories, sales quota, remuneration, travelling expenses, the probation period, and so on.

Review Questions

1. What steps are involved in the selection process?
2. Why is it important for an organisation to have a well-planned programme?
3. Which tool is more important in the selection process, application forms or personal interviews? Why?
4. What are the basic tests that can be in the sales personnel process? Explain the purpose of each of each test.
5. Can you eliminate the personal biases and prejudices of interviewers so that they will conduct an interview impartially? Explain?

Chapter 7

Training the Sales Force

Introduction

The training programme is a vital link in the process of converting a recruit into a productive salesperson. It should be emphasised that the money spent on recruiting and selecting salespeople may be wasted if their hiring is not followed up with the proper training programme. Furthermore, experienced salespeople may not improve or even maintain their productivity if they are not provided with an adequate amount of continual training. In this chapter, we discuss developing and conducting a sales training programme. The two basic types of training programmes are initial training for new recruits and continuous training programmes for experienced salespeople. The decisions an executive makes regarding training vary with the type of training being considered.

This chapter discusses the many aspects of training the sales force. It covers the issues of the importance and objectives of sales training, the assignment of responsibility for sales training, training programme content, the methods for sales training, and the evaluation of training.

The Importance of Sales Training

The purpose of sales training is to achieve improved job performance. Training substitutes for, or supplements, experience; salespeople who are given training reach high job performance levels earlier. If sales training helps new salespeople to perform their jobs satisfactorily, the rates of sales force turnover declines, recruitment and selection costs fall, and the overall efficiency of the personal selling operation goes up.

Designing the Sales Training Programme

Designing a sales training programme depends on five major decisions. The specific training aims must be defined, the content decided, the training methods selected, the execution arrangements made, and the procedures set up to evaluate the results. These decisions are sometimes referred to as the O-C-M-E-E decisions—objective, content, methods, execution, and evaluation. Therefore, the following discussion relates to the elements of the O-C-M-E-E decisions.

Defining Training Objectives

Defining the specific objectives of the sales training programme is the first step in its planning. The objectives should be stated in realistic, quantifiable terms with respect to a specific time period. They should also be stated in written form, so that they can be used later in evaluating the programme's effectiveness. The specific objectives must be directly derived from the training needs as seen by the sales management. Training needs, then, must be identified.

Although the specific objectives of sales training may vary from firm to firm, there is some agreement on the broad objectives. Sales training is undertaken to increase productivity, improve morale, lower turnover, improve customer relations, and produce better management of time and territory. Each of these is explained next, as summarised by Churchill et al. (2000).

1. **Increase Productivity**. One objective of sales training is to provide trainees with the necessary skills so that their selling performance makes a positive contribution to the firm. In a relatively short time, sales training attempts to teach the skills possessed by the more experienced members of the sales force.

2. **Improve Morale**. An objective of sales training is to prepare trainees to perform tasks so that their productivity increases as quickly as possible. If sales trainees know what is expected of them, they will be less likely to experience the frustrations that arise from trying to perform a job without adequate preparation.

3. **Lower Turnover**. If sales training can lead to improved morale, then that should result in lower turnover. Turnover can result in customer problems, since many customers prefer continuity in their sales representatives. A customer who is called on by a sales representative who then suddenly quits may transfer business to other suppliers rather than wait for a new representative. Sales training alleviates such problems, by leading to lower turnover.

4. **Improve Customer Relations**. One benefit of sales training that accompanies lower turnover is continuity in customer relations. Having the same sales representative call on customers on a regular basis promotes customer loyalty, especially when the salesperson can handle customer questions, objections, and complaints. Customers place orders for their own benefits. Inadequately trained salespeople are usually not able to provide these benefits, and customer relations suffer.

5. **Manage Time and Territory Better**. Time and territory management is a subject in many sales training programmes. How much time should be devoted to calls on existing accounts, and how much time should go to calls on potential new accounts? How often should each class of account be called on? What is the most effective way of covering the territory to ensure that routes travelled are the most efficient with respect to miles driven and time spent?

Many sales training programmes provide salespeople with answers to these questions.

As indicated earlier, before deciding on the content of the training programme, there is the need to identify the initial and continuing training needs of the sales force. We look at these next.

Identifying Initial Training Needs

Determining the need for and specific objectives of an initial training programme requires analysis of three basic factors: (1) job specifications, (2) an individual trainee's background and experience, and (3) sales-related marketing policies. Each of these basic factors is explained next.

Job Specifications

The specifications needed to perform the job are outlined in the job specification. Not everybody possesses these qualifications at the time of hiring. The set of job specification requires being scrutinised for clues to the points on which new people would most likely need training. Other questions to be answered that will help in identifying specific training needs of newly recruited sales force include: How should salespeople apportion their time? Which duties require the greatest proportion of time? Which are neglected? Why? Which selling approaches are most effective?

Individual Trainee's Background and Experience

Each individual enters an initial sales training programme with a unique educational background and experience record. The gap between the qualifications in the job specifications and those already possessed by a trainee represents the nature and amount of needed training. Determining recruits' real training needs will be essential to developing initial training programmes of maximum benefit to both the company and the trainee.

Sales-Related Marketing Policies

Sales-related marketing policies must be analysed to determine initial training needs. Differences in products and markets mean differences in selling practices and policies, which, in turn, point to differences in training programme needs. Differences in promotion, price, marketing channel, and physical distribution all have implications for initial sales training.

Identifying Continuing Training Needs

Determining the specific aims for a refresher, or continuing, sales training programme requires identification of specific training needs of experienced sales force. Basic changes in product and markets give rise to the need for training, as do changes in company sales-related marketing policies, procedures, and organisation. Refresher, or continuing, training can help the sales force understand and adapt to changes quickly, increasing the sales force's overall selling effectiveness.

As Donaldson (1990) suggests, training should cover the gap between what a salesperson needs to know and what is known at present. According to him, the training gap will vary when:

- new people are recruited,
- a salesperson takes on a new territory,
- new products are introduced,
- new business or new market segments are to be won,
- new company procedures or policies are introduced,
- an individual is being considered for promotion, or
- selling habits are poor or inappropriate.

Deciding Training Content

Initial sales training programmes are broader in scope and coverage than continuing, or refresher programmes are. Initial training programmes provide instruction covering all the important aspects of performance of the salesperson's job, including product knowledge, knowledge of competitors and the overall industry, customer and market knowledge, company knowledge, and knowledge of the selling progress. Continuing training programmes concentrate on specific aspects of the job where experienced salespeople have deficiencies. Therefore, the following discussion relates to the content of initial sales training programmes. Generally, a salesperson should be trained in the following areas.

Product Knowledge

Some product training is crucial to any initial sales training programme. New salespeople must know about the products and how they are use by customers, as well as believe in the products' merits and the products' usefulness in solving customers' problems. After trainees are informed about the products and their uses, they should be allowed to see or use the products in order to gain as much technical understanding of them as possible. Product knowledge is essential to a salesperson's self-confidence and enthusiastic job performance. New salespeople learn how to relate to company products to the fulfilment of customers requirements, thus equipping themselves for effective selling.

Knowledge of Competitors and the Industry

Sales trainees should be informed about industry trends and competitive tactics and need to understand how these may affect demand for the company's products. Salespeople need to know the important characteristics of competitors' products and their uses and applications. They should know the strengths and weaknesses of competitive products. Through this knowledge, the salespeople can structure sales presentations to emphasise superior features of the company's products.

Customer and Market Knowledge

Sales trainees need to know who the customers are, their locations, the particular products in which they are interested, their buying habits and motives, and the financial condition of customers. In effect, salespeople need to know who buys what, as well as why and how they buy. Consequently, effective sales training programmes must offer salespeople the opportunity to be trained to create cooperative partnerships with their customers.

Company Knowledge

The salesperson needs to be aware of the company's policies in general, as well as the company's specific selling policies. The sales training programme should include coverage of all sales-related marketing policies and the reasoning behind them. The salesperson must have knowledge about company pricing policy, for instance, to answer customers' questions. The salesperson must be fully informed on other policies, such as those relating to product services, spare parts and repairs, credit extension, and customer relations.

The initial training programme also teaches the salesperson about the company's specific policies concerning selling practices, such as how many sales calls to make per day, how to handle returns, and how to write up orders.

Knowledge of the Selling Process

New salespeople need basic instruction in the steps involved in selling as well as in selling techniques that can be applied in different circumstances. The basic steps of the selling process involve prospecting, planning the call, approaching the prospect, making the sales presentation, meeting objections, closing the sale, and following up.

Selecting Training Methods

The planners next select training methods. There is a variety of training methods that can be employed to train the new sales recruits, but the programme content often limits those that are appropriate. It is essential to select those training methods that most effectively convey the desired content. The most commonly used training methods are discussed in the next section.

Lectures

Lectures are used extensively in sales training. Lectures are used because they can present more information to a large number of trainees in a short period of time than any other teaching method. However, only a limited amount of lecturing should be employed in sales training programmes, because the lecture features passive, rather than active, trainee participation. For effective lecturing, the sessions should be short and interspersed with demonstrations and visual aids. As Donaldson (1990) submits, most sales training by lectures incorporates other backup methods such as slides, flip charts, and audio- and videocassettes.

Personal Conferences

Training can take place in personal conferences in which the trainer and the trainee discuss and analyse problems in selling. In the personal conference, the trainer, usually a sales executive or a sales supervisor, and trainee jointly analyze problems, such as effective use of selling time, route planning and call scheduling, and handling unusual selling problems. Personal conferences are held in such places as offices, bars, restaurants, motel rooms, and other places.

Personal conferences should provide opportunities for two-way communication. Salespeople should have the chance to bring up problems and seek advice or counselling. These sessions should also present opportunities for the sales manager to offer positive reinforcement to the salesperson through praise and recognition for well-performed duties. The personal conference can be a very effective learning tool, and it can establish good rapport between the trainee and the sales executive or trainer (Anderson et al. 1992).

Demonstrations

Demonstrations are appropriate for conveying information on such topics as new products and selling techniques. Demonstrating how a new product works and its uses is effective—much more so than lecturing on the same material.

Role-Playing

Role-playing is learning by doing. In role-playing, trainees act out parts in planned problem situations. With this technique, artificial sales situations are constructed to educate salespeople what to do and what not to do in a given situation. The role-playing session begins with the trainer describing the situation and the different personalities involved. The trainer provides required props and then designates trainees to play the salesperson, prospect, and other characters. Each plays his or her assigned role. After that, they, together with other group members and the trainer, appraise each player's effectiveness and suggest how the performance of each might have been improved.

Role-playing can help trainees learn to handle unforeseen developments that often arise in selling situations. It also gives the trainer a chance to work with trainees on voice, poise, mannerisms, speech, and movements. Through role-playing, trainees can be made aware of weak points. They also learn the importance of being knowledgeable about the product, the company, the competition, customers, and the industry (Anderson et al. 1992).

Group Discussions

Group discussions can be used in sales training programmes. The simplest form is one in which the trainer leads and stimulates talk and participation on the part of the trainees. Case studies have been employed widely as a device to stimulate group discussion. The trainees are given a case to study, and then the trainer leads a group discussion to analyse and solve the problems involve in the case.

Simulation Games

Simulation games help in learning by allowing the trainees to assume the roles of decision makers in either their own or customers' organisations through successive rounds of play. In simulation games, which are highly structured and based on reality, trainees must make decisions about the timing and size of orders, sales forecasts, advertising, pricing, and so forth. The trainees are then given feedback concerning the outcomes of their decisions.

On-the-Job Training

On-the-job, or coach-and-pupil, training occurs when an experienced salesperson is assigned to a trainee to teach him or her about the job and how to sell. This method combines telling, showing, practising, and evaluating. The coach begins by describing particular selling situations, explaining various techniques and approaches that might be used effectively. Next, accompanied by the pupil, the coach makes actual sales calls, discussing each with the trainee afterward. Then, under the coach's supervision, the trainee makes sales calls, each one being followed by discussion and appraisal. Gradually, the trainee works more and more on his or her own, with less frequent supervision.

Programmed Learning

Programmed learning breaks down subject matter into numbered instructional units called frames, which are incorporated into a book or are microfilmed for use with a teaching machine. Each frame contains an explanation of a specific point, plus question or problem for the trainee to use in testing his or her understanding. Trainees check their answers by referring to another designated frame. If the answer is correct, the trainee is directed to new material; if it is incorrect, additional explanation is provided, and the trainee is retested on the point before going on to new material. Thus, trainees check their own progress as they work through the materials and move through them at their own speeds.

Correspondence Courses

Correspondence courses are used in both initial and continuing sales training. In the insurance field, for instance, this method is employed to acquaint new salespeople with industry fundamentals and to instruct salespeople in basic sales techniques. This method is used also to train non-company sales force, such as distributors' salespeople, to improve their knowledge of the manufacturer's product lines and selling techniques. This method alone is not very effective, but when combined with other training methods, it can be a very helpful learning tool.

Sales Manuals

A sales manual is an easy reference material for the salesperson. It is a textbook that contains information such as company history, organisational responsibilities, and fringe benefits available to the sales personnel.

Job Rotation

Many companies follow a practise of rotating the sales recruits through various departments of a company. They may spend time in the factory learning how the product is made, in the credit and billing department to see how orders are processed, and in the advertising and marketing research departments to understand the services these functions perform for the salespeople. One interesting approach is to have each salesperson spend time with some of the company's customers.

Group versus Individual Training Methods

Of the training methods discussed, lecturing, role-playing, group discussion, and simulation games are group methods. Personal conferences, on-the-job training, programmed learning, correspondence courses, sales manuals, and job rotation are individual methods. The demonstration is either a group or an individual method, depending on whether the audience is a group or an individual.

Executing Sales Training Programmes

The execution step requires organisational decisions. Who will be the trainees? Who will do the training? When will the training take place? Where will the training site be? The trainers should be notified, necessary travel arrangements made, and living accommodations arranged. Effective execution of the programme will also depend upon instructional skills as well as coordination of planning and housekeeping details. Discussion in this section focuses on these issues.

Organisation for Sales Training

The execution step requires five main organisational decisions:
(1) Who will be the trainees?; (2) Who will do the training?; (3)
When will the training take place?; (4) Where will the training
site be?; and (5) What instructional materials and training aids
should be used? Each of these decisions is discussed next.

Who Will Be the Trainees?

A majority of companies identify the trainees for their initial
sales training programme when they put sales job descriptions
into forms and hire sales job applicants. The general practice
with continuing sales training programmes is to select trainees
according to some criteria, which commonly include: (1) reward
for good performance, (2) punishment for poor performance,
(3) convenience (of trainee and trainer), and (4) seniority.

Who Will Do the Training?

The main issues to consider here include: (1) initial sales
training, (2) continuing sales training, (3) sales training staff,
(4) training the trainers, and (5) outside experts. Each of these
is looked at next.

Initial Sales Training

While initial sales training is a line function in some
companies, in others it is a staff function. In a situation
where it is a line function, responsibility for initial sales
training is assigned to the human resource director,
and sales management has an advisory role.

Continuing Sales Training

It is the top sales executive's responsibility for
continuing sales training. The top sales executive is in
the best position to recognise the need and to design
and execute appropriate sales training programmes
dealing with issues, including introduction of
new products, adoption of revised sales policies,
perfection of improved selling techniques, and similar
developments.

Sales Training Staff

Top sales executives normally delegate sales training performances to subordinates. Many a large company has a sales training director, reporting to the top sales executive. The director conducts some training and coordinates it on a decentralised basis by regional and/ or district sales managers.

Training the Trainers

For effective training programmes, many companies have training programmes for sales trainers. The starting point is to identify the subjects the trainers should know thoroughly, including the company and its policies, the products, the customers and their problems, the salesperson's job, and sales techniques.

Outside Experts

Most companies hire outside experts (consultants) to conduct portions of sales training programmes. Several outside training consultants present sessions on sales techniques and, through broad and long experience, achieve high effectiveness.

When Will the Training Take Place?

The main issues to consider here include: (1) timing group versus individual training, (2) timing initial sales training programmes, and (3) timing continuing sales training programmes. We focus on each of these next.

Timing Group versus Individual Training

There are arguments about the timing of group and individual training. The majority of sales executives argue that newly recruited trainees should be given formal group training before starting to sell. A minority group, however, assigns trainees to selling jobs before sending them on to sales school.

Timing Initial Sales Training Programmes

The timing of initial sales training depends upon the number of new personnel trained each year, which, in turn, depends upon the size of the sales force, sales force turnover, and management's plans for changing the sales force size.

Timing of Continuing Sales Training Programmes There is the belief that effective sales management requires continuous training and learning. Issues concerning new products, new refinements of selling techniques, new product application and uses, new customer problems, new selling aids, and new selling suggestions require that each salesperson's training continues as long as he or she is on the job.

Where Will the Training Site Be?

The location of a training programme is determined by the extent to which it should be centralised. Some companies hold initial sales training programmes at the central offices; others conduct separate programmes that usually involve organised training schools, periodic conventions, or seminars held in a central location such as the home office. Decentralised training can involve one or more types of training, such as office instruction, use of experienced salespeople, on-the-job training, or travelling sales clinics.

Training Aids and Instructional Materials

Successful execution of sales training programmes depends upon training aids and instructional materials. These vary for different companies as well as for different aims, contents, and methods. The training aids used by most companies include manuals, other printed materials, and sight or sound equipment. Manuals or workbooks are used in most formal group sales training programmes. Good manuals contain outlines of the main presentations, related reading materials, statements of learning objectives for each session, thought-provoking questions, cases and problems, and directions for sessions that involve role-playing or simulation games.

Training aids are supplementary devices capable of transmission of sight and/or sound stimuli used in sales training programmes. Blackboards, posters, motion picture projectors, tape recorders, videotape recorders, and other playback equipment can be effective aids in training programmes.

Evaluating Sales Training Programmes

The evaluation step focuses on measuring programme effectiveness. It is important that, once a sales training programme has been carried out, the programme's effectiveness be evaluated. That is, the sales manager must determine how well overall objectives and specific goals have been met.

An essential aspect of the sales manager's job is determining how a sales training programme is to be evaluated. Four levels at which training programmes can be evaluated, as summarised by Stevenson (1989), are illustrated in Table 7.1. First, at the reaction level the trainees' attitudes and feelings toward the training programme are measured. Second, evaluation at the knowledge level assesses how well the trainees learned basic principles, facts, and so on during the training programme. Third, evaluation at the attitude level measures changes in behaviour as a result of the training. Such evaluation is usually achieved by collecting questionnaires from supervisors, subordinates and even customers. However, such assessments are often subjective, because of the personal relationships that frequently develop during training. Finally, at the results level, changes in performance are measured. This is done by plotting salespeople's performance before and after training and comparing the results against training programme objectives.

Table 7.1 Training Evaluation Levels

Levels	Measures	Methods
Reaction	Attitudes and feelings	Survey, comment sheets, exit interview, and discussion

Knowledge	Principles, facts, and techniques	Tests
Attitude	Changes in behaviour	Questionnaires and observation
Results	Changes in performance	Change in sales, profits, expenses, etc

An example of an evaluation form that would be distributed to trainees in order to assess their reaction to the sales training programme is presented in Table 7.2. The sample evaluation form in Table 7.3 would be used by trainers to assess trainees' changes in attitude and behaviours throughout the training programme. As organisations spend more and more money on sales training each year, they are becoming more interested in evaluating their training programmes. Research suggests that a majority of organisations today use some form of evaluation for their sales training programmes (Anderson et al. 1992).

Table 7.2 Training Programme Evaluation Form

	Strongly Agree	Agree	Neutral	Disagree	Strongly Disagree
The instructor was well prepared.	--------	-------	---------	----------	---------
The material was relevant.	--------	---- ---	---------	----------	---------

| The instructor's objectives were made clear. | ---------- | ---- --- | --------- | --------- | --------- |
| Visual aids were effectively used. | ---------- | ---- --- | --------- | --------- | --------- |

Table 7.3 Field Evaluation and Career Development Report

CONFIDENTIAL	**4 Superior 1 Satisfactory**
Date ……………………..	**3 Excellent 0 Needs 2 Average Improvement**

Salesperson --------------------------------
Regional Manager --------------------------------

		0	1	2	3	4
1.	***Sales Profile***					
	Knowledge of product					
	Product-line representation and stock balance					
	New accounts opened and follow-up of leads					
	Knowledge of advertising and sales promotion procedures					
	Sales conference preparation and participation					
	Creative selling techniques					
	Ability to meet assigned goals					

2. ***Time and Territory Management***
   Account analysis
   Workload analysis
   Allocation of time for maximum
   productivity
   Customer sales planning
   Territory coverage
   Territorial control

3. ***Customer Relations***
   Is familiar with all company
   policies and procedures
   Creates confidence with accounts
   Handles complaints locally where
   possible
   Has rapport with customers
   Is in control of credit problems

4. ***Personal Traits***
   Appearance
   Reliability
   Attitude, job, and company

5. ***Growth Development***
   Potential for advancement
   Motivation level
   Desire for advancement

Source: R. E. Anderson, J. F. Hair, Jr., and A. J. Bush, *Professional Sales Management* (New York: McGraw-Hill, 1992), 290. Reprinted with permission of McGraw-Hill.

Review Questions

1. Why should sales training and sales force development be thought of as a long-term, ongoing process?

2. Briefly discuss the planning decisions that must be made by sales managers in designing sales training programmes.

3. Name and discuss the five basic elements that initial sales training programmes must cover. Are these elements any different from elements of refresher training programmes?

4. How can the sales manager keep top-notch sales representatives interested in continual training programmes?

5. How can sales managers prove the cost-effectiveness of their sales training programmes?

Chapter 8

Sales Territories

Introduction

Establishing sales territories helps in matching selling efforts with sales opportunities. Salespeople are assigned the responsibility for serving particular groupings of customers and prospects and for providing contact points with the markets. Effective assignment of sales personnel to territories lends direction to the planning and control of sales operations.

This chapter explains the sales territory concept and the alternative approaches for assigning and managing sales territories to achieve sales objectives efficiently and effectively. It explains the procedures for setting up and revising sales territories and for scheduling and routing to optimise sales coverage and minimise wasted time.

The Sales Territory Concept

As Still et al. (1988) point out, the emphasis in the sales territory concept is on customers and prospects rather than on the area in which an individual salesperson works. A sales territory may be defined as a group of present and potential customers who are assigned to a salesperson, branch, dealer, or distributor for a given period. Good sales territories are made up of customers who have money to spend and the willingness to spend it. In general, a sales territory is a grouping of present and potential customers who can be called upon conveniently and economically by an individual salesperson.

Reasons for Establishing or Revising Sales Territories

Sales territories are established, and subsequently revised as market conditions dictate, to facilitate the planning and control of sales operations. But, typically, the more specific reasons sales managers have for establishing territories include the following.

Provide Proper Market Coverage

If sales management does not have proper market coverage because it has not matched selling efforts with sales opportunities effectively, competitors have a better match, and they obtain the orders. In effect, if sales territories are established intelligently and if assignments of sales personnel to them are carefully made, it is possible to obtain proper market coverage. Sales territories should be big enough to represent reasonable workloads for the salesperson while assuring that all prospects that are potentially profitable can be visited as often as needed.

Control Selling Expenses

A well-designed sales territory combined with a careful salesperson assignment would result in low selling expenses and high sales volumes. Sales personnel spending fewer nights away from home reduces or eliminates a lot of charges for lodging, food, and transportation. These savings, in addition to high sales volumes, would minimise the ratio of selling expenses to sales.

Assist in Evaluating Sales Force

Good territorial design assists the sales manager in evaluating sales force performance. The sales manager can evaluate the salespeople on the basis of their performance compared with the territory's potential.

Contribute to Sales Force Morale

As Anderson et al. (1992) emphasise, well-designed sales territories can stimulate and motivate sales personnel, improve morale, increase interest, and build a more effective sales force.

Setting up sales territories defines jobs objectively, assigns each salesperson a reasonable workload, and encourages the sales force to perform well.

Aid in the Coordination of Personal Selling with Other Marketing Functions

Well-designed sales territories can aid management in improving the coordination of personal selling and other marketing functions. Generally, a sales and cost analysis can be done more easily on a territory basis than on an entire-market basis.

Strengthen Customer Relations

Well-designed sales territories enable salespeople to spend more time with present and potential customers and less time travelling. As Anderson et al observe, the more salespeople can learn about their customers, the better they can understand the customers' problems and the more comfortable their relationship becomes. Properly designed sales territories would need to result in regularly scheduled sales calls on customers.

Determining the Sales Force Size

The need to consider sales, costs, productivity, and turnover makes sales force size a difficult decision. Fortunately, some analytical tools are available to help management process relevant information and evaluate sales force size alternatives more fully. Four commonly used approaches are: (1) breakdown, (2) workload, (3) increment, and (4) turnover. The details of each of these analytical tools are explained in the next section.

The Breakdown Method

A relatively simple approach for calculating sales force size is the breakdown method. It assumes that an accurate sales forecast is available. This forecast is then "broken down" to determine the number of salespeople needed to generate the forecasted level of sales. With the breakdown method, an average salesperson is treated as a salesperson unit, and each salesperson unit is assumed to possess the same productivity potential. To determine the size of the sales force needed, divide total forecasted sales for the firm by the sales likely to be produced by each individual. Mathematically,

$$N = \frac{S}{P}$$

Where:

N = number of sales personnel needed

S = forecasted sales volume

P = estimated productivity of one salesperson unit.

Illustrated Example

Assume that a firm forecasts sales of GH¢5 million for next year. If salespeople generate an average of GH¢250,000 in annual sales, then the firm needs 20 salespeople to achieve the GH¢5 million sales forecast. Thus:

GH¢5,000,000/GH¢250,000 = 20 salespeople (sales force size)

The basic advantage of the breakdown method is its ease of development. The approach is straightforward, and the mathematical calculations are simple. However, the approach is weak conceptually. The concept underlying the calculations is that sales determine the number of salespeople needed. This puts "the cart before the horse," because the number of salespeople employed by a firm is an important determinant of firm sales. A sales forecast should be based on a given sales force size. The addition of salespeople should increase the forecast, and the elimination of salespeople should decrease it (Ingram et al. 2004).

The Workload Method

The basic premise underlying the workload approach (or build-up method) is that all sales personnel should carry an equal amount of work. Management estimates the work required to serve the entire market. The workload method allows the number of salespeople needed to be calculated, given that the company knows the number of calls per year it wishes its salespeople to make on different classes of customer. The method consists of first determining how much selling effort is needed to cover the firm's market adequately. Then the number of salespeople required to provide that amount of selling effort is calculated. The basic formula is

Number of salespeople = $\dfrac{\text{Total selling effort needed}}{\text{Average selling effort per salesperson}}$

Illustrated Example

Assume that a firm determines that 40,800 sales calls are needed in its market area and that a salesperson can make an average of 600 annual sales calls—then 68 salespeople are needed to provide the desired level of selling effort. Thus:

40,800/600 = 68 salespeople

The key factor in the workload approach is the total amount of selling effort needed. Several workload methods can be used, depending on whether single-factor, portfolio, or decision models were used for determining the allocation of effort to accounts. Each workload method offers a different way to calculate how many sales calls to make to all accounts and prospects during any time period. When the sales call allocation strategies are summarised across all accounts and prospects, the total amount of selling effort for a time period is determined. Thus, the workload approach integrates the sales force size decision with account effort allocation strategies.

The workload approach is relatively simple to develop, although this simplicity depends on the specific method used to determine total selling effort needs. The approach is also sound conceptually, because sales force size is based on selling effort needs established by account effort allocation decisions. It is worthy to note, however, that the workload approach is presented in a simplified manner here by considering only selling effort. A more realistic presentation would incorporate non-selling time considerations. (e.g., travel time and planning time) in the analysis. Although incorporating these considerations does not change the basic workload concept, it does make the calculations more complex and cumbersome (Ingram et al. 2004). The main drawbacks of this method are that salespeople are not alike in their abilities and that all customers do not have similar characteristics and requirements. For example, all salespeople would not be able to average an equal number of daily calls. However, the method can be used in conjunction with management's knowledge of its market.

The workload approach is suited for all types of selling situations. Sales organisations can adapt the basic approach to their specific situation through the method used to calculate total selling effort. The most sophisticated firms can use decision models for this purpose, whereas other firms might use portfolio models or single-factor approaches.

The Incremental Method

The most rigorous approach for determining sales force size is the incremental approach. Its basic concept is that sales representatives should be added as long as the incremental profit produce by their addition exceeds the incremental costs. An example of these calculations is provided in Table 8.1. At 100 salespeople, marginal profits exceed marginal costs by GH¢10,000. This relationship continues until sales force size reaches 102. At 102 salespeople, the marginal profit equals marginal costs, and total profits are maximised. If the firm added one more salesperson, total profits would be reduced, because marginal costs would exceed marginal profits by GH¢5,000. Thus, the optimal sales force size for this example is 102.

The major advantage of the incremental approach is that it quantifies the important relationships between sales force size, sales, and costs, making it possible to assess the potential sales and profit impacts of different sales force sizes. It forces management to view the sales force size decision as one that affects both the level of sales that can be generated and the costs associated with producing each sales level.

The incremental method is, however, somewhat difficult to develop. Relatively complex response functions must be formulated to predict sales at different sales force sizes (sales = *f* [sales force size]. Developing these response functions requires either historical data or management's judgment. Thus, the incremental approach cannot be used for new sales forces where historical data and accurate judgments are not possible (Ingram et al. 2004).

Table 8.1 Incremental Approach

Number of Salespeople	Marginal Salesperson Profit Contribution	Marginal Salesperson Cost
100	GH¢85,000	GH¢75,000
101	GH¢80,000	GH¢75,000
102	GH¢75,000	GH¢75,000
103	GH¢70,000	GH¢75,000

Turnover

As Ingram et al. (2004) observe, all the analytical tools incorporate various elements of sales and costs in their calculations. Therefore, they directly address productivity issues but do not directly consider turnover in the sales force size calculations. When turnover considerations are important, management should adjust the recommended sales force size produced by any of the analytical methods to reflect expected turnover rates. For example, if an analytical tool recommends a sales force size of 100 for a firm that experiences 20 percent annual turnover, the effective sales force size should be adjusted to 120. Recruiting, selecting, and training plans should be based on the 120 sales force size.

Procedures for Setting Up Sales Territories

After the number of sales territories has been determined, the sales manager will be able to address territory design questions. In setting up or in revising sales territories, there are five steps: (1) select a basic geographic control unit, (2) make an account analysis, (3) develop a salesperson workload analysis, (4) combine geographic control units into territories, and (5) assign sales personnel to territories. Each of these steps is discussed next.

Select a Basic Geographic Control Unit

The starting point in setting up territories is the selection of a basic geographic control unit. The most commonly used control units are towns, cities, code areas, metropolitan areas, and regional and trading areas. There are two reasons for selecting a small control unit. One reason is that a small unit will help management in identifying the exact geographic location of sales potential. Secondly, the use of small geographic control areas will make management's task of adjusting the territories much easier.

Make an Account Analysis

The next step is to conduct an audit of each geographic control unit. The purpose of this audit is to identify customers and prospects and determine how much sales potential exists for each account. First, accounts must be identified by name, making use of such sources as trade directories, professional association membership lists, directories of companies, etc. Having identified potential buyers (accounts), management next estimates the sales potential for all accounts in each geographic control unit.

Develop a Salesperson Workload Analysis

A salesperson workload analysis is an estimate of the time and effort required to cover each geographic control unit. This estimate is based on an analysis of the number of accounts to be called on, the frequency of the calls, the length of each call, the travel time required, and the non-selling time. The outcome of the workload analysis estimate is the formation of a sales call pattern for each geographic control unit.

Combine Geographic Control Units into Sales Territories

The sales manager next combines adjoining basic control units into larger geographic sales territories of roughly equal sales potential. Adjoining units are combined to prevent salespeople from having to crisscross paths while skipping over geographic areas covered by another representative. Formerly, the sales manager developed a list of tentative sales territories by manually combining adjoining units, which, in most cases, resulted in uneven split of control units and territories. This could result in disputes about territory boundaries. Today, computers are handling this task in a much shorter time period.

Assign Sales Personnel to Territories

When an optimal territory alignment has been obtained, it is time for the sales manager to assign salespeople to territories. Sales personnel vary in physical condition, ability, initiative, and effectiveness and will represent the range of available selling talent. It is suggested that management assign each salesperson to the particular territory where his or her relative contribution to profit is the highest. A reasonable and desirable workload for one salesperson may overload another and cause frustration.

Revising Sales Territories

A sales territory should not be considered a permanent unit. The following factors may suggest the need for territory revision:

- **Growth in Firm.** As a company grows, it will normally need a large sales force to cover the market adequately. If the firm does not hire additional sales personnel, the sales force will probably only move lightly over the territory, instead of covering it intensely.

- **Overestimation of Sales Potential.** Territories may also need revision because of an overestimation of sales potential. For instance, a territory might be too small for a good salesperson to earn an adequate income.

- **Environmental Changes.** Certain environmental changes could also warrant the revision of a sales territory. In a situation of drastic price increases of a product, such as oil, many consumers may become cautious with their purchasing decisions. The resultant fall of sales in the market will cause companies to revise sales territories accordingly.

- **Overlapping Territories.** Overlapping territories are another reason for territory revision. This problem usually happens when territories are split, and it can cause a great amount of friction in the sales force.

- **Territory Jumping.** When one salesperson jumps into another salesperson's territory in search of business, territory revisions may be necessary. This is an unethical practice that will cause problems within the sales force. Generally, territory jumping leads to higher costs, selling inefficiencies, bitterness, and low morale in the sales force.

Scheduling and Routing Sales Personnel

Another important element of time and territory management is scheduling calls and planning movement around the sales territory. Scheduling and routing plans aim to maintain the lines of communication, to optimise sales coverage, and to minimise wasted time.

Scheduling refers to establishing a fixed time (day and hour) for visiting a customer's business. Routing is the travel pattern used in working a territory. Some sales companies prefer to determine the formal path or route that their salespeople travel when covering their territory. In such cases, management will need to develop plans that are feasible, flexible, and profitable to the company and the individual salesperson and that are satisfactory to the customer.

Advantages of Routing

Well-designed routing systems enable the company to:

1. **reduce travel time and selling costs.** A careful routing plan can reduce time and costs, thereby giving the salesperson more time to spend productively with customers. Much backtracking, travel time, and other non-selling time is eliminated, and scheduled call frequency fits customers' needs.

2. **improve territory coverage.** A routing and scheduling plan should also help improve the coverage of territory; it minimises wasted time.

3. **improve communication.** It helps to establish communication between management and the sales force in terms of the location and activities of individual salespeople. When the sales manager is informed at all times of salespeople's whereabouts in the field, it is easier to contact them to provide needed information or last-minute instructions.

In developing route patterns, management must know the salesperson's exact day and time of sales calls for each account; approximate waiting time; sales time; miscellaneous time for contacting people like the promotional manager, for checking on inventory, or for handling returned merchandise; and travel time between accounts.

Using Computers in Territory Management

It is significant to acknowledge how computers have taken over the time-consuming task of designing and aligning territories. Many sales managers are increasingly employing computers and mapping software in designing and revising their sales territories. This is much faster and more comprehensive than plotting and analyzing territories manually by the traditional breakdown or build-up method. The computer technology is known as a geographic information system (GIS). GIS provides an in-depth understanding of sales territories by bringing multiple layers of information about that territory and then presenting it in an easy-to-understand graphic or map. The recent development of TIGER (Topographically Integrated Geographically Encoded Records) and its related software is one example. A complete GIS consists of the following four elements, as summarised by Spiro et al. (2008):

1. **Software.** GIS requires software that can store, analyse, and graphically display information about the sales territory.

2. **Hardware.** A standard desktop computer, running a Windows operating system, is typically sufficient. A quality, colour printer is also necessary.

3. **Data.** Generally, the GIS output will be more valuable as the amount of inputted data about the territory (i.e., the layers of information) increases. The data include image data such as aerial photographs or satellite images as well as data about customer locations, call frequencies, sales, potentials, and so on.

4. **Trained People.** An individual with training, or at least practical experience, with GIS must operate the system. GIS has become such a critical part of strategic planning that some companies have created a new position: geographic information officer.

In recent years, electronic spreadsheet programmes have become widely used for sales analysis, planning, and control. Other programmes allow sales managers to keep track of prospects, leads, and product enquiries all the way through to the after-sale follow-up. As Collins (1984) submits, software can evaluate the quality and cost of leads according to the various media that produced them or to the performance of individual sales reps.

Review Questions

1. Why is it important to establish sales territories that are equal?

2. Why is it important to match the right salesperson with the right territory?

3. What are some of the signals indicating that a company's territorial structure may need revising?

4. What are some advantages and disadvantages of routing?

5. Explain the function of routing as a managerial device for planning and controlling the activities of the sales force.

Chapter 9

Sales Quotas

Introduction

Sales quotas are quantitative objectives assigned to sales organisational units. Quotas are used as standards for appraising selling effectiveness. They specify desired performance levels for sales volume; such budgeted items as expenses, gross margins, and net profit; selling and non–selling-related activities. They help in planning and evaluating sales force activities. Thus, sales quotas are an important device in the strategic planning, control, and evaluation of a marketing unit's sales activities. When setting sales quotas, the sales manager should consider the goals and strategies developed in the marketing planning. The effectiveness of quotas depends on both the information used in setting them up and management's administration of the system. Sales quotas are based on the company's sales forecasts and cost estimates and on the market's sales potential. Therefore, accurate data, as well as administrative expertise, are required for an effective quota system.

This chapter addresses the different types of sales quotas; their purposes; and how they are developed, measured, and administered.

The Purpose of Quotas

Quotas facilitate the planning and control of the field selling effort in a number of ways. They serve several purposes. They provide goals and incentives for the salespeople. They are also used to evaluate the performance of the salespeople, control the salesperson's activities, and uncover strengths and weaknesses

144

in the selling structure. Furthermore, they help improve the effectiveness of the compensation plan, control selling expenses, and enhance sales contests. These purposes are discussed in the next section.

Providing Goals and Incentives

In business, as in any other walk of life, individuals usually perform better if their activities are guided by standards and goals. A quota furnishes salespeople with a standardised measure of sales ability. It provides a goal for them to strive for and inspires them to reach that goal. To enhance the motivational effect of a quota, it needs to be realistic and attainable. The salespeople should feel very positive about their ability to attain the quota so that they do not quit when times get tough. They must also feel that attainment of the quota is imperative to maintaining their position with the company and that performance above and beyond the quota will be recognised (Anderson et al. 1992).

Evaluating Performance

Quotas provide a means for determining which salespeople, other units of the sales organisation, or distributive outlets are doing an average, below-average, or above-average job. For example, territorial sales volume quotas are standards for measuring territorial sales performance.

Controlling the Salesperson's Activities

Quotas provide the means for management to direct and control the activities of the sales force. Salespeople's activity quotas—for example, calling on new accounts and giving a minimum number of demonstrations—are designed to make sure that salespeople perform their duties and stress those duties that are most important to the company. If the salesperson does not attain these quotas, then management will be able to take corrective action immediately, before the situation deteriorates.

Uncovering Strengths and Weaknesses in the Selling Structure

By using a quota system, the company can see certain strengths and weaknesses within its selling structure and work toward improving the one and rectifying the other. A significant sales shortfall for the quota in a particular territory will call for the cause to be determined. If the quota is easily exceeded, the reasons for that must also be analyzed.

Improving the Compensation Plan's Effectiveness

A quota can play a significant role in the company's sales compensation plan. Quotas can furnish incentives to salespeople who are paid straight salary. Salespeople in some companies must exceed the quota before they start to earn any commission. A salesperson knows, too, that a creditable performance in meeting assigned quotas reflects favourably on him or her when it is time for a salary review (Spiro et al. 2008).

Controlling the Selling Expenses

Quotas are also designed to keep selling costs at a minimum. Management can often encourage expense control by the use of expense quotas alone, without tying them to the compensation plan. By the imposition of a limit on the amount of money that sales force may spend on meals, lodging, etc., management can control the costs of selling.

Enhancing Sales Contests

Sales quotas are used frequently in conjunction with sales contests. Sales contests can be powerful incentives and motivating forces for salespeople. Companies often use "performance against quota" as the main basis for determining awards in sales contests. Sales contests are more powerful incentives if all participants feel that they have a more or less equal chance of winning.

Types of Quotas

There are four basic types of quotas, including:

- sales volume quotas,
- financial quotas,
- activity quotas, and
- combination quotas.

Sales Volume Quotas

The sales volume quota is the most commonly used type of quota. It is a significant standard for appraising the performances of individual salespeople, other units of the sales organisation, and distributive outlets. A sales volume quota communicates the expectations of management as to "how much for what period." Sales quotas are set for geographical areas, product lines, or marketing channels or for one or more of these in combination with any unit of the sales organisation, the exact design depending upon what facets of the selling operation management wants to appraise or motivate.

Types of Sales Volume Quotas

Three commonly used sales volume quotas are:

- monetary sales volume quotas,
- unit sales volume quotas, and
- point sales volume quotas.

Monetary Sales Volume Quotas

Companies selling broad products lines set sales volume quotas in monetary terms (e.g., dollars) rather than in units of products. These companies meet complications in setting unit quotas and in evaluating sales performance for individual products. A key advantage of sales volume quotas expressed in terms of cash is that they provide the convenience of being easily understood by the salespeople and commonly recognised as a measure for all products. The salespeople are fully aware of what is expected in the way of sales and can gauge their performance directly against a monetary figure. Again, monetary volume sales quotas relate easily to other performance data, such as selling expenses, through ratios and percentages. Monetary sales volume quotas are also frequently used because they can be calculated and adjusted quickly and easily from year to year.

Unit Sales Volume Quotas

Unit sales volume quotas are useful when the salesperson is responsible for only a few products. Thus, a quota may be set in terms of the number of gallons of oil or the number of personal computers sold. Unit sales volume quotas are also attractive when prices fluctuate rapidly; in this situation, unit sales volume quotas are better yardsticks than are dollar sales volume quotas. For instance, if a product is now priced at GH¢80 per unit, 600 units sold means GH¢48,000 in sales, but if the price rises by 25 percent (to GH¢100 per unit), only 480 units sold produces the same Cedi value. A per-unit quota is also advisable for psychological reasons if unit prices are high. For example, a salesperson may regard a GH¢1,000,000 quota as a higher hurdle than a 20-unit quota for items priced at GH¢50,000 each.

Point Sales Volume Quotas

Some companies use sales volume quotas expressed in points. A company using point sales volume quotas might consider each GH¢100 sales as worth one point, it might value unit sales of product X at five points and of product Y at one point, or it might convert both monetary and unit sales into points. Companies generally use point sales volume quotas because of problems they have in using dollar sales or unit sales volume quotas.

Procedures for Setting Sales Volume Quotas

The six common procedures for setting sales volume quotas are explained as follows.

Quotas Based on Territorial Sales Potentials

It is quite logical that a sales volume quota should be derived from the sales potential present, such as potential in a territory. A sales volume quota sums up the effort a particular selling unit should put forth, while the sales potential represents the maximum sales opportunities open to the same selling unit.

The assumption is that the sum of all territorial sales volume quotas should equal the total company sales potential.

Quotas Based on Total Market Estimates

Some companies have neither statistics on territorial sales potentials nor sales force estimates. These companies depend on market estimates, from which they forecast a company's sales estimate. Management may either:

- break down the total company sales estimate and then make adjustments to arrive at territorial sales volume quotas (that is, how much would each territory contribute?); or
- take the company estimate, adjust it according to expected company changes in price, product, and promotion, and then break down the adjusted estimate into territorial estimates and adjust accordingly.

Quotas Based on Past Sales Experience

A procedure of basing sales volume quotas on past sales experience is the easiest method of establishing quotas. The procedure in this situation would be to determine the percentage by which the market is expected to increase and then to add that onto the previous year's quota.

Quotas Based on Executive Judgment

At times, sales volume quotas are based solely on executive judgment. This should be justified when there is little information to use in setting quotas.

Quotas Related to Compensation Plan

Sometimes, companies base sales volume quotas solely upon the projected amount of compensation that management believes salespeople should receive. No consideration is given to territorial sales potentials, total market estimates, or past sales experience, and quotas are tailored exclusively to fit the sales compensation plan.

Quotas Set by Salespeople

Some companies allow the salespeople to set their own quotas. The rationale for this move is that salespeople are closest to the market and are therefore thought to be the ones who know the most about its potential. Setting their own quotas also allows the salespeople to reflect their individual abilities. Finally, if salespeople make the decisions about their own goals, they will have higher morale and strive more to attain the quotas. Although salespeople should have some input in the quota-setting process, assigning total responsibility to the salesperson is shirking responsibility on the part of management. Salespeople cannot be expected to set responsible, realistic quotas on their own. Optimistic salespeople often tend to overestimate their capability and set unrealistically high quotas for themselves. When these salespeople realise that they cannot reach the goal, their morale is damaged (Spiro et al. 2008).

Financial Quotas

Financial quotas make salespeople conscious of the cost and profile implications of what they sell. Financial quotas are set for various units in the sales organisation to control expenses, gross margin, or net profit. These quotas can be applied to salespeople, regions, and product lines. Financial quotas are most applicable when the firm's market penetration approaches saturation levels. In such instances, it is hard to increase sales or market share, and an emphasis on selling efficiency and cost control becomes a logical mechanism for increasing profit (Churchill et al. 2000).

Types of Financial Quotas

Financial quotas are often stated in terms of direct selling expenses, gross margin, or net profit. These three common types of financial quotas are highlighted below.

Expense Quotas

Expense quotas are designed to make salespeople conscious of the cost involved in their selling efforts. These quotas emphasise keeping expenses in line with sales volume, thus indirectly controlling gross margin and net profit contributions. One method is to tie reimbursement for expenses directly to the sales volume or compensation plan. For instance, salespeople might be allowed to spend four percent of their sales for expenses (for food, travel, and lodging). If they exceed this quota, the difference is taken out of their salary or commissions.

Gross Margin Quotas

Companies consider gross margin quotas useful when there are significant differences in gross margins by product, since they can be set so salespeople will concentrate on items with higher returns. Unfortunately, problems are met both in setting and administering gross margin quotas. Some firms simply do not wish to disclose production cost information to sales personnel. Even among those that do, it is difficult for salespeople to tell how they are doing with respect to their own gross margin quotas at any given time, and thus the quotas do not produce the desired motivation effects (Churchill et al. 2000).

Net Profit Quotas

Companies use the net profit quotas to emphasise to the salespeople that the company would prefer profitable sales volume and not sales volume for its own sake. The rationale is that salespeople perform more efficiently if they recognise that sales increases, expense reductions, or both are important only if profits result. Net profit quotas can be superior to gross margin quotas when products with high gross margins require extensive effort and thereby produce higher field selling expenses and lower net profit.

Activity Quotas

Activity quotas attempt to recognise the investment nature of a salesperson's efforts. Many companies, in an effort to ensure that salespeople conduct their activities diligently, require that their salespeople meet activity quotas. Activity quotas are designed to control the many different activities the salesperson is responsible for. They are directly related to factors that salespeople can actually control.

A company setting activity quotas starts by determining the important activities salespeople perform; then it sets target performance frequencies. Some common types of activity quotas are total sales calls made, calls made to particular classes of customers, calls made to prospects, number of new accounts opened, proposals submitted, field demonstrations arranged, equipment installations supervised, meetings and conventions attended, dealer sales meetings held, and displays arranged.

Combination Quotas

Combination quotas are used to control the performance of both selling and non-selling activities of the sales force. These quotas normally use points, that is, percentage points, as a common yardstick to overcome the difficulty of using different measurement units to evaluate different aspects of performance.

Administering the Sales Quota System

A well-designed sales quota system needs to be skilfully administered. In order for the quota system to effectively plan, control, and evaluate the sales effort, the sales force should be willing to cooperate with the system. Few salespeople take kindly to having their performance strictly monitored and measured. Most salespeople oppose quotas, and they question anything that suggests the quotas may be unfair, inaccurate, or unattainable, thus reducing the system's effectiveness.

Setting Accurate, Fair, and Attainable Quotas

Good quotas must be accurate, fair, and attainable. Obtaining accurate quotas is a function of the quota-setting procedure. The more closely quotas are related to territorial potentials, the greater the chances for accuracy. Accurate quotas result from skilful blending of planning and operating information with sound judgment. Setting a fair quota involves determining the proper blend of sales potential and previous experience.

Creating Understandable Quotas

Management must ensure that the salespeople understand the quota plan. This is critical in securing salespeople's cooperation in and acceptance of the quotas, so the quota-setting procedure must be carefully explained to them. If salespeople do not understand the procedure used in setting quotas, they may feel, for example, that the quotas are a managerial technique to extract more effort from them without any reward for it. That attitude would destroy the effectiveness of the quota as an incentive. Additionally, if the salespeople understand the quota system, they are more likely to consider it accurate, fair, and attainable. The following are some of the ways management can help the sales force understand the quotas.

Participation by Sales Force in Quota-Setting

If management allows salespeople to participate in the quota-setting procedure, the task of explaining quotas and how they are determined is eased. This would enhance salespeople's understanding and considerably reduce questions of inaccuracy, unfairness, and un-attainability.

Keeping the sales force informed

It is vital that management keep the sales force informed of its progress relative to the quotas. The salespeople would need to receive regular reports detailing their performance to-date. This allows salespeople to analyze what they are doing right and what they are doing wrong and take corrective action so that they can improve their performance.

Maintaining Control

In administering the quota system, there is the need for management to continuously monitor performance. Arrangements must be made to gather and analyze performance information with minimum delay. A lot of companies are increasingly producing periodic charts to show each salesperson's progress toward his or her quota. These charts may be filled in weekly or monthly, and they sometimes include a ranking of the entire sales force on the basis of actual performance compared with the quota. Table 9.1 is a typical chart for comparing sales quotas with actual performances.

Table 9.1 Sales Quota and Actual Performance for Month, Year

Sales-person	Current Month				Year-to-Date			
	Quota	Sales	Percent	Rank	Quota	Sales	Percent	Rank
A								
B								
C								
D								
E								
F								
G								
H								
I								
J								
K								
L								
M								
N								
O								
P								
Q								
R								
S								
T								
U								
V								
W								
X								
Y								
Z								
Total								

Review Questions

1. Is it necessary to establish equal quotas for territories of equal potential?

2. Can you establish a quota without a sales forecast? A sales budget? An estimate of the territory's potential?

3. Why would a luggage manufacturer use volume quotas for its sales force?

4. Why would a company adopt the approach of setting different sales volume quotas?

5. Should quotas be used for a missionary or promotional representative for candy bars?

Chapter 10

Motivating the Sales Force

Introduction

Salespeople operate in a highly dynamic, stressful environment outside of the organisation. There are many factors that influence the salesperson's ability to perform. One of the most critical factors is motivation. It is essential that sales managers understand the process of motivation and be able to apply it to each individual in the sales force in such a manner as to maximise his or her performance potential. All motivation is self-motivation. Salespeople cannot be motivated unless they want to be. The challenge for management is to identify, understand and channel the motivation that their salespeople possess. A sales manager acts as a catalyst, providing both the stimulation for salespeople to feel motivated and the proper rewards so that they continue to feel motivated.

This chapter focuses on motivating the sales force. It initially explains the nature and meaning of motivation and the importance of motivation. It then describes the behavioural concepts in motivation and the various theories of motivation and considers non-financial as well as financial rewards. It also discusses how the sales manager can use the motivational tools of sales contests and sales meetings effectively.

The Meaning of Motivation

Motivation is referred to as a goal-directed behaviour, underlying which are certain needs or desires. The composite of needs and desires that stem from within individuals leads them to act so as to satisfy those needs and desires. According to Futrell (1999), motivation is the arousal, intensity, direction, and persistence of effort directed toward job tasks over a period.

Specifically as applied to sales force, motivation is the amount of effort the salesperson desires to expend on the activities associated with the sales job. Expending effort on each activity that makes up the sales job leads to some level of achievement on one or more dimensions of job performance. As Still et al. (1988) emphasise, most salespeople require motivational help from management to reach and maintain acceptable performance levels. They require motivation as individuals and as group members. Thus, in terms of motivation, the sales manager's job is twofold:

- Keep the salesperson's morale up in the face of adversities.
- Motivate the salesperson to continually work at some level close to, if not at, potential.

Patty (1979) has observed that the morale of a sales force is very closely linked to the satisfaction the salespeople obtain from their jobs. Morale goes up when the job is going well—customers are buying or reacting in an otherwise positive manner—and relations are harmonious within the work environment. When any one of these factors is negative, morale typically decreases. Of course, morale can also be affected by factors outside the work environment, such as family problems, financial problems, etc.

Theories of Motivation

Research studies in the behavioural sciences show that all human activity, including the salesperson's job behaviour, is directed toward satisfying certain needs and reaching certain goals. How salespeople behave on the job is directly related to their individual needs and goals. Some salespeople, in other words, are more successful than others because of the different motivational patterns and amounts and types of efforts they exert in performing their jobs.

As Weaver (1985) emphasises, the sales manager is responsible not only for motivating the sales force per se but also for counselling each salesperson individually to find the source of that person's motivation. The discussion in this section focuses on some of the several contemporary theories of motivation to further help sales managers in their understanding of needs and motivation.

There are a number of theories of motivation. In this session, however, seven major contemporary theories of motivation will be discussed in relation to selling. These are:

1. Maslow's Hierarchy of Needs Theory,
2. Herzberg's Motivator-Hygiene Theory,
3. achievement-motivation theory,
4. Vroom's Expectancy Theory,
5. equity theory,
6. attribution theory, and
7. goal-setting theory.

Maslow's Hierarchy of Needs Theory

Abraham Maslow (1970) propounded a theory of motivation based on the assumption that individuals seek to fulfil personal needs according to some hierarchy of importance.

First, human beings are motivated by the desire to satisfy certain needs—related to physiology, safety, belongingness, self-esteem, and self-actualisation. These needs energise the individual to take action to satisfy the needs. Once a need has been satisfied, it is no longer capable of motivating behaviour (until it becomes reactivated). Second, the needs of individuals are universal and appear in hierarchical form (see Figure 10.1).

Maslow's suggestion is that, as the lower needs are satisfied, behaviour is motivated toward satisfying the next higher needs. In other words, the physiological needs are the most important. As those needs are satisfied, their ability to motivate diminishes, and the individual is motivated by safety and security needs, and then by belongingness and social relations needs. This process continues until the self-actualisation needs are satisfied. Thus, relative gratification of the needs at one level activates the next higher order of needs.

The question, then, is: What motivates salespeople? Salespeople's motives for working vary according to the nature and potency of the unsatisfied portion of their individual hierarchies of needs. It must also be recognised, however, that some of the salespeople's needs are fulfilled off the job as well as on it. One salesperson may work because of the need for money to feed a family, another because the job is seen as a means for gaining the esteem of others, still another because of a need to achieve (self-actualisation) to the maximum of one's abilities, seeing job performance as a means to that end.

Figure 10.1 Maslow's Hierarchy of Needs

Self-Actualization Needs

Esteem Needs

Belongingness and Social Relations Needs

Safety and Security Needs

Physiological Needs

Implications of Maslow's Hierarchy of Needs Theory for Sales Management

Sales managers applying need theory should be mindful of its two major premises, which are the following:

- The greater the deprivation of a given need, the greater its importance and strength.
- Gratification of needs at one level in the hierarchy activates needs at the next higher level.

The sales manager would need to keep track of the levels of needs that are most important to each salesperson. Before salespeople stagnate at one level, they must be given the opportunity to activate and satisfy higher level needs, if they are to be successfully motivated toward greater performance. Since various salespeople are at different need levels at any given time, the sales manager has to retain his or her sensitivity to the evolving needs of individual sales representatives through close personal contact with each member of the sales force.

Herzberg's Motivator-Hygiene Theory

Fredrick Herzberg (1966), the American psychologist, developed the motivator-hygiene theory, which is also known as the two-factor theory and the dual-factor theory. Basically, the motivator-hygiene theory suggests that the factors involved in producing job satisfaction (and motivation) are quite different from those factors producing job dissatisfaction. Job satisfaction is not the opposite of job dissatisfaction; a person is either satisfied or not satisfied, dissatisfied or not dissatisfied.

According to this theory, two types of factors are associated with the satisfaction of employees. Factors of satisfaction are called motivators, because they are necessary to stimulate individuals to superior efforts. These factors relate to the nature or content of the job itself and include achievement; recognition, responsibility, and opportunities for growth and advancement. Factors of dissatisfaction are called hygiene factors, because they are necessary to keep employee performance from dropping or becoming unhealthy. They relate to the working environment and include salary, fringe benefits, types of supervision, and company policy.

Implications of Motivator-Hygiene Theory for Sales Management

Herzberg's Motivator-Hygiene Theory has two fundamental implications for sales managers. First, sales managers must see that hygiene factors (pleasant work environment) are maintained—that is, that the job provides the conditions that prevent dissatisfaction. This means the sales manager must provide an acceptable working environment, fair compensation, adequate fringe benefits, fair and reasonable supervision, and job security. Secondly, the sales manager must provide motivators (job enrichment) for the sales force, involving opportunities for achievement, recognition, responsibility, and advancement. The following are some examples of ways to provide job enrichment, as identified by Anderson et al. (1992):

- Give salespeople a complete, natural unit of work responsibility and accountability (e.g., specific customer category assignment in a designated area).
- Grant greater authority and job freedom to the salespeople in accomplishing assignments (e.g., let salespeople schedule their time in their own unique way as long as organisational goals are met).
- Introduce salespeople to new and more different tasks and to challenges not previously handled (e.g., opening new accounts, selling a new product category, or being assigned a large national account).
- Assign salespeople specific or specialised tasks, enabling them to become experts (e.g., train new salespeople on "how to close a sale").
- Send periodic reports and communications directly to the salesperson, instead of forwarding everything via the sales supervisor. (Of course, it is necessary for the supervisor to be informed about what information the salespeople are receiving).

Achievement-Motivation Theory

McClelland and his associates developed the achievement-motivation theory. They confirmed that some people have higher achievement needs than others; they labelled such persons "achievement oriented." According to the achievement theory, if a person spends considerable time thinking about doing his or her job better, accomplishing something unusual and important, or advancing his or her career, that individual has a high need for achievement (*nAch*). People who have high needs for achievement (i.e., achievement-oriented people) are characterised as people who:

- want to take personal responsibility for solving problems;
- are goal oriented (they set moderate, realistic, attainable goals);
- seeking challenges, excellence, and individuality;
- take calculated, moderate risks; and
- desire concrete feedback on their performance.

In effect, people with high *nAch* readily accept individual responsibility, seek challenging tasks, and are willing to take risks doing tasks that may serve as stepping stones to future rewards. These individuals receive more satisfaction from accomplishing goals and more frustration from failure or unfinished tasks than the average person.

Implications of the Achievement-Motivation Theory for Sales Management

Sales managers need to target recruiting toward individuals with high *nAch*. They would need to identify the achievement-motivated salespeople and then give them personal responsibility for solving definable problems or achieving certain goals. Regular, specific feedback is also important so that these salespeople would be able to know whether or not they are successful.

Expectancy Theory

Vroom's Expectancy Theory holds that people are motivated to work toward a goal when they expect that their efforts will pay off—that is, when achievement of the goals is both profitable and desirable. This theory views people as intelligent, rational individuals who make conscious decisions about their present and future behaviour. Each one of us estimates the probability of success in our work endeavours and the relative value of the payoff if we succeed. One aspect of the expectancy theory is that the effort to do something depends on the valence (anticipated satisfaction) in accomplishing it and the expectancy (probability) that an action will yield the expected result.

Performance within a sales organisation, as Patty (1979) suggests, is a result of at least three factors: (1) the motivational levels of the individuals belonging to the organisation, (2) the abilities and traits that those particular individuals possess, and (3) the perceived role each individual has within the organisation. An individual must not only want to perform well; he or she must also have the ability to perform well. In addition, the job requirements must be accurately understood, otherwise the desire and abilities could be expended in doing the wrong things.

Expectancy Illustration

The following formula expresses expectancy theory:

Motivation = Expectancy x Instrumentality x Valence

Here is an example of applying the expectancy theory formula to a salesperson's motivation.

Expectancy = A salesperson strongly believes that an increased number of calls per week will generate higher sales. This person would have a high effort-performance expectancy, such as a 95 percent chance of this occurring (Effort).

Instrumentality = If this same person also believes that such a sales increase will result in winning a sales contest, the person has a high performance-outcome expectancy. Assume a 99 percent chance of this outcome happening (Result).

Valence = If winning the contest is extremely important, a prize worth 0.90, for example, on scale of 1.00, then the person is highly motivated. However, if the contest prize were of little value for the salesperson, say 0.20, then the motivational force would be much lower (Value).

As shown in Table 10.1, if any one of the three factors of expectancy, instrumentality, or valence, is low, a person's motivational level may drop dramatically. Thus, all three motivational components must be high for high motivational levels to exist.

Table 10.1 Salesperson A Values the Contest and has a High Motivational Level; Salesperson B will not Work Hard

Salesperson	Expectancy		Instrumentality		Valence		Motivational Level
Salesperson A	.95	X	.99	X	.90	=	.846
Salesperson B	.95	X	.99	X	.20	=	.188

Implications of Expectancy Theory for Sales Management
Although expectancy theory is complex, it helps the sales manager to focus on key leverage points for influencing motivation. Three implications are crucial for the manager (Futrell 1998) who needs to:

1. **Increase expectancy.** Provide a work environment that facilitates the best performance, and set realistically attainable performance goals. Provide training, support, and encouragement so salespeople are confident they can perform at the levels expected of them.

2. **Make performance instrumental toward positive outcomes.** Make sure good performance is followed by personal recognition and praise, favourable

performance reviews, pay increases, and other positive results. Make sure as well that working hard and doing tasks well will have as few negative results as possible. Again, ensure that poor performance has fewer positive and more negative outcomes than good performance.

3. **Identify positive valence outcomes.** Understand what salespeople want to get out of their work. Think about what their jobs provide them and what is not but could be provided. Consider how people may differ in the valences they assign to outcomes.

According to the expectancy theory, sales management needs to create the expectation in the sales force that their efforts will be more than adequately rewarded. In most cases, to become motivated, salespeople should expect that the rewards for extra efforts will be greater than the costs so that they will profit personally.

Equity Theory

The equity theory of motivation assumes that people compare their relative working contributions and rewards with those of other individuals in similar situations. Inequity is experienced when people feel either under-rewarded or over-rewarded for their contributions relative to those of others. The stronger the feeling of inequity, the stronger the drive to reduce tension. Generally, most people who feel under-rewarded relative to others who are making similar contributions tend to decrease their work efforts. People may also reduce their rewards and contributions versus those of others. Ultimately, people may leave a perceived inequity situation by quitting the job or changing the comparison group.

In practice, if inequity is perceived, the salesperson may be motivated to restore equity using one of four methods, as summarised by Futrell (1999).

- First, the salesperson may increase or decrease the level of input that may, in turn, influence outcomes.

In other words, the salesperson may see other people working harder and receiving higher rates, so he or she may work harder.

- Second, the salesperson could distort the facts by convincing himself or herself that equity really does exist, even though it may not.
- Third, the salesperson could choose another salesperson with whom to compare the ratio of outcome to input.
- Fourth, the salesperson could influence other salespeople to decrease the amount of effort they are putting into their jobs. For example, the salesperson might ask the super salesperson to slow down.

Equity theory asserts that the salesperson would leave the job if he or she could not achieve an equitable relationship. Thus, the salesperson chooses a work/salary level that is equitable in comparison to that of some other salespeople.

Implications of Equity Theory for Sales Management

It is important that sales managers be aware of equity theory, because it points to a real need for management to evaluate salespeople's performance effectively and to reward accordingly. The salesperson is concerned not only with the level of salary received but also with how that relates to fellow salespeople's salaries, including those of salespeople outside the company who work in similar situations.

Thus, as the equity theory asserts, it is important that sales managers learn how individual salespeople feel about the equity of their contributions and rewards compared to those of others. If inequity is perceived by some of the salespeople, the sales manager needs to correct the situation if inequity really does exist or help the salespeople reduce tension by altering their perceptions of the comparison group's relative contributions and rewards.

Attribution Theory of Motivation

Attribution theory contends that people are motivated not only to maximise their own rewards but also to understand their environment or surroundings. This means people are motivated to know why an event occurs and why they succeed or fail at a certain task. The explanations for success and failure lead individuals to make causal attributions for the outcomes they experience. The causal attributions (or perceived causes of success and failure) usually include ability, effort, strategy, luck, and the difficulty of the tasks.

These attributions, or perceptions, influence motivation. For instance, a top-performing salesperson might be motivated to continue a certain selling activity if he or she attributes the success to that activity or behaviour. Similarly, a person who attributes failure to a certain selling activity or strategy is likely to be motivated to change that work habit so that he or she has a better chance of succeeding the next time.

The outcome of the attribution process is that salespeople can choose either to work harder or to work smarter. Motivation to increase the amount of effort on the job involves working harder—calling on more clients or putting in more hours is working harder. On the other hand, motivation to change the type or direction of effort pertains to working smarter— altering a sales presentation to match the customer is a way to work smarter. For certain selling situations, working smarter may produce greater benefits than working harder (Sujan 1986). Even though sales managers have traditionally endeavoured to motivate their sales forces to work harder, Sujan's work suggests that they should concentrate on motivating the salespeople to work smarter—that is, to make better choices in the activities they perform.

Goal-Setting Theory

Goal-setting theory seeks to increase motivation by linking rewards directly to individuals' goals. This theory suggests sales managers and subordinates should set specific goals for the individual salesperson on a regular basis. These goals should be moderately difficult to achieve, but they should be the type of goals that the salesperson would want to accomplish. According to Anderson et al, because goal-setting theory helps sales managers to develop individualised reward systems, it provides a means of clarifying any role ambiguities or conflicts that may arise.

Motivation and Leadership

Effective sales managers are leaders of the sales force. As Still et al observe, they earn the voluntary cooperation of members of the sales organisation, motivating them—individually and as a group—to reach the sales department's goals. They know the motivations, desires, and ambitions of those they lead, and they use this knowledge to guide their followers into the necessary activities.

The handling of relationships with the sales force is seen as one of the main aspects of leadership related to motivation. Effective sales managers need to treat the sales force fairly, particularly as regards assignments, promotions, and changes in pay. They need to commend salespeople for jobs well done, but if performance is poor, they call that to the subordinate's attention privately.

Motivational Tools

Sales management can select from a number of motivational tools for the implementation of their approaches to motivating the sales force. Apart from offering attractive financial compensation and properly designed training programmes, sales management can consider several motivational tools. Two main mechanisms are sales meetings and sales contests. These promotional tools are explained next.

Sales Contests

Sales contests are temporary programmes that offer financial and/or non-financial rewards for attaining specified, usually short-term, objectives. Thus, sales contests are special selling campaigns that offer incentives in the form of prizes or rewards beyond those in the compensation plan. Popular incentives, as indicated by the extent to which they are awarded to salespeople, include merchandise, gift certificates, cash, electronics, and travel (Ingram et al. 2004).

In terms of Herzberg's Motivator-Hygiene Theory, sales contests aim to fulfil individual needs for achievement and recognition. Salespeople must periodically gain reinforcement that comes from attaining an objective. The rewards and recognition that come from winning a short-term contest can provide that immediate reinforcement. The use of incentives programmes continues to grow. Sales contests may involve group competitions among salespeople, individuals' competitions whereby each salesperson competes against past performance standards or new goals, or a combination of group and individual competitions.

Successful contests require:
- clearly defined, specific objectives,
- an exciting theme,
- reasonable rewards, and
- promotion and follow-through.

Each of these requirements is explained in the next section.

Contest Objectives

Most sales contests aim to motivate the sales force in terms of:

1. obtaining new customers;
2. securing larger orders per sales call;
3. pushing slow-moving items, high-margin goods, or new products;
4. overcoming a seasonal sales slump;
5. selling a more profitable mix of products;
6. improving the performance of distributors' sales personnel;
7. promoting seasonal merchandise;

8. obtaining more product displays by dealers;
9. getting reorders; and
10. promoting special deals to distributors, dealers, or both.

Contest Formats

Contest formats are classified as direct or novelty. A direct format has a contest theme describing the specific objective, such as obtaining new accounts. A novelty format uses a theme that focuses upon a current event, sport, or the like, as in "Let's hunt for hidden treasure" (find new customers).

Contest Prizes

To ensure that the desired motivational effects are created, contest prizes must include items that the majority of participants want. Four main kinds of contest prizes are cash, merchandise, travel, and special honours or privileges. Cash and merchandise are the most common prizes. Many sales contests feature more than one kind of prize—for example, travel for large awards and merchandise for lesser awards.

How Many Prizes and How Should They be Awarded? To stimulate widespread interest in the contest, it is important to make it possible for participants to win—meaning the basis for awards should be chosen carefully. Recommendation by contest planners is that performance level should be taken into account and the basis of award be improvement rather than total performance.

Contest Duration

Contest duration is essential to maintaining the interest of sales force. Contests normally last more than one month and less than five months. In general, salespeople should have enough time in the contest to make at least one complete pass through their territories. The longer the contest, the bigger the prize should be.

Contest Promotion

Effective contest promotion is important. No matter how good a product is, it will not sell if it is not promoted. So it is with an incentive programme. It too must be promoted and sold if it is going to meet its objectives of increased volume, profitability, and so on. Contests should be introduced in a surprise announcement followed by a barrage of promotional material. It is essential that the exact nature and rules of the contest be announced to all salespeople at the same time as a dramatic surprise. Explanatory posters should be put up after announcing the contest, and some device showing everyone's relative progress should be prominently exhibited.

Advantages of Sales Contests

Sales contests can be very effective tools in motivating salespeople to meet short-term objectives and to re-instil enthusiasm for meeting longer-term goals. Contests are exciting; they can perk up interest and generate enthusiasm for the job itself. Contests can be very successful in providing fast and frequent reinforcement. But most of all, at least from the standpoint of the salesperson, a contest can bring recognition.

Disadvantages of Sales Contests

The greatest disadvantages arising from the use of contests are the result of poor management. Contests can encourage salespeople to go to great lengths to win—even cheat, if necessary. Salespeople have been known to save up sales and turn them in during the contest period. They have also been known to overstock customers with the promise that if the merchandise doesn't sell, it can be returned. If a person wants to cheat badly enough, there are numerous ways. However, close supervision can usually prevent such tactics. Some companies are continually running contests, and since few people can work at full steam week after week, contests eventually lose their ability to excite and motivate. Again, this is indicative of poor management.

Managerial Evaluation of Sales Contests

Management should perform both pre- and post-evaluation of a sales contest. Pre-evaluation aims to detect and correct weaknesses. Post-evaluation seeks insights helpful in improving future contests.

Guidelines for Optimizing the Use of Sales Contests

As Ingram et al. (2004) point out, there is always a concern about whether sales contests have any lasting value or simply boost short-term sales. If sales contests merely pull sales from a future period into the contest period, little is gained—and the expenses of running contests can be substantial. To optimise the use of sales contests, the following guidelines, as summarised by Kalra and Shi (2001), are recommended:

1. Minimise potential motivation and morale problems by allowing multiple winners. Salespeople should compete against individual goals and be declared winners if those goals are met. To increase motivation, base the amount of the reward on relative rank achieved so that those ranking higher achieve larger amounts.

2. Recognise that contests will concentrate efforts in specific areas, often at the temporary neglect of other areas. Plan accordingly.

3. Consider the positive effects of including non-selling personnel in the sales contests.

4. Use variety as a basic element of sales contests. Vary timing, duration, themes, and rewards.

5. Ensure that sales contests' objectives are clear, realistically attainable, and quantifiable to allow performance assessment.

Sales Meetings

Sales meetings, be they national, regional, or local, are important both for communication and for motivational purposes. Sales meetings provide for two-way communication and interaction among all members of the sales team.

The most widely used vehicle for training salespeople is still the sales meeting. While many types of information can be sent into the field by cassette or workbook, when two-way communication is needed, sales meetings are important. Sale meetings may be very large (a sales convention) or very small (a seminar). They may last anywhere from an hour to a week. Whatever the length, sales meetings need to be well planned and the meeting sites chosen in light of the objectives of the meetings.

Integrative Sales Meetings

As Ingram et al. (2004) point out, one of the best opportunities for sales managers to demonstrate leadership ability comes when they plan and execute an integrative sales meeting. An integrative sales meeting is one in which several sales and sales management functions are achieved. As the authors observe, although multiple objectives are accomplished at such meetings, their overall purpose is to unite the sales force in the quest for common objectives.

Such meetings may combine training, strategic planning, motivational programmes, recognition of outstanding sales performance, and recreation and entertainment for the attendees. In large organisations, the entire sales force may attend a major integrative sales meeting each year to review the past year's performance and unite for the upcoming year (Ingram et al. 2004).

Planning Sales Meetings

Detailed advanced planning is required for effective sales meetings. In planning sales meetings, five main tasks are required, including the following:

(1) **Define the specific training aims.**
(2) **Decide on the meeting content.** Determining the meeting's content involves planning its agenda, which is a list or an outline of things to be considered or done during the meeting.
(3) **Determine the methods for conducting the**

meeting. The methods used depend upon the aim and content as well as upon the time available and meeting place.

(4) **Decide how to execute (hold) the meeting.** Decisions are reached on speakers, seminar leaders, meeting site, and time.

(5) **Decide how to evaluate the results.** The basis for the evaluation should be whether the meeting accomplished its aims.

Suggestions from Salespeople on Conducting Sales Meetings

As Ingram et al. (2004) observe, one of the opportunities for sales managers to demonstrate leadership ability comes when they plan and execute an integrative sales meeting—one in which several sales and sales management functions are achieved. As is true with all leadership functions, the needs and wants of the sales force should be given some consideration in the planning and execution of integrative sales meetings. The following are some suggestions from salespeople, as summarised by Ingram et al. (2004):

1. Keep technical presentations succinct, and use visual aids and breakout discussion groups to maintain salespeople's interest.

2. Keep salespeople informed of corporate strategy and their roles in it.

3. Minimise operations reviews, unless they are directly related to sales. Use a combination of face-to-face exchanges and handouts to introduce key people in advertising and customer service.

4. Set a humane schedule. Over-scheduling can deter learning. Allow time for salespeople to share experiences, so they can learn from each other.

5. Let salespeople know what is planned. Be sure they can be briefed on the purpose and content of the meeting. Distribute a written agenda.

6. Ask salespeople for their ideas on topics, speakers, and preferred recreational activities, if applicable.
7. Generate excitement with a contest. Reward efforts and results so that all participants enjoy the chance to win.

Types of Sales Meetings

Some of the common types of sales meetings are national, regional, and local meetings. These different types of meetings are discussed next.

National Sales Meetings

National sales meetings are often held once a year. They may include the entire sales force or only a select group of top-performing personnel. The expenses for bringing the entire sales force to national meetings are considerable, but they are sometimes appropriate. For instance, if comprehensive changes in marketing or sales polices are being made, a national meeting can introduce the changes rapidly and uniformly, providing standardised explanations and answers to questions.

Regional Sales Meetings

Regional sales meetings are usually planned with programmes designed to give emphasis to peculiar problems of the region. The smaller attendance should increase participation time per person attending. In place of the field sales force coming together at the central office, headquarters' sales executives and personnel attend the regional meetings, which reduces total travel costs and lowers lost selling time.

Local Sales Meetings

Local sales meetings are conducted weekly or biweekly by district sales managers. As Anderson et al. (1992) submit, these meetings are important for bestowing timely recognition on salespeople, providing group interaction, and focusing sales training on solving territorial problems and creating selling opportunities.

Site Selection

The meeting site should be selected in light of the meeting's objectives. A key factor in choosing a meeting site is the personality of the group involved and its needs. Choose the site that will best advance the purposes of the meeting while staying within budget constraints. Small, once-a-week meetings are usually held on the company premises. Natural and regional sales meetings are best held away from the company, either in a hotel in the same city as company head office or perhaps in a resort area.

Review Questions

1. Define motivation and explain why it is particularly important for salespeople.

2. Why is motivation such an important concept for sales managers to understand and learn how to use?

3. Which of the contemporary theories of motivation would you use to help motivate your sales force? Why?

4. What do you feel is the difference between expectancy theory and equity theory? Which one do you feel motivates you the most?

5. Discuss the reasons for using sales contests. What makes a good sales contest?

Chapter 11

Sales Force Compensation

Introduction

As indicated in chapter ten, compensation is the most widely used method of motivating salespeople. It is the key to changing salespeople's behaviour. Yet over the years, numerous studies have indicated that the majority of companies do not rate their sales force compensation plan as very successful. In view of changes in the environment, companies should review their compensation plans regularly to ensure that they are consistent with the organisation's direction.

This chapter focuses on sales force compensation, suggesting ways in which sales executives can design effective compensation plans. It deals with the importance and purposes of and basic objectives for an effective compensation plan. It also examines various compensation plans and how they need to be modified with changing market conditions.

Motivational Roles of the Sales Compensation Plan

Money, as our review of motivation theories in chapter ten indicated, has limited potential as a motivator. Nonetheless, the sales compensation plan is an important part of the overall programme for motivating the sales force. As Still et al. (1988) suggest, a sales compensation plan, if properly designed, has three motivational roles:

1. It provides a living wage.
2. It adjusts pay levels to performance, thereby relating job performance and rewards (in line with Vroom's

Expectancy Theory).

3. It provides a mechanism for demonstrating the congruence between attaining company goals and individual goals (also in line with Vroom's Expectancy Theory).

As the Still et al. emphasise, a properly designed sales compensation plan fits a company's special needs and problems, and from it flows attractive returns for both the company and its sales force. Sales and growth goals are reached at low cost, and profits are satisfactory. Sales force receives high pay as a reward for effective job performance, and loyalty among the members is high.

Purposes of Compensation

Compensation has six basic ways of influencing motivation, which are highlighted below.

- **Connects the individual with the organisation.** Generally, compensation provides salespeople with a means to bridge the gap between sales force objectives and the individual salesperson's expectations and aspirations. The reward system must satisfy the individual needs of sales force members and must be tied directly to performance to maximise the possibility of attaining sales force objectives.

- **Influences work behaviour.** Compensation can directly motivate salespeople to behave in ways they otherwise would not behave. A sales manager often considers pay a major means of influencing salespeople's work behaviour to improve their sales performance in the organisation. Thus, this is the main purpose of compensation.

- **Impacts organisational choice.** A good compensation plan should serve to help in recruiting and hiring qualified salespeople. It must also help in retraining salespeople. The choice of joining or leaving an organisation is often influenced by expectations of compensation.

- **Influences satisfaction.** Compensation can affect a salesperson's satisfaction. Satisfaction with pay is both fairly simple and straightforward and complex.
- **Gives feedback.** Pay serves as direct feedback about the organisation's performance. Assume a sales manager tells a salesperson that he or she is doing a good job. As a result of this, the manager offers the salesperson a substantial pay raise per month. The salesperson would have little doubt about how well he or she is doing in the job.
- **Reinforces behaviour.** Pay can be viewed as reinforcing salespeople's behaviour if it is tied to performance.

Basic Questions in Designing Effective Compensation Programmes

To ensure success, sales managers must first provide answers to certain basic questions that are central in designing effective compensation programmes. The following are such questions, as summarised by Churchill et al. (2000):

(a) Which compensation method among the variety available from straight salary to a combination of salary and incentive bonuses, to 100 percent commission is best for motivating specific kinds of selling activities in specific situations?

(b) What proportion of a salesperson's total compensation should be determined by incentive pay?

(c) What is the appropriate mix of financial and nonfinancial incentives for motivating salespeople?

Requirements of a Good Sales Compensation Plan

There are seven distinct requirements that a good sales compensation plan must meet.

1. It provides a good, living wage, preferably in the

form of a secure income.

2. The plan fits with the rest of the motivational programme; it does not conflict with other motivational factors, such as the intangible feeling of belonging to the sales team.

3. The plan is fair; it does not punish salespeople because of factors beyond their control.

4. It is easy for salespeople to understand; they are able to calculate their own earnings.

5. The plan adjusts pay to changes in performance.

6. The plan is economical to administer.

7. The plan helps in attaining the objectives of the sales organisation.

Specific Objectives for a Good Compensation Plan

Patty (1979) submits that the specific objectives for a good compensation plan depend on the peculiar need of both the company and the salespeople. The specific objectives of compensation plans from the salespeople's perspective and from the company's perspective are examined next.

Needs of the Salespeople

The specific objectives of compensation plans from salespeople's perspectives, as Patty suggests, are the following.

Equitable

From the standpoint of the individual salesperson, any compensation plan must be equitable in at least three ways. First, it must be equitable internally—i.e., in relation to compensation plans of other company employees. If other divisions' salespeople or non-sales employees of comparable work levels receive significantly higher compensation, morale will suffer. Second, the compensation must be comparable to that received by salespeople working for direct competitors. Last, the compensation received must be commensurate with both the amount of effort expended and the result obtained.

Stable

Any compensation plan should protect salespeople from a loss of income (at least to some degree) due to circumstances beyond the salesperson's control. In some way, the "famine" periods should be eliminated. Almost every salesperson has regular monthly expenses that must be paid—house payments, food, utilities, doctor bills, etc. A stable income will enable the salesperson to live comfortably.

Provide Incentive

Every salesperson should have the opportunity, through greater and/or more effective effort, to earn compensation beyond that provided by a regular, stable income plan. Superior performance should have its rewards.

Understandable

Any compensation plan should be understood by the salesperson, at least enough that expected income can be calculated simply and accurately. It is emphasised that salespeople look for these requirements, and they are motivated to perform the more the compensation plan meets their needs.

Company Needs

The company must also satisfy its need when it offers good compensation to its sales force. We now examine some of the objectives companies seek, in the design of compensation plans, to achieve.

Attract and Retain Desirable Salespeople

Since good salespeople are one of a company's most important resources, the income-generating arm, it is vital that the company attract and retain men and women with the characteristics and abilities needed in that company for successful selling. Both the amount of income and the method in which it is received are important considerations for anyone taking on a new job.

Encourage Specific Activities

If left completely on their own, many salespeople will ignore many of the functions deemed essential to the company's success—for example, pushing difficult-to-sell products, responding to customer needs, providing essential feedback, calling on out-of-the-way or new prospects, or attending essential meetings.

The compensation plan may be used by the company to encourage (1) selling to particularly profitable customers, (2) selling products or services with wider profit margins, (3) selling a balanced mix of products, (4) selling equipment on lease instead of making outright sales, (5) performing essential sales tasks, and (6) cultivating a minimum number of new accounts each month.

Reward Outstanding Performances

When salespeople are implementing the specific activities desired by company management, then the compensation plan should provide the framework for quick and effective rewards.

Provide the Optimum Balance between Costs and Results

Earlier, we discussed that salespeople are among the company's most important resources. They also appear as costs on the company's accounting statements. Consequently, one of the objectives of any compensation plan is to provide rewards that are commensurate with results.

However, results are not always easily or effectively measured. How does a sales manager measure the results, at least in the short run, of the training given by the company's salespeople to the salespeople of its dealers or distributors? Sometimes prospects may be worked on for months before a sale is consummated. The most obvious method of balancing costs and results is through a straight commission plan. However, as will be seen later, there are often serious problems involved in such a plan.

Develop Long-Term Relationships with Customers

Although this objective relates closely to some of those discussed above, it is worthy of separate treatment. One of the difficult-to-measure intangibles is the relationship between customers and salespeople. There is some proof, for example, that turnover in salespeople can injure the company's relationship with its customers—i.e., the relationship between the customer and the company. Certainly, the old adage "the customer is king" has a degree of validity.

Provide Easy Administration

Any compensation plan should be easy to explain, easy to understand, easy to implement, and easy to adjust when necessary. The compensation plan should be understood by both the sales manager and the salespeople. The plan should also be flexible such that temporary adjustments can be made without compromising the plan's integrity.

Developing a Sales Compensation Plan

There are ten distinct steps in the process of developing a systematic compensation plan:

1. Define the sales job.
2. Consider the company' general compensation structure.
3. Consider compensation patterns in the community and the industry.
4. Determine the compensation level.
5. Provide for the various compensation elements.
6. Allow for special company needs and problems.
7. Consult the present sales force.
8. Commit the tentative plan to writing, and pretest it.
9. Revise the plan.
10. Implement the plan and provide for follow-up.

Step One: Define the Sales Job

There needs to be a re-examination of the nature of the sales job. Detailed, meaningful job descriptions are needed for developing a compensation plan. These job descriptions need to be logically compared to other sales positions in terms of their importance to the company.

Step Two: Consider the Company's General Compensation Structure

A majority of companies use job evaluation to determine the comparative value of individual jobs, the purpose of which is to arrive at fair compensation relationships among jobs. Four commonly used job evaluation methods are:

(i) **Simple Ranking.** In simple ranking, a sales executive committee sorts job descriptions in the order of worth. This job evaluation is done without considering the individuals currently in the jobs or their compensation levels.

(ii) **Classification or Grading**. The classification or grading method uses a system of grades and grade descriptions, against which jobs are compared. The grades, or classes, are described in terms of job responsibility, skills required, supervision given and received, exposure to unfavourable and dangerous working conditions, and similar characteristics. Job descriptions are then classified into appropriate grades. All jobs within a grade are treated alike with respect to base compensation.

(iii) **Point System**. The point system involves defining the factors common to most jobs that represent key elements of value inherent in all jobs. Generally the specific factors include mental and physical skills, responsibility, supervision given and received, personality requirements, and minimum education required. Each factor is assigned a minimum and maximum number of points. Next, appraised factor scores are combined into a total point value. Finally, different bands of points are decided upon and become the different compensation classes.

(iv) **Factor Comparison Method.** The factor comparison method is similar to the point system. It uses a scheme of ranking and cross-comparisons to reduce error from fault judgment. This method employs selected factors and evaluation scales. The selected number of key jobs, typical of similar jobs throughout the company, is then evaluated, factor by factor. This is done by arranging them in rank order from highest to lowest for each factor.

Step Three: Consider Compensation Patterns in the Community and the Industry

It is important for sales management to consider prevailing compensation patterns in the community and industry. Management needs to answer four basic questions: (1) What compensation systems are being used?; (2) What is the average compensation for similar positions?; (3) How are other companies doing with their plans?; and (4) What are the pros and cons of departing from industry or community patterns? An effective programme for setting compensation of salespeople considers the relation of external compensation practices to those of the company.

Step Four: Determine the Compensation Level

Management should determine the amount of compensation a salesperson should be offered on average. It is essential that the general level of compensation be sufficiently competitive to attract and retain competent salespeople. The most significant factors to be considered to determine the basic level of pay for the sales force include:

- the skills, experiences, and education required to do the job successfully;
- the level of income for comparative jobs in the company; and
- the level of income for comparative jobs in the industry.

The importance of each of these factors would differ from one company to another.

Step Five: Provide for the Various Compensation Elements

The four basic elements of a sales compensation plan include:

1. a fixed element, either a salary or a drawing account to provide some stability of income;
2. a variable element (for example, a commission, bonus, or profit-sharing arrangement) to serve as an incentive;
3. an element covering the fringe or "plus factor," such as life insurance and pension; and
4. an element providing for reimbursement of expenses or payment of expense allowances.

Not all four elements are included in all situations. Management normally selects the combination of elements that best fits the selling situation.

Step Six: Allow for Special Company Needs and Problems

Although a sales compensation is no panacea for marketing ills, it is often possible to construct a plan that increases marketing effectiveness. Several possibilities exist for using the sales compensation plan to help solve special company problems. Compensation plans may assist in securing new customers and new business, improving the quality of salespeople's reports, controlling expenses of handling complaints and adjustment, eliminating price shading by the sales staff, reducing travelling and other expenses, making collections, and gathering credit information.

Step Seven: Consult the Present Sales Force

Management should consult the present salespeople about the compensation plan, owing to the fact that a lot of complaints stem from the salespeople. Management needs to encourage salespeople to express their likes and dislikes about the current plan and to suggest changes in it. Criticisms and suggestions should be evaluated relative to the plan or plans under consideration.

Step Eight: Commit the Tentative Plan to Writing, and Pretest It

The tentative plan is put in writing to ensure clarification and to eliminate inconsistencies. The plan, then, is pretested. The amount of testing needed will depend upon how much the new plan differs from the existing one. To identify the probable impact on profits, the sales and potential earnings (for the new plan) for each salesperson over the past several years should be computed.

Step Nine: Revise the Plan

The plan is then revised to eliminate any existing deficiencies. If changes are extensive, the revised plan should go through further pretests and perhaps another pilot test. But further testing would not be necessary if there have been minor changes.

Step Ten: Implement the Plan and Provide for Follow-up

When the new plan is implemented, it is explained to the sales force. Management needs to convince the salespeople of its basic fairness and logic. The sales force is made to understand what management wishes to accomplish through the new plan and how it is to be done. As indicated earlier, a good compensation plan must be fair, easy to understand, and simple for the salespeople to calculate.

Provisions for follow-up are made. The compensation plan should be evaluated on a frequent, regular basis. As time and circumstances change, objectives change. Frequently, this means that some aspect of the compensation plan must be adjusted to motivate salespeople to meet new objectives.

Types of Compensation Plans

There are four basic types of compensation plans: straight salary, straight commission, bonus, and a combination of salary and variable elements.

Straight Salary Plan

Under the straight salary compensation plan, salespeople receive a fixed amount of money at regular intervals—such as weekly or monthly—representing total payments for their services. Salary is a regular, fixed sum that is time-related rather than output-related. According to Donaldson (1990), the jobs salespeople are expected to perform under this plan are not volume-related or even quantifiable—for example, the jobs of providing market information or technical advice and handling complaints. New staff in training will also need to have salary-related rather than performance-related compensation. A recent study suggests that straight—salary compensation plans are more common among industrial goods companies than among consumer goods companies.

When to Use Straight Salary Plans

As Anderson et al. (1992) suggest, straight salary is most appropriate in the following situations:

- **Team-Selling Situations.** Several people—for example, a coordinating salesperson, a technical engineer, a marketing service representative, and a member of marketing management—cooperate as a team in making a sale.
- **Long Negotiating Periods.** A year or more may be needed to make a complex sale of a system of products and services.
- **Mixed Promotional Situations.** Advertising sometimes plays a vital role in selling, and the relationship between a salesperson's effort and advertising may be difficult to evaluate. This situation would apply to both inside and outside sales forces.
- **Learning Periods.** During the first year, a salary is usually required to attract new recruits into selling and to compensate the trainee at least until commissions are large enough to provide

188

an adequate living standard. For example, some insurance firms pay a salary during the first year. After one year, the salesperson is placed on a straight commission plan.

- **Missionary Selling.** These are non-selling jobs, such as developing goodwill among customers by providing them with advice, service, and assistance in merchandising (e.g., setting up displays or developing local advertisements).
- **Special Conditions.** Special activities include introducing a new line of products, opening up new territories, calling on new customer accounts, or selling in unusual market conditions.

Other characteristics of straight salary companies, as summarised by Futrell (1999), are the following:

- Dominant market share in a mature, stable industry
- Highly defined and stable customer base
- Strongly centralised and closely managed selling effort
- Significant number of house accounts
- Highly team-oriented sales efforts
- Service versus selling emphasis

Advantages of the Straight Salary Plan

The straight salary compensation plan has the following advantages:

- It provides security to salespeople, because they know that their basic living expenses will be covered. For the sales force, the stability of income offered by the straight salary plan provides freedom from the financial uncertainties inherent in other compensation plans.
- It helps develop a sense of loyalty to the company.
- It increases flexibility in territorial assignments, because salespeople are less likely to become attached to certain sales territories and customers.

- It gives management a higher degree of control over salespeople's activities. It provides strong financial control over sales personnel, and management can direct their activities along the most productive lines.
- It permits a rapid adaptation of sales force efforts to changing market demands and company objectives.
- It is economical to administer, because of its basic simplicity. Additionally, because of its basic simplicity, salespeople have no difficulty in understanding straight salary plans.

Weaknesses of the Straight Salary Plan

The straight salary compensation plan, however, has several potentially undesirable features, including the following:

- It provides no financial incentive to put forth extra effort. Since there are no direct monetary incentives, many salespeople do only an average rather than an outstanding job.
- It may increase selling costs, because salaries go on when sales are not being made. Even though sales revenue is not produced, due to either inadequate effort on the part of the sales force or to other circumstances, salaries still go on. Selling costs consequently go up in relation to sales revenues.
- It often leads to income inequities, since the least productive salespeople tend to be overpaid, and the most productive underpaid.
- It leads to adequate, but not superior, performance. There is a tendency for salespeople to perform only enough to maintain their jobs.

Straight Commission Plan

Under the straight commission plan, the salesperson receives an amount that varies with results, usually sales or profits. Some straight commission plans provide for differential commission rates for sales of different products, to different categories of customers, or during given selling seasons. The straight compensation plan provides strong incentives rather than security, and it tends to result in higher productivity and earning levels for salespeople than salary-based commission does in similar organisations. It is likely to be used in industries such as real estate, furniture sales, or door-to-door sales.

The straight commission plan is a completely incentive-based compensation plan. Commissions are paid only for measurable achievements (usually sales volume). If salespeople do not sell anything, they do not earn anything. Application of straight commission systems requires sales managers to determine:

1. the base, or unit, upon which the commissions will be paid (units sold or gross profits);
2. the rate to be paid per unit (usually expressed as a percentage of sales or gross profit);
3. the point at which commissions start (after selling the first unit or after reaching a sales quota); and
4. the time when the commissions are paid (when the order is obtained, when it is shipped, or when it is paid for).

When to Use Straight Commission Plans

Situations where straight commission plans are most appropriate follow:

*   Little non-selling, missionary work is involved.
*   The company cannot afford to pay a salary and wants selling costs to be directly related to sales.
*   The company uses independent contractors and part-timers.

Other characteristics of straight commission firms, as summarised by Futrell (1999), are the following:

*   Low barriers to entry into the job
*   Limited corporate cash resources
*   Small entrance into an emerging market or market segment
*   High risk reward sales force culture

- Undefined market opportunity or customer base
- Inability to set quotas or other performance criteria
- Volume-oriented business strategy

Advantages of the Straight Commission Plan

Straight commission plans have some advantages, including the following:

- Income is directly related to productivity. It provides maximum direct monetary incentive for the salesperson to strive for higher-level volume. The high-performing salesperson is paid more than he or she would be under most salary plans, and low producers are not likely to be overcompensated.
- Commission is easy to calculate, so salespeople may keep track of their earnings.
- There is no ceiling on potential earnings.
- Money is not tied up in salaries, because commissions are paid only when revenues are generated.
- Costs are proportional to sales. Straight commission plans also provide a means for cost control; almost all direct selling expenses fluctuate directly with sales volume changes and sales compensation becomes virtually an all-variable expense.
- Salespeople have maximum work freedom.
- Poorly performing salespeople eliminate themselves by quitting.
- Income is based strictly on accomplishments and not on subjective evaluations by sales managers.

Weaknesses of the Straight Commission Plan

Disadvantages of the straight commission plan include the following (Anderson et al., 1992):

- Excessive emphasis may be placed on sales volume rather than profitable sales. Additionally, unless differential commission rates are used, salespeople push the easiest-to-sell, high-margin items.

- Salespeople have little loyalty to the company.
- Because of the extreme fluctuations in earnings, such plans create uncertainty for many salespeople about meeting daily living expenses for their families. Additionally, some salespeople's efficiency may diminish because of income uncertainties.
- There may be high sales force turnover rates when business conditions are slow.
- Non-selling activities (service, missionary sales, displays, etc) are neglected.
- Salespeople may overload customers with inventory, thereby straining long-term customer relationships.
- Windfall earnings may come about under good business conditions, which may be disturbing to sales management.
- Flexibility to split territories or transfer salespeople is diminished, because of limited means of control over the sales force. Thus, commission provides little financial control over salespeople's activities.
- Sales managers may become perfunctory in recruiting, selecting, and supervising, since they may consider marginal salespeople acceptable under this compensation plan.

Bonus Compensation Plan

Bonuses are different from commissions. A bonus is an amount paid for accomplishing a specific sales task; a commission varies in amount with sales volume or other commission base. A bonus consists of a lump sum of money paid for some form of outstanding performance. The bonus is a payment for achievement that is not strictly volume- or individual performance-related. As a means of stimulating the salespeople, it may be offered and paid for meeting or exceeding quotas, for selling a given product mix, for opening a new account, or for any other conceivable activity that the company may want to encourage. Individuals can achieve bonuses for reaching their individual targets. A bonus may be paid weekly, monthly, biannually, or annually.

Bonuses are never used alone; they always appear with one of the other three main sales compensation methods of straight salary, straight commission, and a combination of salary and variable elements. If used with the straight salary, the plan resembles the commission plan. If used with straight commission, the result is a commission plan to which an element of managerial control and direction has been added. If used with the combination salary and commission plan, the bonus becomes a portion of the incentive income that is calculated differently from the commission.

Flexibility is the main advantage of a bonus. It can provide quick and positive behaviour reinforcement when needed. When offered to groups, a bonus can create solidarity and motivate a combined team effort. The main disadvantage of the bonus plan is that it can be costly if sales executives are not able to set realistic objectives and evaluate performance quickly. With group bonuses, there is also the propensity of some salespeople to ride on the achievements and efforts of other group members.

Certain administrative actions that are crucial when a bonus is included in the compensation plan, as summarised by Still et al. (1988), include the following:

1. The bonus conditions should thoroughly be explained, as all sales personnel must understand them.
2. The necessary records must be set up and maintained.
3. Procedures are needed for keeping sales personnel abreast of their current standings relative to the goals.
4. Any bonus misunderstandings or grievances arising should be dealt with fairly and tactfully.

Combination Compensation Plans

Most sales compensation plans are combinations of two or three of the basic compensation methods. Commissions and bonuses are usually used to achieve volume or profit goals, while salary helps achieve less quantifiable goals, such as customer service, expense control, and long-run sales development. Combination plans are the most widely used of all compensation methods. They are mostly developed as attempts to capture the advantages and to offset the disadvantages of the salary, commission, and bonus systems.

Types of Combination Compensation Plans

Combination compensation plans are the most flexible of all systems. The following are some combination compensation plans that fit a variety of situations (Anderson et al. 1992).

1. **Salary Plus Commissions.** This combination is best when management wants to get high sales without sacrificing customer service. It is good for new salespeople, since it provides more security than straight commission.

2. **Salary Plus Bonus.** This is best for achieving long-term objectives, such as selling large installations or product systems or achieving a desired customer mix.

3. **Salary Plus Commission Plus Bonus.** This combination is best for seasonal sales, when there are frequent inventory imbalances and when management wants to focus on certain products or customers.

4. **Commission Plus Bonus.** This combination is normally employed for group efforts, whereby some salespeople call on central buyers while others call store managers.

When to Use a Combination Salary Plan

The characteristics of companies that offer combination plans, as summarised by Futrell (1999), are the following:

- Established company with growth potential, many products, and active competition
- Company has a need to direct a complex set of behaviours
- Company has a need for a variable pay component that will ensure top performers are rewarded commensurately

Advantages of a Combination Compensation Plan

Some of the identified advantages of a combination compensation plan are the following:

- It provides the greatest flexibility and control over salespeople in that all desirable activities can be rewarded
- It provides security plus incentive. The plan has the capability of providing at the most favourable ratio of selling expenses to sales security plus incentive.
- It allows frequent, immediate reinforcement of desired sales behaviour.

Disadvantages of a Combination Compensation Plan

Some of the identified disadvantages of a combination compensation plan are the following:

- It can be complex and misunderstood.
- It can be expensive to administer, particularly if not computerised.
- It may fail to achieve management objectives if not carefully conceived.

Nonfinancial Compensation

As Ingram et al. (2004) observe, compensation for effort and performance may include nonfinancial rewards. Examples of nonfinancial compensation include career advancement through promotion, a sense of accomplishment on the job, opportunities for personal growth, recognition of achievement, and job security. As the authors point out, sometimes, non-financial rewards are coupled with financial rewards (for example, a promotion into sales management usually results in a pay increase), so one salesperson might view these rewards as primarily financial, whereas another might view them from a nonfinancial perspective. Details of nonfinancial compensation rewards are discussed in the next section.

Promotion

Opportunity for promotion is a highly valued reward among salespeople. Among younger salespeople, as Cron et al. (1988) observe, it often eclipses pay as the most valued reward. Giving the increasing number of young to middle-aged people in the workforce, the opportunities for promotion may be limited severely in non-growth industries. Growth industries, such as financial services and direct sales, offer reasonably good opportunities for advancement through promotion (Ingram et al. 2004).

Sense of Accomplishment

A sense of accomplishment, unlike some rewards, cannot be delivered to the salespeople from the organisation. As Ingram et al observe, because a sense of accomplishment originates from the salesperson's mind, all the organisation can do is facilitate the process by which it develops.

Steps that can be taken to facilitate a sense of accomplishment in the sales force, as summarised by Ingram et al. (2004), include the following:

1. Ensure that the sales force members understand the critical role they fulfil in revenue production and other key activities within the company.

2. Personalise the causes and effects of salesperson performance. This means that each salesperson should understand the link between effort and performance, and between performance and rewards.

3. Strongly consider the practice of management by

> objectives (MBO) or goal setting as a standard management practice.
> 4. Reinforce feelings of worthwhile accomplishment in communication with the sales force.

Opportunity for Personal Growth

Opportunities for personal growth are regularly offered to salespeople. Common examples are educational tuition reimbursement programmes and seminars and workshops on topics like physical fitness, stress reduction, and personal financial planning.

Recognition of Achievement

As Ingram et al (2004) emphasise, recognition (both informal and formal) forms an integral component of the sales force reward system. Informal recognition refers to "nice job" praises and similar public admiration and glory usually delivered in private conversation or correspondence between a sales manager and a salesperson. Informal recognition is easy to administer, costs practically nothing, and can reinforce desirable behaviour immediately after its occurrence.

Formal recognition programmes, as the authors observe, are typically based on group competition or individual accomplishments that represent improved performance. Formal recognition may also be associated with monetary, merchandise, or travel awards. It is, however, distinguished from other rewards by two characteristics. First, formal recognition implies public recognition for accomplishment in the presence of peers and superiors in the organisation. Second, it includes a symbolic award of lasting psychological value, such as jewellery or a plaque.

Guidelines for Formal Recognition Programmes

There are guidelines for conducting effective formal recognition programmes. Formal recognition programmes have a better chance of success, if sales managers consider the following, as summarised by Ingram et al. (2004):

> 1. Remember that recognition programmes should

produce results well beyond the expected and that the programme should make sense from a return-on-investment perspective.

2. Publicise the programme before it is implemented. Build momentum for the programme while it is under way with additional communiqués, and reinforce the accomplishments of the winners with post-programme communications both inside and outside the company.

3. Ensure that the celebration for winners is well conceived and executed. Consider the possibility of having customers and team mates join in with brief congratulatory testimonials or thanks.

4. Arrange for individual salespeople or sales teams to acknowledge the support of others who helped them win the award. This builds the teamwork orientation.

5. Strive for fairness in structuring recognition programmes so that winners are clearly superior performers, not those with less difficult performance goals.

Job Security

As Ingram et al. (2004) observe, job security, although valued highly by salespeople nearing retirement age, is the least valued among other sales force rewards. High-performing salespeople may sense that they have job security, if not with their present employer then with another employer.

It cannot be overemphasised that the current wave of mergers, acquisitions and general downsizing of companies is making it more difficult to offer job security as a reward. In the past, job security was easier to assure, at least as long as performance contingencies were met. Another factor that will make it difficult to offer job security with a given company is the lack of unionisation of the salespeople in most fields.

Review Questions

1. What are the three ways to compensate performance? Which of these has the most impact and why?

2. What critical factors must managers consider when designing a sales force compensation package?

3. What are the essential criteria for designing and implementing a sound bonus incentive programme?

4. Which salary plan allows an organisation the most control over sales personnel, and which is better for motivation of high sales?

5. What compensation mix do you think is best for a missionary salesperson calling on physicians?

Chapter 12

Leading the Sales Force

Introduction

For the sales manager, leadership is the focus of activity through which sales objectives are attained. Effective leadership is the one critical asset that significantly differentiates successful organisations from unsuccessful organisations. This chapter presents an analysis of the nature of leadership, leadership influences on salespeople's behaviour, and important leadership activities.

This chapter focuses on leading the sales force. It explains the nature of leadership and the distinction between leadership and management and the sources of leader power. Major leadership theories are described and evaluated. It also deals with analysis of the appropriate style of sales management leadership and the important activities of the sales manager that direct the behaviour of the sales force.

The Nature of Leadership

Leadership can mean different things. An effective leader is one who motivates, influences, and gives direction. One can define the three basics of leadership as people, influence, and goals— leadership occurs among people, involves the use of influence, and is used to attain goals. One of the formal definitions of leadership is the ability to influence other people's behaviour toward the attainment of goals.

In a context of sales management, leadership deals with the relationship between a sales manager or sales superior and the salespeople. The dynamics of leadership include the sales

201

manager (leader), the salespeople (followers), and the specific situation.

Leadership and Management

It is appropriate for the sales manager to understand that, although leadership and management are related, they are very different. Management is primarily a learned process whereby subordinates are guided in the performance of formally prescribed duties toward the achievement of organisational goals. Leadership, on the other hand, is a process whereby people are moved in some direction through non-coercive means. Thus, a person can be a manager, a leader, both, or neither. A sales manager is a person whose job is the management of salespeople and budgets. Leading is part of the manager's directing function.

Leader Influence and Power

Central to understanding leadership influence over an organisation is the concept of power. Power is the ability to influence the behaviour of others. Within the organisation, leaders may draw upon power from various sources—legitimate power, reward power, coercive power, referent power, and expert power (Busch 1980; Futrell 1999). These sources of power are explained next.

- **Legitimate Power.** Legitimate power comes from a formal management position in an organisation and the authority delegated to that position and is recognised by others as necessary in achieving organisational objectives. For example, once a salesperson has been selected as a district manager, most salespeople understand they are obligated to follow the new manager's direction with respect to work activities. Salespeople accept this source of power as legitimate, which is why they comply.
- **Reward Power.** Reward power stems from the leader's authority to provide subordinates with

various rewards. These rewards may include money, praise, and recognition. Leaders can use rewards to influence the behaviour of salespeople.

- **Coercive Power.** Coercive power comes from the leader's ability to punish or withhold rewards. It is based on obtaining compliance through fear of punishment. A leader has coercive power when he or she has the right to dismiss or demote employees, to withdraw pay increases, or to criticise. For example, if Fianko, a salesperson, does not perform as expected, his manager has the coercive power to criticise him, reprimand him, put a negative letter in his file, and hurt his chance for a raise.

- **Referent Power.** Referent power stems from the leader's personality characteristics that command followers' identification, respect, and admiration, so they wish to emulate the leader. When a salesperson admires and respects a manager because of the way the manager deals with him or her, the influence is based on referent power. Referent power depends on the leader's personal characteristics rather than on a formal title or position.

- **Expert Power.** Expert power depends upon the leader's skills, special knowledge, or special abilities. When the leader is a true expert, salespeople go along with recommendations because of the manager's superior knowledge (Futrell 1999).

The majority of sales managers have access to all of these power sources, and they attempt to use each at the appropriate time and situation to influence salespeople to attain desired goals.

Leadership Theories

The three main theories of leadership are the trait theory, behavioural theory, and contingency theory. Each of these theories uses a different set of characteristics to assess different styles of leadership. We consider each of these theories in the next section.

Trait Theory

The first systematic approach to understanding leadership was the attempt to identify the personal characteristics, or traits, of leaders. The proponents of this theory assumed that great leaders possessed a set of stable and enduring leadership traits or characteristics that set them apart from followers. The goal was to identify these traits so that they could be made use of as a basis for selecting leaders (Von Fleet 1991).

In searching for measurable leadership traits, researchers took two approaches: (1) comparing the traits of those who emerged as leaders with the traits of those who did not; and (2) comparing the traits of effective leaders with those of ineffective leaders. The first category tends to be the most common approach, but it has largely failed to reveal any traits that consistently set leaders apart from followers (Weiss and Adler 1984). As a group, leaders have been found to be taller, brighter, more extroverted, and more self-confident than non-leaders. However, a lot of people have these traits and do not achieve leadership positions, while many people acknowledged as leaders do not possess these traits. Both Alexander the Great and Napoleon, for example, were of below-average height; Abraham Lincoln was moody and an introvert. Studies that have taken the second category of leadership trait approach have also failed to isolate traits that are strongly associated with successful leadership.

Because of the many weaknesses associated with the trait theory, it has lost popularity. Research efforts have turned to the relationship between leader behaviour and desired goals, such as job performance and employee morale.

Implications of Trait Theory for Sales Management

While no single profile of traits can identify an effective sales force leader, many researchers believe that certain traits, or characteristics, are needed to become an effective sales manager. For example, some believe that an effective sales force leader must be a hard worker and be people-oriented. Others believe that a sales manager must have the innate ability to take risks and be a decision maker (Bethel 1985). The personal qualities needed to be a successful leader in any endeavour, as summarised by Futrell (1998), are the following:

- **Leaders have a strong, defined sense of purpose.** They know what needs to be done.
- **Leaders are effective communicators.** They communicate their visions of the future. They let people know what is expected and how they are doing.
- **Leaders are persistent.** They are willing to invest whatever time or effort is required to achieve results. Success for the leader is 1 percent inspiration and 99 percent perspiration.
- **Leaders are self-knowledgeable.** They know their strengths, weaknesses, skills, and abilities.
- **Leaders are learners.** They stay informed and develop new skills and strengthen old ones.
- **Leaders love their work.** They see work as an adventure and are constantly renewed by it.
- **Leaders attract others.** They are able to draw and unite people in a consolidated effort.
- **Leaders establish human relationships based on trust, respect, and caring.**
- **Leaders are risk takers.** They are willing to explore and experiment with any resources that can serve their ultimate purposes.
- **Leaders are willing to help others attain their goals.** They reduce roadblocks to subordinates' goals and help them reach success in their jobs.
- **True leaders are not just managers or supervisors.** They are in a class by themselves. The true leader has

the ability to motivate and inspire people to grow and learn while they translate a dream into reality.

Behavioural Theory

Unlike the trait approach, which sought to identify characteristics that differentiate leaders from non-leaders, the behavioural approach attempted to determine behavioural patterns (styles) that set effective leaders apart from ineffective leaders. The Ohio State University Studies is one of the most important sets of studies on the behavioural leadership approach. This is summarised below.

The Ohio State University Studies

At Ohio State University, researchers identified two critical dimensions of leadership behaviour: initiating structure (i.e., the extent to which leaders organise and define the relationship between themselves and their followers—sometimes called a "task orientation") and consideration (i.e., friendship, mutual trust, respect, and warmth—sometimes called the "employee-orientation") behaviour. The researchers found that initiating structure focused on getting the job done. Conversely, consideration behaviour focused on the employee (Fleishman 1953). These dimensions were investigated in terms of their degree of presence; the resulting four leadership styles are shown in Figure 12.1. Research focused on determining the association of these styles with job performance and employee satisfaction. The research evidence was that employee turnover rates were lowest and employee satisfaction highest under leaders who were rated high in consideration. On the other hand, leaders who were rated low in consideration and high in initiating structure had high grievance and turnover rates among their employees.

Although "high initiating structure, high consideration" (quadrant two) tended to yield high employee satisfaction and performance, no single leader behaviour surfaced as best for all situations. Moreover, few managers can be both task- and employee-oriented. Nevertheless, the behavioural approach continues to appeal to many a manager, because it is understandable, and there is widespread belief that specific leader behaviours can be learned and put into practice (Anderson et al. 1992).

Figure 12.1 Dimensions of Leadership Style: Ohio State Leadership Studies

	LOW ← Initiating structure → HIGH	
HIGH Consideration **LOW**	1 High consideration Low structure Leader focuses on achieving group harmony and individual need satisfaction	2 High consideration High structure Leader strives to accomplish the job while maintaining a harmonious work group
	3 Low consideration Low structure Leader becomes largely passive and allows the situation to take care of itself.	4 Low consideration High structure Leader focuses on getting the job done

Source: Adapted from Ohio State Leadership Studies, "Dimensions of Leadership Style," In *Current Developments in the Study of Leadership,* edited by Edwin A. Fleishman and James G. Hunt, (Southern Illinois University Press: Carbondale, Illinois, 1973), 153 .

Implications of Behavioural Theory for Sales Management
Several behaviour styles may be effective for sales managers in different situations. Figure 12.2 makes use of the four basic leadership styles identified by the Ohio State University researchers to illustrate how certain leadership styles can work for sales managers, as summarised by Anderson et al. (1992).

Figure 12.2   Behavioural Styles for Various Sales Management Tasks

HIGH

1. Experienced, high-performing salespeople who tend to be too competitive with one another	2. Newly hired, inexperienced sales trainees
3. Experienced, high-performing salespeople doing work they know and enjoy	4. Experienced salespeople required to do unpleasant, unfamiliar work

Consideration

LOW

LOW   HIGH

Initiating Structure

Source: R. E. Anderson, J. F. Hair, Jr., and A. J. Bush, *Professional Sales Management,* (New York: McGraw-Hill, 1992), 460. Reprinted with permission of McGraw-Hill.

- Quadrant One: A high-consideration, low-structure style is appropriate if the sales force consists of highly motivated individuals who are dedicated to the task at hand but require social support from superiors. For example, experienced, high-performing salespeople who tend to be too competitive with one another.

- Quadrant Two: A high-consideration, high-structure style is appropriate if the sales force consists of individuals who require social support from superiors, are not cohesive, and lack a strong identification with the task at hand. For example, newly hired, inexperienced sales trainees.

- Quadrant Three: A low-consideration, low-structure leadership style is appropriate if the sales force consists of highly motivated individuals who are socially mature and dedicated to the task at hand. For example, experienced, high-performing sales representatives who are doing work they know and enjoy.

- Quadrant Four: A low-consideration, high-structure leadership style is appropriate if the sales force consists of individuals who are socially mature and highly cohesive but who do not understand or identify with the task at hand. For example, an experienced sales force that is required to do unpleasant, unfamiliar work such as collecting payments on overdue customer accounts.

The behavioural theories, like the trait theories, by themselves may not be adequate to explain leadership. The belief is that a theory of leadership should combine traits and situations. Some traits may be unique to certain leaders, while other traits may be common to all leaders.

Contingency Theory

The trait and behavioural leadership theories focus primarily on the leader. The contingency leadership theory emphasises the contingencies surrounding the leader, the followers, and the situation. Figure 12.3 illustrates how this contingency theory may apply to the sales manager. This theory assumes that successful leadership is dependent (or contingent) on various factors related to the salesperson (or follower) and the situation. Therefore, the sales manager's traits and behaviour can directly influence both the sales force and the situation. Moreover, as the double-headed arrows used in the figure indicate, salespeople and the situation can also influence the leader (or sales manager). For example, a supervisor who has been constantly unsuccessful in trying to get an employee to improve his or her performance will eventually decrease his or her efforts to work with that employee.

Fiedler is considered to have developed the first and, perhaps, best-known contingency model of leadership. The model incorporates both the leadership style and the nature of the leadership situation. As Anderson et al. (1992) point out, since 1951, Fiedler has been conducting research on the relationship between organisational performance and leader attitudes. He believes that a leader's performance depends on two interrelated factors: (1) the degree to which the situation gives the leader control and influence and (2) the leader's basic motivation—whether toward accomplishing the task or toward having close, supportive relations with others. Leaders are either task-motivated or relationship-motivated. These two orientations are roughly equivalent to initiating structure and consideration from the Ohio State University studies mentioned under behavioural theory.

Figure 12.3 A Contingency Approach to Sales Force Leadership

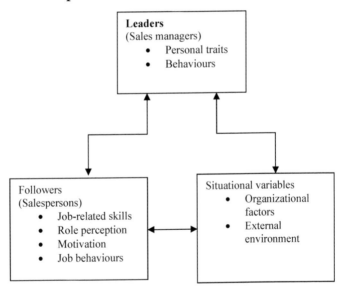

Source: R. E. Anderson, J. F. Hair, Jr., and A. J. Bush, *Professional Sales Management* (New York: McGraw-Hill, 1992), 461. Reprinted with permission of McGraw-Hill.

Specifically, Fiedler has tried to discover which leaders are most likely to develop high-producing groups: leaders who are very lenient or those who are highly demanding and discriminating in evaluating subordinates. His results indicate that the most effective type of leadership depends upon three situational variables:

1. The quality of the leader's personal relationships with members of the group
2. The formal power or authority provided by the leader's position
3. The degree to which the group's task is structured

Situations high on all three components are considered favourable, because (1) leaders can usually expect support from group members; (2) leaders can enforce their will with the legitimate power or formal authority of their positions; and (3) more structured tasks can be more clearly defined, delegated, controlled, and evaluated by all members of the organisation.

The most favourable situation (cell I in Figure 12.4) for a leader is one in which he or she is well liked by the members (good leader-member relations), has a powerful position (high position power), and is directing a well-defined job (high task structure). Conversely, the most unfavourable situation is one in which the leader is disliked, has little position power, and faces an unstructured task (cell III).

Fiedler discovered that a discriminating, task-oriented leader attitude is effective in either highly favourable or highly unfavourable situations. But when the situation is moderately favourable or moderately unfavourable, a more lenient and considerate leader attitude is best for higher group performance, as suggested in cell II of Figure 12.4. When relations with group members are moderately poor, position power is low, and a highly structured task is at hand, the leader should be permissive and accepting in behaviour and attitude.

Fiedler's contingency model of leadership effectiveness suggests that group performance can be improved either by modifying the leader's style or by modifying the group's task and situation. However, he believes that most organisations cannot afford expensive selection techniques to find talented leaders who fit specific job requirements. Nor does training provide adequate answers to the problems of leadership (Fiedler 1973). The most reasonable approach is to tailor the job to fit the manager. Since the type of leadership needed depends on the favourableness of the situation, the organisation can more easily alter the job than the members. Such factors as the power associated with the leader's position, the task assigned to the group, or the composition of the group's membership can be changed (Behling and Schriesheim 1976).

Implications of Fiedler's Theory for Sales Management

As Anderson et al. (1992) observe, Fiedler's contingency theory offers several important implications for sales managers. Most importantly, it should be understood that both relationship-oriented and task-oriented sales managers can perform well under some situations but not others. For example, a high-performing salesperson who is promoted to sales manager may fail, because his or her task-oriented leadership style does not match the demands of the situation. In the past, this person may have had very clearly defined performance goals (e.g., to increase sales revenue by 15 percent) and may have known exactly how to achieve them. In the new situation as sales manager, this person may face tasks that are more complex and less routine, such as motivating an older sales representative or building confidence in younger salespeople. Thus, the new task-oriented sales manager will not be an effective leader unless he or she adopts a more relationship-oriented style.

Figure 12.4 Fiedler's Contingency Theory

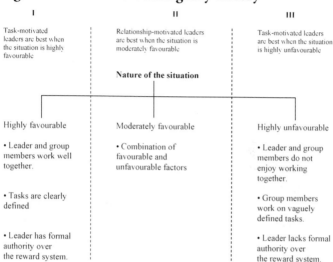

I	II	III
Task-motivated leaders are best when the situation is highly favourable	Relationship-motivated leaders are best when the situation is moderately favourable	Task-motivated leaders are best when the situation is highly unfavourable

Nature of the situation

Highly favourable	Moderately favourable	Highly unfavourable
• Leader and group members work well together.	• Combination of favourable and unfavourable factors	• Leader and group members do not enjoy working together.
• Tasks are clearly defined		• Group members work on vaguely defined tasks.
• Leader has formal authority over the reward system.		• Leader lacks formal authority over the reward system.

Source: R. Kreitner and M. A. Sova, *Understanding Management: A Problem-Solving Process* (Boston: Houghton Mifflin, 1980), 396. Reprinted with permission of Houghton Mifflin.

Substitutes for Leadership

A new perspective on leadership that has recently attracted a great deal of attention is the concept of substitutes for leadership. As Kerr and Jermier (1978) submit, this model was developed because existing leadership models and theories do not account for situations in which leadership is not needed. The concept applies to situations in which leadership is neutralised or replaced by characteristics of the subordinate, the task, and the organisation. First, such characteristics of the subordinate such as experience, need for independence, and professional orientation may serve to neutralise leadership behaviour. For example, productive employees with a high level of professionalism may not have to be told what to do. Second, characteristics of the task itself may substitute for leadership. For example, individuals whose tasks are challenging or intrinsically satisfying may not need or want direction from a leader. Finally, organisational characteristics that may serve as substitutes for leadership include formalisation, group cohesion, inflexibility and a rigid reward structure. For example, leadership may not be needed when company policies and practices are formal and inflexible. Preliminary research on substitutes for leadership has provided support for this concept as a viable leadership perspective (Mang and Sims 1987).

Implications for Sales Management

The substitutes for leadership perspective offers several important insights to sales managers. Most importantly, it points out that there are many instances in which leadership may not be needed. In many selling situations, leadership behaviours are neutralised or replaced by the characteristics of the individual salesperson, the selling task being performed, and the organisation itself. For example, salespeople with a great deal of experience or a great need for independence may not require as much direction as younger, less confident salespeople. Additionally, many individuals go into sales as a career because of the challenge and flexibility it offers them. Thus, it appears that the personal selling environment is very applicable to the concept of substitutes for leadership. According to this concept, sales managers, in some situations, can be better leaders if they know when *not* to lead (Anderson et al. 1992).

Sales Management Leadership in Practice

The leadership role for sales managers is one with many facets that must result in attaining organisational goals. Perhaps, the most critical facet of the leadership role revolves around staffing, which ensures that recruiting, selecting, and training are carried out well. The eventual success or failure of an organisation depends, to a large extent, upon the quality of the people it hires and retains.

The demands of sales management call for leadership in many different situations. These may involve reassuring a struggling salesperson and standing up for the sales team before superiors. Leadership also requires that the sales manager motivate salespeople through integration of their personal goals with those of the organisation. Furthermore, evaluating and controlling the activities of salespeople in order to take timely corrective action where and when needed continuously challenges the sales manager's leadership.

Leadership Styles

All sales managers exhibit a leadership style, whether or not they are conscious of it. The sales manager's personality, characteristics, needs, motives, power, and past experiences directly influence the person's natural leadership style. No one style of leadership is appropriate for all situations. Effective leaders match their style of leadership with the maturity and duties of the sales force. A range of leadership styles from task-oriented to human relations-oriented can be successful as long as the style is matched correctly with the situation. The real task of the successful sales manager is to select the style of leadership most appropriate for the individual salesperson, for the sales force as a whole, and for the particular sales situation.

The Sales Manager's Behaviour Influences Salespeople

The study of leadership has identified two forms of behaviour that sales managers can use to influence their salespeople. Indications are that the manager should exhibit both task and relationship behaviour in different situations.

Task behaviour involves the leader in describing the duties and responsibilities of an individual or group. This includes telling people what to do, how to do it, when to do it, where to do it, and who is to do it. In addition, the people are closely supervised to make sure the job is done correctly.

Relationship behaviour is people-oriented. It involves the extent to which the leader uses two-way communication not one-way as in task behaviour. It includes listening, providing clarification, getting to know the individuals motives and goals, and giving positive feedback to help reinforce characteristics such as a person's self-image, confidence, and ego. Relationship behaviour can involve delegating a high degree of authority and responsibility to salespeople for developing their own goals and plans for how to meet these goals. The sales manager is available to assist and give guidance if necessary. However, it is up to the salesperson to accomplish the job's various goals. This is a very democratic leadership approach toward motivating people (Futrell 1999).

To help illustrate the use of leadership styles in different situations, four different styles were developed, based on past research. These four styles form the leadership continuum shown in Figure 12.5. On one extreme, the leadership approach is task-oriented, and on the other extreme it is people-oriented. Next, four quadrants were developed to position these four basic leadership styles (Figure 12.6). The following examples, as summarised by Futrell (1999), illustrate different situations in which these styles can be used.

Figure 12.5 Four Basic Leadership Styles that Influence Salespeople

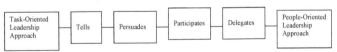

Source: C. M. Futrell, *Fundamentals of Selling* (Boston: McGraw-Hill, 1999), 537. Reprinted with permission of McGraw-Hill.

Figure 12.6 The Leadership Styles in Terms of Task and Relationship Behaviour

High	Sales manager and salesperson decide together on why **Style Three: Participates** Low Task High People	Sales manager makes decision with discussion **Style Two: Persuades** High Task High People
	Low Task Low People **Style Four: Delegates** Salesperson makes decision	High Task Low People **Style One: Tells** Sales manager makes decision
Low	Low	High

(Vertical axis: Concern for people; Horizontal axis: Concern for Task)

Concern for Task

Source: C. M. Futrell, *Fundamentals of Selling* (Boston: McGraw-Hill, 1999), 537. Reprinted with permission of McGraw-Hill.

Style One: Tells. Above-average levels of task behaviour and below-average levels of relationship behaviour characterise this leadership.

- Example of an appropriate use: A new salesperson is unsure of how to develop a sales presentation. The manager instructs the person.
- Example of an inappropriate use: The manager tells an experienced, high-performing salesperson how to develop a sales presentation.

The sales manager makes all the decisions here, exhibiting task-oriented behaviour.

Style Two: Persuades. This leadership style is characterised by above-average amounts of both task and relationship behaviour. The sales manager makes the decision but seeks the salesperson's cooperation by explaining what needs to be done and then persuading the salesperson to carry out the decision.

- Example of appropriate use: A salesperson is

promoted to a key account position and is motivated to do the new job but is presently unable to carry out the job's various activities. The manager instructs the salesperson on the procedures to use.

- Example of an inappropriate use: A new product will be introduced on the market. The salespeople are experienced at selling new products. However, at the sales meeting the manager instructs people on the procedures they should use to sell the new products and gives them an opportunity to ask questions and clarify the instructions.

Style Three: Participates. Above-average levels of relationship behaviour and below-average levels of task behaviour characterise this leadership style.

- Example of appropriate use: A salesperson needs to do more service work in the sales territory but does not see how it will improve sales. The manager provides reasons for increased service and discusses the idea with the salesperson. The salesperson presents his or her viewpoint and, based on what is discussed, is allowed to continue with present activities without increasing the level of service work.
- Example of an inappropriate use: Salespeople are experiencing declining sales due to the introduction of a competitor's product. At a sales meeting, the manager asks people how to handle the problem, praises their past work, and encourages their future efforts. The manager provides little direction and few suggestions on what should be done to improve sales.

Style Four: Delegates. Below-average levels of both task behaviour and relationship behaviour characterise this leadership style.

- Example of appropriate use: The salesperson is a high-performing, seasoned veteran who is highly motivated to be a top performer. The sales manager lets the person do the job with little direction.

- Example of an inappropriate use: A new salesperson asks for help with selling to several customers and asks what would be the best way to routinely contact customers within the territory. The manager says, "You handle it. It is your responsibility."

This delegating type of leadership provides little direction, low levels of personal contact, and little supportive behaviour. Styles three and four are different from styles one and two, where the sales manager provides the directions and makes the decisions. As you can see, quite often the chosen leadership style is based on the salesperson.

The Sales Manager's Activities Influence Salespeople

Three important activities of the sales manager that direct the behaviour of sales personnel are: (1) supervision, (2) coaching, and (3) counselling. These activities are discussed in the next section.

The Supervision Activity

Supervision refers to the actual overseeing and directing of the day-to-day activities of salespeople. It is the aspect of leadership concerned with the direct relationship between the manager and the sales force. A sales manager can supervise salespeople both indirectly and directly.

Indirect Supervisory Methods

Most sales organisations employ the following methods to indirectly help their managers stay abreast of their salespeople's day-to-day activities (Futrell 1998):

1. Call reports let the manager know which customers and prospects were contacted and on what day. Many call reports have a brief description of the salesperson's activities and accomplishments for each sales call.

2.   Expense reports show where the salesperson
     spent the night, how much travelling was done,
     entertainment activities used, and how much money
     was spent.
3.   Compensation plan directs sales personnel's
     activities. Commissions, bonuses, and contests
     influence the time and effort salespeople invest in
     their jobs.
4.   Sales analysis reports show what was sold and how
     much was sold.

These indirect supervisory methods influence people to work toward reaching their job goals. The way to supervise people, however, is with direct methods.

Direct Supervisory Methods

Three common direct supervisory methods employed for supervising people are through the telephone or e-mail, sales meetings, and working with each salesperson (Futrell 1998).

1.   Telephone and e-mail are essential tools for
     contacting salespeople and for salespeople
     to talk with the manager. Both are faster and
     cheaper than travelling to see a salesperson.

2.   Sales meetings take place frequently, often
     once a month. This is a great time to provide
     information, training, and inspiration.

3.   Working with each salesperson, often once a
     month, refers to the manager's routine visits
     with each salesperson. The manager meets
     with each person in his/her sales territory for
     reasons such as:

     •   calling on a specific account to handle
             a specific problem;
     •   joining the sales professional in a
             team effort in which both combine
             their selling talents to close a certain

account;
- breaking in a new salesperson;
- training a seasoned sales professional to sell a new product or an established product in a new way; and
- introducing a seasoned salesperson to a new territory.

The Coaching Activity

Coaching is an important leadership activity that has been described as the single most important training technique available to the sales manager. Coaching refers to training someone on the job intensely through instruction, demonstration, and practice. The purpose of coaching is to help the person to be more efficient. As Futrell emphasises, nothing will improve performance more than a manager's regular on-the-job coaching.

The joint sales call is the main element of a coaching session. This is where the manager accompanies a salesperson on a sales call. By observing what occurs face-to-face with customers, the manager can discuss, immediately after the sales call, any strengths and opportunities to improve. With regular coaching sessions, the manager can reinforce good selling habits and improve selling skills.

Coaching involves special objectives and techniques. It is specifically planned for strengthening selling skills, re-emphasizing or reinforcing formal training exposure, pointing out opportunities to improve, or expanding on selling skills already developed. As Futrell (1998) observes, coaching, then, is the most important link in the continuous sales training process. Coaching involves these four important activities: (1) presession preparation, (2) the joint sales call, (3) postcall discussion, and (4) summary and critique. These activities are explained as follows (Futrell 1998):

1. **Presession Analysis and Planning.** Before actually making calls with anyone, the sales manager should

familiarise him/herself with all significant aspects of the customer's past and current performance. This preparation is done for the same reason that a good salesperson prepares for every important call.

2. **The Joint Sales Call**. When the sales manager has completed his/her presession discussion, he/she is ready for the first sales call. Before making it, however, he/she should review the precall planning. Usually, he/she can do this on the way to the customer's place of business.

    A call planning sheet will be helpful to both the manager and the salesperson. It should be used to plan what should be said and done; then it should be used as a checklist as he/she reviews the precall preparation. In fact, the items on the call planning sheet can be made a part of his/her coaching checklist. The items include the following:

    -   Choosing an objective for the call
    -   Selecting the major appeal to help achieve the objective
    -   Analysing the prospect's needs
    -   Determining the most attractive benefits
    -   Anticipating objections
    -   Deciding on closing tactics

3. **Postcall Discussions**. After a joint sales call, it is important for the sales manager to discuss what took place. Certainly, the salesperson expects some comment from the manager. Nevertheless, the sales manager's comments need not be lengthy or involved.

4. **Summary and Critique**. After all the joint sales calls have been completed, it is time to sit down with the salesperson and review the entire coaching session. In this review, the manager should:

    -   define the sales representative's problems or

opportunities for development;
- outline the action that is expected to be taken to overcome the problem or to take advantage of opportunities;
- set up a time schedule, where applicable, for taking corrective action that is suggested; and
- state the results that are expected to be achieved.

The manager should write down his/her suggestions. To make certain the salesperson understands exactly what is to be done, he/she should prepare a copy. The manager can further check understanding by having salespeople tell him/her in their own words what they think the sales manager has asked them to do.

The Counselling Activity

The purpose of counselling is to help salespeople to be more efficient. Counselling helps a person to become a better-adjusted human being within the work environment. All managers are involved in counselling their employees. Often managers must deal with the persistent complainer, the abrasive troublemaker, the self-important know-it-all, the isolated loner, and so on.

Types of Counselling

Five main types of counselling that sales managers often employ, as summarised by Futrell (1998), are the following:

1. **Performance Counselling.** When a salesperson is lacking in motivation or when attitudes are negative, counselling is called for. Aimless and goalless salespeople who have superior talents are also appropriate candidates for counselling. Another good subject for performance counselling is the employee whose view of and reactions to the firm's normal regimen or its authority figures are self-damaging in the long run.

2. **Career Counselling.** Some of the most confused salespeople are those who have so many talents that

they are unable to decide which way they should advance. Helping such a person formulate a practical career plan may well be the best way to keep the person with the firm.

3. **Job Adjustment Counselling.** Every firm has built-in organisational frustrations in the form of requirements, policies, rules, procedures, customs, and taboos. Pressures—some of them unfair—exist in every sales force. If salespeople are to derive any psychological benefit from daily work, they must learn to adjust to such realities within the limits of personal convictions.

4. **Social Adjustment Counselling.** Organisations involve groups of people with whom one must interact. A great deal of the sales manager's time will be spent helping people relate to one another. The manager's task is to build a cohesive, cooperating work team.

5. **Personal Adjustment Counselling.** Managers must decide the extent to which they can or should become involved in the strictly personal frustrations and conflicts of people in terms of the appropriate counselling approach. It must be stressed, though, that managers should provide counselling only in areas in which they are qualified.

Review Questions

1. What are the personal characteristics necessary for an effective leader?

2. Explain the distinction between sales management and sales leadership.

3. Leaders may draw upon power from a variety of sources. Identify and explain these sources.

4. Explain your understanding of the behavioural model of leadership. What are the implications of this model for sales managers?

5. Discuss what kind of leadership style a sales manager should use when working with a salesperson who is highly motivated and enjoys making calls on customers.

Chapter 13

Evaluating the Effectiveness of Sales Organisation

Introduction

Evaluations of salesperson performance are confined to the individuals themselves not the sales organisation or sales organisation levels. The results of these evaluations are typically tactical in nature. In other words, they lead a sales manager to take specific actions to improve the performance of an individual salesperson. Generally, different actions are warranted for different salespeople, depending on the areas that need improvement.

This chapter focuses on the evaluation of sales organisation effectiveness, and chapter fourteen deals with the evaluation of salesperson performance. This chapter begins with a discussion of a sales organisation audit and examines benchmarking. It then describes more specific analyses of sales, costs, profits, and productivity to determine sales organisation effectiveness.

Sales Organisation Audit

Although the term *audit* is most often used in reference to financial audits performed by accounting firms, the audit concept has been extended to different business functions in recent years. A sales organisation audit is a comprehensive, systematic, diagnostic, and prescriptive tool. As Dubinsky and Hansen (1989) observe, the purpose of a sales organisation audit is "to assess the adequacy of a firm's sales management process and provide direction for improved performance and prescription for needed changes. It is a tool that should be used by all firms whether or not they are achieving their goals." This type of audit is the most comprehensive approach for evaluating sales organisation effectiveness.

A framework for performing a sales organisation audit, as suggested by Dubinsky and Hansen (1989), is presented in Figure 13.1. As indicated in the figure, the audit addresses four major areas: sales organisation environment, sales management evaluation, sales organisation planning system, and sales management functions. The purpose of the audit is to investigate, systematically and comprehensively, each of these areas to identify existing or potential problems, determine their causes, and take the necessary corrective actions. For example, ADP Systems Company used an audit to gain insights into customer relationships and trouble areas that were not being expressed or received any other way. The company credits a sales increase from GH¢50 million to GH¢140 million in less than two years to the implementation of recommendations resulting from the audit.

Table 13.1 presents some sample questions that should be addressed in a sales organisation audit. Answers to these types of questions typically come from members of the sales organisation and company records.

Figure 13.1 Sales Organization Audit Framework

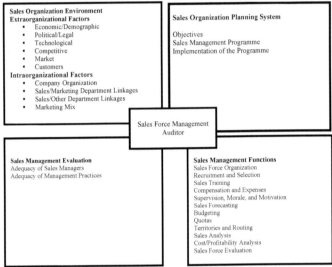

Source: Adapted from Alan J. Dubinsky and Richard W. Hansen, "The Sales Force Management Audit," *California Management Review, 24.2* (1981), 86-95: Copyright © 1981, by The Regents of the University of California. Reprinted by permission of The Regents.

Benchmarking

As submitted by Ingram et al. (2004), although the sales audit can help identify areas in the sales organisation that need improvement, an increasingly popular technique for improving sales organisation effectiveness is benchmarking. Benchmarking is an ongoing measurement and analysis process that compares an organisation's current operating practices with the best practices used by world-class organisations. It is a tool for evaluating current business practices and finding a way to do things better, more quickly, and less expensively to better meet customer needs (Smith et al. 1993).

Figure 13.2 outlines steps in the benchmarking process. A pivotal part of this process is identifying the company or sales force to benchmark against. Literature search and personal contacts are means for identifying companies that perform a process in an exceptional manner. Winning an industry award, being recognised for functional excellence, and receiving a national quality award are three indicators of excellence.

A benchmarking study should provide several outputs. First, it should provide a measure that compares performance for the benchmarked process relative to the organisation studied. Second, it should identify the organisation's performance gap relative to benchmarked performance levels. Third, it should identify best practices and facilitators that produced the results observed during the study. Finally, the study should determine performance goals for the process studied and identify areas in which action can be taken to improve performance.

Table 13.1 Sample Questions from a Sales Organisation Audit

iv. Sales Management Functions
A. *Sales Force Organisation*
1. How is our sales force organised (by product, by customer, by territory)?
2. Is this type of organisation appropriate, given the current intraorganisational and extraorganisational conditions?
3. Does this type of organisation adequately service the needs of our customers?

B. *Recruitment and Selection*
1. How many salespeople do we have?
2. Is this number adequate in light of our objectives and resources?
3. Are we serving our customers adequately with this number of salespeople?
4. How is our sales force size determined?
5. What is our turnover rate? What have we done to try to change it?
6. Do we have adequate sources from which to obtain recruits? Have we overlooked some possible sources?

7. Do we have a job description for each of our sales jobs? Is each job description current?
8. Have we enumerated the necessary sales job qualifications? Have they been recently updated? Are they predictive of sales success?
9. Are our selection screening procedures financially feasible and appropriate?
10. Do we use a battery of psychological tests in our selection process? Are the tests valid and reliable?
11. Do our recruitment and selection procedures satisfy employment opportunity guidelines?

C. Sales Training

1. How is our sales training programme developed? Does it meet the needs of management and sales personnel?
2. Do we establish training objectives before developing and implementing the training programme?
3. Is the training programme adequate in light of our objectives and resources?
4. What kinds of training do we currently provide our salespeople?
5. Does the training programme need revising? What areas of the training programme should be improved or de-emphasised?
6. What methods do we use to evaluate the effectiveness of our training programme?
7. Can we afford to train internally, or should we use external sources for training?
8. Do we have an ongoing training programme for senior salespeople? Is it adequate?

D. Compensation and Expenses

1. Does our sales compensation plan meet our objectives in light of our financial resources?
2. Is the compensation plan fair, flexible, economical, and easy to understand and administer?
3. What is the level of compensation, the type of plan, and the frequency of payment?
4. Are the salespeople and management satisfied with

the compensation plan?

5. Does the compensation plan ensure that the salespeople perform the necessary sales job activities?

6. Does the compensation plan attract and retain enough quality sales performers?

7. Does the sales expense plan meet our objectives in light of our financial resources?

8. Is the expense plan fair, flexible, and easy to administer? Does it allow for geographical, customer, and/or product differences?

9. Does the expense plan ensure that the necessary sales job activities are performed?

10. Can we easily audit the expenses incurred by our sales personnel?

Source: Reprinted by permission of Sales and Marketing Executives International, Inc. (http:/www.smei.org). "SMEI certified Professional Salesperson" and "SCPS" are registered trademarks of Sales and Marketing Executives International, Inc.

Figure 13.2 Benchmarking Process

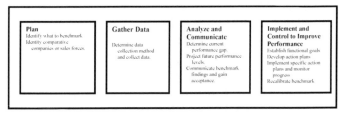

Plan
Identify what to benchmark.
Identify comparative companies or sales forces.

Gather Data
Determine data collection method and collect data.

Analyze and Communicate
Determine current performance gap.
Project future performance levels.
Communicate benchmark findings and gain acceptance.

Implement and Control to Improve Performance
Establish functional goals
Develop action plans
Implement specific action plans and monitor progress
Recalibrate benchmark

Keys to Successful Benchmarking

The keys to successful benchmarking, as identified by Brewer (2000), involve the following:

- Clearly identify critical activities that will improve quality or service or reduce cost.
- Properly prepare and benchmark only one activity at a time.
- Make sure that you thoroughly understand your

own process first.

- Create a "seek, desire, and listen" environment by choosing curious and knowledgeable people for your benchmark team.
- Verify that your benchmark partner company is the best in its class, and clearly understand your partner's process.
- Provide adequate resource, not only financial but, most importantly, knowledgeable personnel.
- Be diligent in selecting the correct partner—be sure not to use a company that may not provide advantages to you.
- Implement the benchmarking action plan.

Sales Organisation Effectiveness Evaluations

Sales organisations have multiple goals and objectives, and thus, multiple factors must be assessed as a measure of sales organisation effectiveness. As illustrated in Figure 13.3, four types of analyses are typically necessary to develop a comprehensive evaluation of any sales organisation. The four types of analyses of sales organisation are:

1. sales analysis,
2. cost analysis,
3. profitability analysis, and
4. productivity analysis.

As Futrell (1999) emphasises, conducting analyses in each of these areas is a complex task for two reasons. First, many different types of analyses can be performed to evaluate sales, costs, profitability, and productivity results. For example, a sales analysis might focus on total sales, sales of specific products, sales to specific customers, or other types of sales and might include sales comparisons to sales quotas, to previous periods, or to sales of competitors or other types of analyses. Second, separate sales analyses need to be performed for the different levels in the sales organisation. Thus, a typical evaluation would include separate sales analyses for sales zones, regions, districts, and territories.

According to Brewer (2000), many sales organisations focus their sales organisation assessments on sales analysis. Customer satisfaction is also heavily relied upon to determine sales organisation effectiveness. This involves surveying customers to determine their level of satisfaction with the company's products, service, and salespeople among other things. Now we discuss how sales, cost, profitability, and productivity analyses can be conducted to evaluate sales organisation effectiveness.

Figure 13.3 Sales Organization Effectiveness Framework

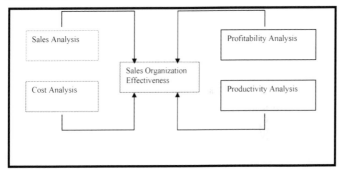

Sales Analysis

Sales analysis may be described as the collection, classification comparison, and evaluation of an organisation's sales figures. Because the basic purpose of a sales organisation is to generate sales, sales analysis is an obvious and important element of evaluating sales organisation effectiveness. All organisations collect and classify sales data as the framework upon which their accounting records and statements are constructed. The difficulty, however, is in determining exactly what should be analyzed.

As Ingram et al. (2004) suggest, one key consideration is in defining what is meant by a sale. Definitions of a sale include a placed order, a shipped order, and a paid order. Most organisations consider a sale to have taken place at the time an order ships, but some organisations keep records for all three definitions of a sale to analyze what volume and type of orders make it through each of the three stages. Whatever the definition used, the sales organisation must be consistent and develop an information system to track sales based on whatever sales definition is used. This is important if sales comparisons across time periods are to be meaningful.

Another consideration is whether to focus on *sales dollars* or *sales units*. This can be extremely important during times when prices increase or when salespeople have substantial latitude in negotiating selling prices. The sales information in Table 13.2 illustrates how different conclusions may result from analyses of sales dollars or sales units. If just sales dollars are analyzed, all regions in the exhibit would appear to be generating substantial sales growth. However, when sales units are introduced, the dollar sales growth for all regions in 2006 can be attributed almost entirely to price increases, because units sold increased only minimally during that period. The situation is somewhat different in 2007, because all regions increased the number of units sold. However, sales volume for region two is relatively flat, even though units sold increased. This could be caused either by selling more lower-priced products or by using larger price concessions than the other regions. In either case, analysis of sales dollars or sales units provides different types of evaluative information, so it is often useful to include both dollars and units in a sales analysis.

Given a definition of sales and a decision concerning sales dollars versus units, many different sales evaluations can be performed. Several alternative evaluations are presented in Figure 13.4. As Ingram et al. (2004) submit, the critical decision areas are: (1) the organisational level of analysis, (2) the type of sales, and (3) the type of analysis. Thus, a sales analysis can be performed at different organisation levels and for different types of sales and can use different types of analysis.

Table 13.2 Sales Dollars versus Sales Units

	2005		2006		2007	
	Sales Dollars	Sales Units	Sales Dollars	Sales Units	Sales Dollars	Sales Units
Region 1	$50,000,000	500,000	$55,000,000	510,000	$62,000,000	575,000
Region 2	$55,000,000	550,000	$60,000,000	560,000	$62,000,000	600,000
Region 3	$45,000,000	450,000	$50,000,000	460,000	$56,000,000	520,000
Region 4	$60,000,000	600,000	$65,000,000	610,000	$73,000,000	720,000

Figure 13.4 Sales Analysis Framework

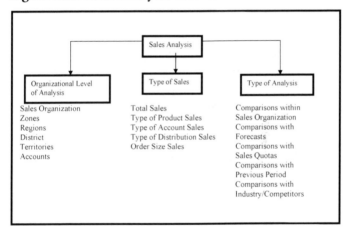

Source: T. N. Ingram, R. W. La Forge, R. A. Avilla, C. H. Schwepker, Jr., and M. R. Williams. Sales Management: Analysis and Decision Making, (Ohio: Thomson/South-Western, 2004), 245. Reprinted by permission of Thomson/South-Western.

Organisational Level of Analysis

Sales analyses should be performed for all levels in the sales organisation for two basic reasons. First, sales managers at each level need sales analyses at their level and the next level below for evaluation and control purposes. For example, a regional sales manager should have sales analyses for all regions as well as for all districts within his or her region. This makes it possible to assess the sales effectiveness of the region and to determine the sales contribution of each district.

Second, a useful way to identify problem areas in achieving sales effectiveness is to perform a hierarchical sales analysis, which consists of evaluating sales results throughout the sales organisation from a top-down perspective. Essentially, the analysis begins with total sales for the sales organisation and proceeds through each successively lower level in the sales organisation. The emphasis is on identifying potential problem areas at each level and then using analyses at lower levels to pinpoint the specific problems. An example of a hierarchical sales analysis for XYZ Systems Company is presented in Figure 13.5.

Figure 13.5 Example of Hierarchical Sales Analysis

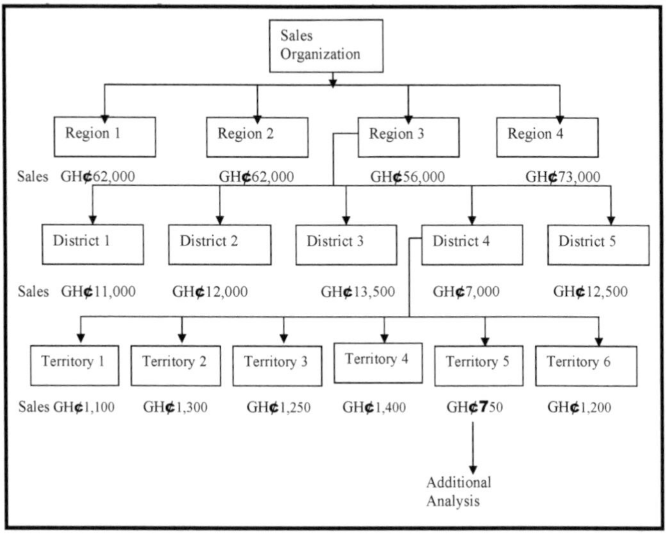

Source: Adapted from T. N. Ingram, R. W. La Forge, R. A. Avilla, C. H. Schwepker, Jr., and M. R. Williams, *Sales Management: Analysis and Decision Making* (Ohio: Thomson/ South-Western, 2004), 246. Reprinted by permission of Thomson/South-Western.

In this example, Region Three has the lowest sales, so all districts in Region Three are examined. District Four has poor sales results, so all the territories in District Four are examined. Additional analysis is indicated for Territory Five to determine why sales are so low for the territory and to take corrective action to increase sales in that territory.

Types of Sales

The analysis in Figure 13.5 addresses only total firm sales at each organisational level. As Ingram et al. (2004) suggest, it is usually desirable to evaluate different types of sales, by looking at the following categories:

- Product Type or Specific Products
- Account Type or Specific Account
- Type of Distribution Method
- Order Size

The hierarchical analysis in Figure 13.5 could have included sales by product type, account type, or other type of sales at each level. Or once the potential sales problem in Territory Five has been isolated, analyses of different types of sales could be performed to define the sales problem more fully. An example of type-of-sales analysis for XYZ Systems Company is presented in Figure 13.6. This example suggests especially low sales volume for Product A and Account Type B. Additional analyses within these product and account types would be required to ascertain why sales are low in these areas and what needs to be done to improve sales effectiveness.

Figure 13.6 Examples of Type-of-Sales Analysis

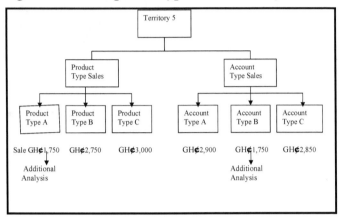

Type of Analysis

The discussion to this point has focused on the actual sales results for different organisational levels and for different types of sales. However, the use of actual sales results limits the analysis to comparisons across organisational levels or sales types. These within-organisation comparisons provide some useful information but are insufficient for a comprehensive evaluation of sales effectiveness. Several additional types of analysis are recommended and presented in Table 13.3.

Comparing actual sales results with sales forecasts and quotas is extremely revealing. A sales forecast represents an expected level of firm sales for defined products, markets, and time periods and for a specified strategy. Based on this definition, a sales forecast provides a basis for establishing specific sales quotas and reasonable sales objectives for a territory, district, region, or zone (methods for establishing sales quotas are discussed in chapter nine). An effectiveness index can be computed by dividing actual sales results by the sales quota and multiplying by one hundred. As illustrated in Table 13.3, sales results in excess of a quota will have index values greater than one hundred, and results lower than quota will have index values lower than one hundred. The sales effectiveness index makes it easy to compare directly the sales effectiveness of different organisational levels and different types of sales.

Another type of useful analysis is the comparison of actual results to previous periods. As illustrated in Table 13.3, this type of analysis can be used to determine sales growth rates for different organisational levels and for different sales types. Incorporating sales data for many periods makes it possible to assess long-term sales trends.

A final type of analysis to be considered is a comparison of actual sales results to those achieved by competitors. This type of analysis can again be performed at different organisational levels and for different types of sales. If the comparison is extended to overall industry sales, various types of market share can be calculated. Examples of these comparisons are presented in Table 13.3.

Table 13.3 Types of Analysis Examples

	District 1	District 2	District 3	District 4	District 5
Sales	GH¢110,000	GH¢120,000	GH¢130,000	GH¢70,000	GH¢120,000
Sales Quota	GH¢110,250	GH¢110,500	GH¢120,750	GH¢100,000	GH¢110,000
Effectiveness Index	98	104	102	70	109
Sales Last Year	GH¢100,700	GH¢110,000	GH¢120,250	GH¢60,800	GH¢100,350
Sales Growth	3%	9%	6%	3%	16%
Industry Sales	GH¢420,000	GH¢420,000	GH¢450,000	GH¢400,000	GH¢450,000
Market Share	26%	29%	29%	18%	27%

Source: Adapted from T. N. Ingram, R. W. La Forge, R. A. Avilla, C. H. Schwepker, Jr., and M. R. Williams, *Sales Management: Analysis and Decision Making* (Ohio: Thomson/South-Western, 2004), 249. Reprinted by permission of Thomson/South-Western.

Cost Analysis

Cost analysis is another major element in the evaluation of sales organisation effectiveness. The emphasis here is on assessing the costs incurred by the sales organisation to generate the achieved levels of sales. The general approach is to compare the costs incurred with planned costs as defined by sales budgets.

Resources of the organisation earmarked for personal selling expenses for a designated period represent the total selling budget. The key sales management budgeting task is to decide the best way to allocate these sales resources throughout the sales organisation and across the different selling activities. The budgeting process is intended to inculcate cost consciousness and profit awareness throughout the organisation, and it is necessary for establishing benchmarks for evaluating selling costs.

As Ingram et al. (2004) point out, selling budgets are developed at all levels of the sales organisation and for all key expenditure categories. The focus of the discussion is on the key selling expense categories and methods for establishing specific expenditure levels within the budget. Table 13.4 shows typical selling budget expense categories.

Table 13.4 Selling Expense Categories in Budget

Classification	Actual 2006	Original 2007 Budget	April Revision	July Revision	October Revision
Compensation expenses					
Salaries					
Commissions					
Bonuses					
Total					
Travel expenses					
Lodging					
Food					
Transportation					
Miscellaneous					
Total					
Administrative expenses					
Recruiting					
Training					
Meetings					
Sales offices					
Total					

Determining expenditure levels for each selling expense category is very tough. Two common approaches for determining these expenditure levels are the percentage of sales method and the objective and task method. The percentage of sales method calculates an expenditure level for each category by multiplying an expenditure percentage times forecasted sales. The effectiveness of the percentage of sales method depends on the accuracy of sales forecasts and the appropriateness of the expenditure percentages. If the sales forecasts are not accurate, the selling budgets will be incorrect, regardless of the expenditure percentages used. If sales forecasts are accurate, the key is to determine the expenditure percentages. This percentage may be derived from historical spending patterns or industry averages. Sales management should adjust the percentage up or down to reflect the unique aspects of their sales organisations.

The objective and task method takes an entirely different approach. Basically, it is a type of zero-based budgeting. In essence, each sales manager prepares a separate budget request that states the objectives to be achieved, the tasks required to achieve those objectives, and the costs associated with performing the necessary tasks. The requests are reviewed, and through an iterative process, selling budgets are approved. Many variations of the objective and task method are used by different sales organisations.

After determining a budget, cost analysis can then be performed. Table 13.5 illustrates examples of two types of cost analysis. The first analysis calculates the variance between actual costs and budgeted costs for the regions in a sales organisation. Regions with the largest variation, especially when actual costs far exceed budgeted costs, should be highlighted for further analysis.

Table 13.5 Cost Analysis Examples

	Compensation Cost			Training Cost		
	Actual Cost	Budgeted Cost	Variance	Actual Cost	Budgeted Cost	Variance
Region 1	GH¢3,660	GH¢3,600	+ GH¢ 60	GH¢ 985	GH¢1,030	- GH¢ 45
Region 2	GH¢3,500	GH¢3,700	- GH¢200	GH¢2,110	GH¢2,040	+ GH¢ 70
Region 3	GH¢3,150	GH¢3,400	- GH¢250	GH¢ 830	GH¢1,060	- GH¢230
Region 4	GH¢4,200	GH¢3,900	+GH¢300	GH¢2,340	GH¢2,160	+ GH¢180

	Compensation Cost		Training Cost	
	Actual % Sales	Budgeted % Sales	Actual % Sales	Budgeted % Sales
Region 1	6.1	6	2.9	3
Region 2	5.8	6	3.1	3
Region 3	5.4	6	2.6	3
Region 4	6.0	6	3.1	3

Source: Adapted from T. N. Ingram, R. W. La Forge, R. A. Avilla, C. H. Schwepker, Jr., and M. R. Williams, Sales Management: Analysis and Decision Making (Ohio: Thomson/South-Western, 2004), 250. Reprinted by permission of Thomson/South-Western.

Profitability Analysis

According to Ingram et al. (2004), sales and cost data can be combined in various ways to produce evaluations of sales organisation profitability for different organisational levels of different types of sales. This section discusses three types of profitability analysis: (1) income statement analysis, (2) activity-based costing, and (3) return on assets managed analysis.

Income Statement Analysis

Schiff (1983) submits that the different levels in a sales organisation and the different types of sales can be considered separate businesses. As a result, income statements can be developed for profitability analysis. One of the major difficulties in income statement analysis is that some costs are shared between organisational levels or sales types.

Table 13.6 illustrates two approaches for dealing with the shared costs. The full cost approach tries to allocate the shared costs to individual units based on some type of cost allocation procedure. This results in a net profit figure for each unit. The contribution approach is different in that only direct costs are included in the profitability analysis; the indirect or shared costs are not included. The net contribution calculated from this approach represents the profit contribution of the unit being analyzed. This profit contribution must be sufficient to cover indirect costs and other overhead and to provide the net profit for the firm.

Table 13.7 illustrates an example that incorporates both approaches. This example uses the direct approach for assessing sales region profitability and the contribution approach for evaluating the districts within the region. Notice that the profitability calculations for each district include only district sales, cost of goods sold, and district direct-selling expenses. A profit contribution is generated for each district. The profitability calculations for the region include district selling expenses, region direct-selling expenses that have not been allocated to the districts, and an allocated portion of shared zone costs. This produces a net profit figure for a profitability evaluation of the region.

Table 13.6 Full Cost versus Contribution Approaches

Full Cost Approach	Contribution Approach
Sales	Sales
Minus: Cost of goods sold	Minus: Cost of goods sold
Gross Margin	Gross margin
Minus: Direct selling expenses	Minus: Direct selling expenses
Minus: Allocated portion of shared expenses	Profit contribution
Net profit	

Table 13.7 Profitability Analysis Example

	Full Cost Approach	Contribution Approach		
	Region	District 1	District 2	District 3
Sales	GH¢300,000	GH¢180,000	GH¢70,000	GH¢50,000
Cost of goods sold	255,000	168,500	58,500	28,000
Gross margin	45,000	11,500	11,500	22,000
District selling expenses	11,000	5,000	3,500	2,500
Region direct selling expenses	10,000	- - -	--- -	------
Profit contribution	24,000	6,500	8,000	19,500
Allocated portion of shared zone costs	16,000			
Net profit	8,000			

Activity-Based Costing

Activity-Based Costing

Activity-based costing (ABC) is perhaps a more accountable method for allocating costs. ABC allocates costs to individual units on the basis of how the units actually expend or cause the costs. Costs are accumulated and then allocated to the units by the appropriate drivers—factors that drive costs up or down (Baker 1994).

Table 13.8 portrays how the profitability picture changed for a building supplies company that shifted to ABC to assess distribution channel profitability (Cooper and Kaplan 1988). It should be noted that, with ABC, selling expenses were no longer allocated to each channel based on a percentage of that channel's sales revenues. Instead, costs associated with each activity that were used to generate sales for a specific channel were allocated to that channel. Using ABC, a clearer picture of operating profits per channel emerged. In particular, the original equipment manufacturer channel appeared to be much more profitable than the firm's prior accounting system indicated.

As Narayanan and Sarkar (2002) point out, ABC placed greater emphasis on more accurately defining unit profitability by tracing activities and their associated costs directly to a specific unit. For example, using ABC analysis, First Choice

Systems was able to determine the profitability of its customers and products. As a result, they raised the prices of some unprofitable products and discontinued other unprofitable products and customers. By doing such, ABC helps foster an understanding of resource expenditures, how customer value is created, and where money is being made or lost.

Table 13.8 Activity-Based Costing Example

Profits by Commercial Distribution Channel (Old System)

	Contract	Industrial Suppliers	Government	OEM	Commercial
Annual Sales (in thousands of dollars)	$79,434	$25,110	$422	$9,200	$114,166
Gross Margin	34%	41%	23%	27%	35%
Gross Profit	$27,375	$10,284	$136	$2,462	$40,256
SG&A Allowance[1] (in thousands of dollars)	$19,746	$6,242	$105	$2,287	$31,814
Operating Profit (in thousands of dollars)	$7,629	$4,042	$31	$174	$11,876
Operating Margin	10%	16%	7%	2%	10%
Invested Capital Allowance[2] (in thousands of dollars)	$33,609	$10,624	$179	$3,893	$48,305
Return on Investment	23%	38%	17%	4%	25%

1 SG&A allowance for each channel is 25 percent of that channel's revenues.
2 Invested capital allowance for each channel is 42 percent of that channel's revenues.

Profits by Commercial Distribution Channel (New System: ABC)

	Contract	Industrial Suppliers	Government	OEM	Commercial
Gross Profit (from previous table)	$27,375	$10,284	$136	$2,461	$40,256
Selling Expenses[3] (all in thousands of dollars)					
Commission	$4,682	$1,344	$12	$372	$6,410
Advertising	132	38	0	2	172
Catalog	504	160	0	0	664
Co-op Advertising	416	120	0	0	536
Sales Promotion	394	114	0	2	510
Warranty	64	22	0	4	90
Sales Administration	5,696	1,714	20	351	7,781
Cash Discount	892	252	12	114	1,270
Total	$12,780	$3,764	$44	$845	$17,433
G&A (in thousands of dollars)	$6,740	$2,131	$36	$781	$9,688
Operating Profit (in thousands of dollars)	$7,855	$4,389	$56	$835	$13,135
Operating Margin	10%	17%	13%	9%	12%
Invested Capital[3]	$33,154	$10,974	$184	$2,748	$47,060
Return on Investment	24%	40%	30%	30%	28%

3 Selling expenses and invested capital estimated under an activity based system.

Source: Reprinted by permission of Harvard Business Review. From "Measure Costs Right: Make the Right Decisions," by R. Cooper and R. S. Kaplan, *Harvard Business Review* (September/ October, 1988), 96–103. Copyright © 1988 by Harvard Business School Publishing Corporation; all rights reserved.

F. O. Boachie-Mensah

Return on Assets Managed Analysis

The income statement approach to profitability assessment produces net profit or profit contribution in dollars or expressed as a percentage of sales. Although necessary and valuable, the income statement approach is incomplete, because it does not incorporate any evaluation of the investment in assets required to generate the net profit or profit contribution.

The calculation of return on assets managed (ROAM) can extend the income statement analysis to include asset investment considerations. The formula for calculating ROAM is:

ROAM as profit contribution as percentage of sales multiplied by asset turnover rate = (profit contribution/sales) x (sales/assets managed).

Profit contribution can be either a net profit figure from a direct approach or profit contribution from a contribution approach. Assets managed typically include inventory, accounts receivable, or other assets at each sales organisational level.

An example of ROAM calculations is presented in Table 13.9. The example illustrates ROAM calculations for sales districts within a region. Notice that District One and District Two produce the same ROAM but achieve their results in different ways. District One generates a relatively high profit contribution percentage, whereas District Two operates with a relatively high asset turnover. Both District Three and District Four are achieving poor levels of ROAM but for different reasons. District Three has an acceptable profit contribution percentage but a very low asset turnover ratio. This low asset turnover ratio is the result of inventory accumulations or problems in payments from accounts. District Four, however, has an acceptable asset turnover ratio but a low profit contribution percentage. This low profit contribution percentage may be the result of selling low margin products, negotiating low selling prices, or accruing excessive selling expenses.

As illustrated in the preceding example, ROAM calculations provide an assessment of profitability and useful diagnostic information. ROAM is determined by both profit contribution percentage and asset turnover. If ROAM is low in any area, the profit contribution percentage and asset turnover ratio can be examined to determine the reason. Corrective action (e.g., reduced selling expenses, stricter credit guidelines, lower inventory levels) can then be taken to improve future ROAM performance (Ingram et al. 2004).

Table 13.9 Return on Assets Managed (ROAM) Example

	District 1	District 2	District 3	District 4
Sales	GH¢24,000,000	GH¢24,000,000	GH¢24,000,000	GH¢24,000,000
Cost of Goods Sold	12,000,000	12,000,000	14,000,000	14,000,000
Gross Margin	12,000,000	12,000,000	10,000,000	10,000,000
Direct Selling Expenses	7,200,000	9,600,000	5,200,000	8,800,000
Profit Contribution	4,800,000	2,400,000	4,800,000	1,200,000
Accounts Receivable	8,000,000	4,000,000	16,000,000	4,000,000
Inventory	8,000,000	4,000,000	16,000,000	4,000,000
Total Assets Managed	16,000,000	8,000,000	32,000,000	8,000,000
Profit Contribution Percentage	20%	10%	20%	5%
Asset Turnover	1.5	3.0	.75	3.0
ROAM	**30%**	**30%**	**15%**	**15%**

Source: Adapted from T. N. Ingram, R. W. La Forge, R. A. Avilla, C. H. Schwepker, Jr., and M. R. Williams, *Sales Management: Analysis and Decision Making* (Ohio: Thomson/ South-Western, 2004), 252.

Productivity Analysis

As Ingram et al. (2004) emphasise, although ROAM incorporates elements of productivity by comparing profits and asset investments, additional productivity analysis is desirable for thorough evaluation of sales organisation effectiveness. Productivity is typically measured in terms of ratios between outputs and inputs. For example, one often-used measure of sales force productivity is sales per salesperson. A major advantage of productivity ratios is that they can be compared directly across the entire sales organisation and with other sales organisations. This direct comparison is possible, because all the ratios are expressed in terms of the same units.

Because the basic job of sales managers is to manage salespeople, the most useful input unit for productivity analysis is the salesperson. Therefore, various types of productivity ratios are calculated on a per-salesperson basis. The specific ratios depend on the characteristics of a particular selling situation but often include important outputs such as sales, expenses, calls, demonstrations, and proposals. An example of a productivity analysis is presented in Table 13.10.

Table 13.10 illustrates how productivity analysis provides a different and useful perspective for evaluating sales organisation effectiveness. As the table reveals, absolute values can be misleading. For example, the highest sales districts are not necessarily the most effective. Although profitability analyses would likely detect this as well, productivity analysis presents a vivid and precise evaluation by highlighting specific areas of both high and low productivity. Take the information concerning District Two. Although sales per salesperson is reasonable and expenses per salesperson is relatively low, both calls per salesperson and proposals per salesperson are much lower than those for the other districts. This may explain why selling expenses are low, but it also suggests that the salespeople in this district may not be covering the district adequately. The high sales may be due to a few large sales to large customers.

Productivity improvements are obtained in one of two basic ways: (1) increasing output with the same level of input and (2) maintaining the same level of output but using less input. Productivity analysis can help determine which of these basic approaches should be pursued.

Table 13.10 Productivity Analysis Example

	District 1	District 2	District 3	District 4
Sales	GH¢20,000,000	GH¢24,000,000	GH¢20,000,000	GH¢24,000,000
Selling expenses	GH¢ 2,000,000	GH¢ 2,400,000	GH¢ 3,000,000	GH¢ 3,000,000
Sales calls	9,000	7,500	8,500	10,000
Proposals	220	180	260	270
Number of salespeople	20	30	20	30
Sales/salesperson	GH¢ 1,000,000	GH¢ 800,000	GH¢ 1,000,000	GH¢ 800,000
Expenses/salesperson	GH¢ 100,000	GH¢ 80,000	GH¢ 150,000	GH¢ 100,000
Calls/salesperson	450	250	425	333
Proposals/salesperson	11	6	13	9

Review Questions

1. What responsibility, if any, do you think a sales manager has to learn more about marketing costs? Why?

2. What is a sales analysis? What is it used for?

3. What is the difference between a full cost approach and a contribution margin approach for determining profitability?

4. Compare a marketing audit with a sales force audit. How are they different? How are they similar?

5. Why do you think sales managers should be concerned about their ROAM?

Chapter 14

Measuring and Evaluating Sales Force Performance

Introduction

Whereas chapter thirteen focused on evaluating sales organisation effectiveness, this chapter examines the task of evaluating salesperson performance. The purpose of this chapter is to investigate the key issues involved in evaluating and controlling the performance of salespeople. The measuring of sales force performance is examined initially. The performance evaluation procedures currently used by sales organisations are then examined. Then, the different purposes of performance evaluations are discussed. This is followed by a comprehensive assessment of the different areas in salesperson performance evaluation. The assessment addresses the approaches used in evaluating salespeople, the methods for evaluating salespeople, and the outcomes of salesperson performance evaluations.

Measuring Sales Force Performance

The primary responsibility of the sales manager is to ensure that sale organisation goals and objectives are being accomplished effectively and efficiently, as planned. This necessitates continuous monitoring of the selected sales performance measures to compare where one is with where one should be in order to take appropriate actions to correct unacceptable deviations.

According to Anderson et al. (1992), effectiveness and efficiency should always be related to a time perspective—that is, the short run, the intermediate run, and the long run.

While skilfully acquiring and employing resources to satisfy its goals and social responsibilities in the short run, the sales organisation needs to adapt to environmental opportunities and threats in the intermediate future. Foremost in the long run, the organisation must survive in a world of uncertainties and increasing competition.

In a systematic approach to sales force measurement and evaluation, the first step is to determine goals and objectives for the sales organisation. Next, the sales plan is developed with specific strategies and tactics for achieving the objectives and goals. Performance standards are set for all sales activities, and the sales manager decides how best to allocate resources and sales force efforts. Then the plan is put into action. Finally, performance is monitored continuously and compared with preestablished standards; if needed, corrective decisions are made by sales managers to minimise or eliminate deviations. The following outline represents the major steps involved in the performance measurement and evaluation process, as summarised by Darlrymple and Parsons (1980):

1. Establish sales force objectives and goals.
2. Develop a sales plan.
3. Set performance standards.
4. Allocate resources and sales force efforts in implementing the sales plan.
5. Measure sales force performance against standards.
6. Determine any deviation from standards.
7. Implement corrective action.
8. Take new action.

It is worth noting here that, for brevity, only the first four items on the list are sequentially presented below. The issues involved in the other four items are variously discussed in the other sections of the chapter.

Establish Sales Objectives and Goals
The performance measurement and evaluation process for the sales organisation begins after company goals and

objectives are passed from top management through the chain of command to the sales manager. The initial step is to formulate the sales goals. For example, the sales organisation goal may be recognition by customers as the most service-oriented sales force in the industry (Anderson et al. 1992). After establishing long-run sales goals, the sales manager may focus on the shorter-run, more quantifiable targets known as sales objectives. For instance, annual objectives might include reaching 100 percent of sales quota, keeping sales expenses within assigned budgets, improving the ratio of selling to non-selling time by 30 percent, or increasing profitability on sales by 20 percent.

After sales management has agreed upon the sales goals and objectives, it is essential to secure the salespeople's understanding, approval, and support through open, two-way communication that connects their personal goals with the broader organisational goals.

Develop a Sales Plan

A sales plan is one of several unit operational plans (e.g., distribution, promotion, new product development) comprising and derived from the marketing plan. The sales plan is then coordinated with other departmental plans (production, finance, research) to complete the organisational plan.

As Anderson et al. (1992) suggest, a sales plan, as depicted in Textbox 14.1, includes four major components: (1) situation analysis, which identifies where the organisation is now; (2) opportunities and problems, which indicate where it should go; (3) action programmes, which outline how to get there; and (4) performance evaluation systems, which measure progress toward the destination (i.e., the goals and objectives).

Textbox 14.1 The Sales Plan

Situation Analysis: "Where Are We Now?"

1. Market situation and competitive environment
   a. Size of the market (by major segments)
   b. Dynamics in the marketplace (e.g., shifts in customer purchasing behaviour and competitive strategy changes)
   c. Market shares (by competitors, products, and customer classes)
   d. Strengths and weaknesses (of each competitor's products and sales organisation relative to ours)
2. Product sales situation
   a. Product types (by line items, sizes, models, etc.)
   b. Sales and distribution data (by geographic regions, territories, customer categories, or sales representatives)
   c. Markets served (by types of customer segments or end users)
   d. Customer profiles (by purchasing patterns and servicing needs)

Opportunities and Problems: "Where Do We Want to Go?"

1. Internal (marketing and sales, R & D and technical, manufacturing/operations, financial, organisation, personnel, etc.)
2. External (market segments, competition, economic, political, legal, social, or international)
3. Planning assumptions and constraints
   a. Internal company environment (estimate stability of objectives, goals, resources, management)
   b. External market environment (estimate short-run and long-run marketing environment conditions)
4. Sales forecasts
5. Contingency planning (based on different sets of assumptions from those in three above)

Action Programmes: "What Is the Best Way to Get There?"
Strategies and tactics (convert sales forecasts into resource, production, service, quotas, and budget needs)

Performance Evaluation Systems: "How Much Progress Are We Making toward Our Destination?"
1. Set standards of performance.
2. Evaluate actual performance versus planned standards.
3. Take necessary corrective action on variances from plan.

Source: R. E. Anderson, J. F. Hair, Jr., and A. J. Bush, *Professional Sales Management* (New York: McGraw-Hill, 1992), 530. Reprinted with permission of McGraw-Hill.

Set Performance Standards

After establishing sales force objectives and goals and having developed the sales plan, the sales manager's next step is to set performance standards for the sales force. Performance standards are planned achievement levels that the sales organisation expects to reach at progressive intervals throughout the year. According to Anderson et al. (1992), an individual performance standard is an agreement between a subordinate and superior as to what level of performance is acceptable in some future period. One of the best ways to formalise this general agreement is to draw up a detailed job description for the subordinate. Textbox 14.2 provides an example of a job description for a resale marketing representative in a major oil company.

Textbox 14.2 Job Description

Position: Resale Marketing Representative
Immediate Supervisor: Area Manager

Purpose of Job: To manage a territory so that assigned objectives are achieved in the following categories: sales/profits, accounts receivable, rent income, and retail efficiency. These objectives can be accomplished by developing a strong network of dealers, salaried service station managers, consignees, agents, and distributors.

Regular Assigned Duties:
1. Plan and organise work in accordance with the team system to achieve sales/profit plan in all categories.
   a. Analyse the accounts in the territory, using the "Quarterly Review and Replanning Guide," to determine the opportunities and problems that can affect sales/profits, accounts receivable, rent income, and retail efficiency; determine what action plans would realise the opportunities and solve the problems.
   b. Prioritise opportunities and problems, determine which should be accomplished each quarter, and set objectives accordingly.
   c. Schedule and plan calls and set target dates to accomplish objectives.
2. Call on accounts on a planned basis.
   a. Solicit orders.
   b. Counsel dealers/managers and wholesalers on money management, hours, planned merchandising, appearance, and driveway service; implement plans, programmes, and methods that will contribute to the territory's objectives.
   c. Keep accounts receivable within established credit limits and collect all monies as required.

     d.   Maintain dealer business in line with company objectives; renew existing dealers' leases with consideration given to the interests of both dealers and/or wholesalers as well as the company.

     e.   Conduct dealer meetings on subjects that can best be handled by group counselling and selling.

3. Recruit and interview lessee dealer/manager prospects following selection procedures; recommend acceptable candidates for management approval; arrange for training; negotiate and propose loans where applicable; install new dealers/managers under installation guide; as required, recruit consignees.

4. Investigate customer complaints; resolve or, where necessary, refer to others for their handling.

5. Recommend appropriate maintenance of corporation-owned buildings and equipment.

6. Keep abreast of competitive activity in territory and, as required, advise dealers and the area manager.

7. Handle correspondence and reports pertinent to the territory and maintain adequate records.

Source: R. E. Anderson, J. F. Hair, Jr., and A. J. Bush, *Professional Sales Management* (New York: McGraw-Hill, 1992), 531. Reprinted with permission of McGraw-Hill.

Key Performance Factors

Successful sales organisations in most cases use a combination of quantitative and qualitative performance standards, chosen from a list such as the one in Table 14.1. The factors involved in these standards are explained next.

Table 14.1 Sales Force Performance Evaluation
Quantitative Measures

Sales Results	Sales Efforts
Orders: Number of orders obtained Average order size (units or dollars) Batting average (orders ÷ sales calls) Number of orders cancelled by customers	*Sales calls*: Number made on current customers Number made on potential new accounts Average time spent per call Number of sales presentations Selling time versus non-selling time Call frequency ratio per customer type

Sales volume:
 Dollar sales volume
 Unit sales volume
    By customer type
    By product category
 Translated into market share
 Percent of sales quota achieved	

Margins:
 Gross margin
 Net profit
    By customer type
    By product category
	Selling expenses:
	 Average per sales call
	    As percent of sales volume
	    As percent of sales quota
	    By customer type
	    By product category
	 Direct selling expense ratios
	 Indirect selling expenses ratios

Customer accounts: Number of new accounts Number of lost accounts Percent of accounts sold Number of overdue accounts Dollar amount of accounts receivable Collections made of accounts receivable	*Customer service:* Number of service calls Displays set up Delivery cost per unit sold Months of inventory held by customer type Number of customer complaints Percent of goods returned

Qualitative Measures

Sales-related activities:
Territory management: sales call preparation, scheduling, routing, and time utilisation
Marketing intelligence: new-product ideas, competitive activities, new customer preferences
Follow-ups: use of promotional brochures and correspondence with current and potential accounts
Customer relations
Report preparation and timely submission

Selling skills:

Knowledge of the company and its policies
Knowledge of the competitors' product and sales strategies
Use of marketing and technical backup teams
Understanding of selling techniques
Customer feedback (positive and negative)
Product knowledge
Customer knowledge
Execution of selling techniques
Quality of sales presentations
Communication skills

Personal characteristics:
Cooperation, human relations, enthusiasm, motivation, judgment, care of company property, appearance, self-improvement efforts, patience, punctuality, initiative, resourcefulness, health, sales management potential, ethical and moral behaviour

Source: R. E. Anderson, J. F. Hair, Jr., and A. J. Bush, *Professional Sales Management* (New York: McGraw-Hill, 1992), 534. Reprinted with permission of McGraw-Hill.

Quantitative Performance Standards
The following factors are some of the quantitative performance standards that most companies consider in the control of sales operations.

Sales Quotas

Sales quotas are normally perceived as motivational targets as well as performance standards for the entire sales organisation, for territorial sales teams, or for individual salespeople. As the most commonly used quantitative standard, sales quotas specify desired levels of accomplishment for sales volume, gross margin, net profit, expenses, performance of non-selling activities, or a combination of these and similar items.

Sales Expense Ratio

Sales managers employ the sales expense ratio to control the relation of selling expenses to sales volume. Many factors cause selling expenses to vary with the territory, so target sales expense ratios should be set individually for each salesperson on the sales force.

Territorial Gross Margin or Net Profit Ratios

For effective control over the relative profitability of the sales mix (of products and customers), sales managers may set a target ratio of gross margin or net profit for the sales force. This encourages salespeople to sell certain products to selected customers to obtain the highest gross margins and to consider relative profitability (of different products, individual customers, and the like).

Territorial Market Share

The territorial market share standard seeks to control market share on a territory-by-territory basis. The sales manager sets target market share percentages for each territory. The manager later compares company sales to industry sales in each territory and measures the effectiveness of sales force or salesperson in obtaining market share.

Sales Coverage Effectiveness Index

The sales coverage effectiveness index standard controls the efficiency with which a salesperson works an assigned territory. This index involves the ratio of the number of customers to the total prospects in a territory. To allocate the salesperson's efforts more among different classifications of prospects, individual standards for sales coverage effectiveness are set up for each class and size of customer.

Call-Frequency Ratio

A call-frequency ratio is calculated by dividing the number of sales on a particular class of customers by the number of customers in that class. By setting different call-frequency ratios for different classes of customers, sales managers direct selling efforts of sales representatives to those accounts most likely to produce profitable orders.

Sales Calls per Day

It is desirable—for example, in consumer product fields where salespeople contact large numbers of customers—to set a standard for the number of calls per day. Standards for calls per day are set individually for different territories, depending on territorial differences in customer density, road, and traffic conditions, and competitors' practices.

Order-Call Ratio

The order call ratio seeks to measure the effectiveness of sales force in securing orders. Sometimes called the "batting average," it is derived by dividing the number of orders received by the number of sales calls made. A salesperson's order-call ratio can vary widely from one customer class to another.

Average Cost per Call

A target for average cost per call is set to emphasise the importance of making profitable calls. Average cost per call standards are used to reduce the call frequency on accounts responsible for small orders.

Average Order Size

Average order size standards control the frequency of calls on different accounts. The common practice is to set different standards for different sizes and classes of customers. Sales managers use average order size standards along with average cost per call standards to control a salesperson's allocation of effort among different accounts and increase the order size obtained.

Non-Selling Activities

Sales managers can establish quantitative performance standards for such non-selling activities as obtaining dealer displays and cooperative advertising contracts, training distributors' personnel, and making goodwill calls on distributors' customers.

Multiple Quantitative Performance Standards

It is common practice for sales managers to assign multiple quantitative performance standards. A sales manager may set many different quantitative standards per operating period for a sales force.

Qualitative Performance Standards

Some qualitative criteria are used by organisations for evaluating the less quantifiable sales-related activities, personal skills, and qualities of individual salespeople. There is a difficulty in defining the desired qualitative characteristics. Some sales managers arrive at informal conclusions as regards the extent to which each salesperson possesses them. Others, on the other hand, consider the qualitative criteria formally. One method being employed is to rate sales representatives against a detailed checklist of subjective factors, such as product knowledge, awareness of customer needs, service follow-up, punctuality, general attitude, diligence, accuracy, adaptability, and reliability. Examples of these qualitative performance criteria can be seen in Table 14.1.

Allocate Resources and Sales Force Efforts in Implementing the Sales Plan

The actual test of sales managers is how well they allocate human, financial, and material resources while implementing the sales plan. If goals are not achieved, it is the sales manager who is blamed, not the salespeople.

At ULX Company, sales managers can sit down at desktop terminals to analyze a database that has profiles of every customer and prospect who has come into contact with the company. From direct-mail responses, prospects who are interested in a new product can be researched, and the salesperson can be provided with a comprehensive profile before making the sales call.

Various objectives and goals must be separated into meaningful components for achievement by individual salespeople. The management by objectives (MBO) process is one practical approach for doing this. Assigning sales territories, routing salespeople, setting sales quotas, and determining sales budgets are the basic tools sales managers use to allocate sales force efforts. Since these topics were covered in other chapters of the book, they will not be discussed further here.

Evaluating Sales Force Performance

All organisations have some form of performance evaluation monitoring system (PEMS). This system may be largely informal in smaller companies, relying on the firsthand observations of supervisors; but larger companies use a more formalised PEMS. Companies differ greatly in their approaches to PEMS. Most companies, however, try to quantify managerial observations and judgments by performance results, behaviour, or personal characteristics. In their drive to develop quantifiable scores, many organisations lose sight of what they want PEMS to do.

Stages in the Implementation of a PEMS

The three successive stages in the effective implementation of a PEMS, as summarised by Anderson et al. (1992), are the following:

1. **Performance Planning** – This allows the salesperson to obtain the advice of the manager in deciding three chief questions: "Where am I going? "How will I get there?" "How will I be measured?"

2. **Performance Appraisal** – Performance appraisal is a continuous interpersonal process whereby sales managers offer individual salespeople immediate

feedback on each specific task, project, or objective accomplished. The sales manager, in his or her supervisory role, needs to provide some kind of recognition, praise, correction, or comment after any salesperson's performance.

3. **Performance Review:** This is a periodic review of the preceding performance appraisals to summarise where the salesperson is in his or her personal development. It should answer the question "How am I doing?" and lead into the next performance planning stage.

Although the three stages in the PEMS overlap, sales managers should not assume that all three can be dealt with simultaneously in once-a-year, overall performance appraisals. As Anderson et al emphasise, performance planning lays out objectives and plans for achieving them and explains how the individual will be evaluated. A well-constructed MBO programme can be extremely useful in this stage. Performance appraisals are day-by-day, mini-evaluations on specific performances. The performance review is a periodic summing up of these daily appraisals so that the salesperson can see where he or she stands.

Purposes of Performance Evaluation

The basic objective of performance evaluations is to determine how well individual salespeople have performed. However, the results of performance evaluations can be used for many sales management purposes, as summarised by Ingram et al. (2004):

1. To ensure that compensation and other reward disbursements are consistent with actual salesperson performance.
2. To identify salespeople who might be promoted.
3. To identify salespeople whose employment should be terminated and to supply evidence to support the need for termination.

4. To determine the specific training and counselling needs of individual salespeople and the overall sales force.
5. To provide information for effective human resource planning.
6. To identify criteria that can be used to recruit and select salespeople in the future.
7. To advise salespeople of work expectations.
8. To motivate salespeople.
9. To help salespeople set career goals.
10. To improve a salesperson's performance.

These diverse purposes affect all aspects of the performance evaluation process. For example, performance evaluations for determining compensation and special rewards should emphasise activities and results related to the salesperson's current job and situation.

Performance Evaluation Approaches

According to Ingram et al. (2004), although it is impossible to determine with precision all the performance evaluation approaches used by sales organisations, several studies have produced sufficiently consistent information to warrant some general conclusions.

1. Most sales organisations evaluate salesperson performance annually, although many firms conduct evaluations semiannually or quarterly. Relatively few firms evaluate salesperson performance more often than quarterly.
2. Most sales organisations use combinations of input and output criteria that are evaluated by quantitative and qualitative measures. However, emphasis seems to be placed on outputs, with evaluations of sales volume results the most popular.
3. Sales organisations that set performance standards or quotas tend to enlist the aid of salespeople in establishing these objectives. The degree of

salesperson input and involvement does, however, appear to vary across firms.

4. Many sales organisations assign weights to different performance objectives and incorporate territory data when establishing these objectives.

5. Most firms use more than one source of information in evaluating salesperson performance. Computer printouts, call reports, supervisory calls, sales itineraries, prospect and customer files, and client and peer feedback are some of the common sources of information.

6. Most salesperson performance evaluations are conducted by the field sales manager who supervises the salesperson. However, some firms involve the manager above the field sales manager in the salesperson performance appraisal.

7. Most sales organisations provide salespeople with a written copy of their performance review and have sales managers discuss the performance evaluation with each salesperson. These discussions typically take place in an office, although sometimes they are conducted in the field.

As the authors observe, these results offer a glimpse of current practices in evaluating salesperson performance. Although performance appraisal continues to be primarily a top-down process, changes are taking place in some companies, leading to the implementation of a broader-based assessment process. Some of the common evaluation approaches are: (1) 360-degree feedback, (2) performance management, and (3) total quality management (TQM). Each of these approaches is briefly explained next.

360-Degree Feedback

An increasingly popular assessment technique, dubbed "360-degree feedback," involves performance assessment from multiple raters, including sales managers, internal and external customers, team members, and even salespeople themselves.

Performance Management

Performance management is another evaluation approach that moves away from the traditional top-down appraisal. This approach involves sales managers and salespeople working together to set goals, give feedback, review, and reward. With this system, salespeople create their own development plans and assume responsibility for their careers. The sales manager acts as a partner in the process, providing feedback that is timely, specific, regular, solicited, and focused on what is within the salesperson's control to change. Salespeople are compensated on the value of their contributions to the organisation's success. To facilitate the review process, sales managers may want to use software applications (such as Performance Now Enterprise Edition), which provide a framework for implementing a comprehensive performance management system (Ingram et al. 2004).

Total Quality Management

As Cravens et al (1993) observe, a performance management approach is consistent with the principles of total quality management (TQM). TQM incorporates a strong customer orientation, a team-oriented corporate culture, and the use of statistical methods to analyze and improve all business processes including sales management. TQM programmes focus on efforts to continuously monitor and improve performance rather than merely evaluate performance over extended periods. This can be accomplished by mapping the processes that lead to desired results and then concentrating effort on improving these processes. As a result, reengineering may occur, resulting in a simpler process with corresponding savings in time and cost and improvements in quality (Wotruba 1996).

Key Issues in Evaluating and Controlling Salesperson Performance

Oliver (1987) suggests a useful way to view different perspectives for evaluating and controlling salesperson performance, as presented in Textbox 14.3. An outcome-based perspective focuses on objective measures of results with little monitoring or directing of salesperson behaviour by sales managers. By contrast, a behaviour-based perspective incorporates complex and often subjective assessments of salesperson characteristics and behaviours with considerable monitoring and directing of salesperson behaviour by sales managers.

According to Ingram et al. (2004), the outcome-based and behaviour-based perspectives, illustrated in Textbox 14.3, represent the extreme positions that a sales organisation might take concerning salesperson performance evaluation. Although the current practice indicates a tendency towards an outcome-based perspective, most sales organisations operate somewhere between the two extreme positions. However, emphasis on either perspective can have far-reaching impacts on the sales force and important implications for sales managers. Several of these key implications are presented in Textbox 14.3, as suggested by Cravens et al. (1993). It should be noted that placing too much focus on outcomes may lead to undesirable behaviour.

Textbox 14.3 Perspectives on Salesperson Performance Evaluation

Outcome-Based Perspective	Behaviour-Based Perspective
• Little monitoring of salesperson	• Considerable monitoring of salespeople
• Little managerial direction of salespeople	• High levels of managerial direction of salespeople
• Straightforward, objective measures of results	• Subjective measures of salesperson characteristics, activities, and strategies

The perspectives that a sales organisation might take toward salesperson performance evaluation and control lie on a continuum. The two extremes are the outcome-based and behaviour-based perspectives.

The more behaviour-based (versus outcome-based) a salesperson performance evaluation is:

- the more professionally competent, team-oriented, risk-averse, planning-oriented, sales support-oriented, and customer-oriented salespeople will be.
- the more intrinsically and recognition-motivated salespeople will be.
- the more committed to the sales organization salespeople will be.
- the more likely salespeople will be to accept authority, participate in decision making, and welcome management performance reviews.
- the less the need for using pay as a control mechanism.
- the more innovative and supportive the culture is likely to be.
- the more inclined salespeople are to sell smarter rather than harder.
- the better salespeople will perform on both selling (e.g., using technical knowledge, making sales presentations) and non-selling (e.g., providing information, controlling expenses ethically) behavioural performance dimensions.
- the better salespeople will perform on outcome (e.g., achieving sales objectives) performance dimensions.
- the better the sales organization will perform on sales organization effectiveness dimensions (e.g., sales volume and growth, profitability, and customer satisfaction).
- the greater salespeople's job satisfaction will be.

Source: D. Cravens, T. Ingram, R. LaForge, and C. Younge, "Behaviour-Based and Outcome-Based Sales Force Control Systems," *Journal of Marketing* 57 (1993): 47–59.

Performance Evaluation Methods

Sales managers can employ a number of different methods for measuring the behaviours, professional development, results, and profitability of salespeople. In an ideal situation, as summarised by Edwards et al. (1984), the method used should be:

- **job-related.** The performance evaluation method should be designed to meet the needs of each specific sales organisation.
- **reliable.** The measures should be stable over time

and exhibit internal consistency.

- **valid.** The measures should provide accurate assessments of the criteria they are intended to measure.

- **standardised**. The measurement instruments and evaluation process should be similar throughout the sales organisation.

- **Practical.** Sales managers and salespeople should understand the entire performance appraisal process and should be able to implement it in a reasonable amount of time.

- **Comparable.** The results of the performance evaluation process should make it possible to compare the performance of individual salespeople directly.

- **Discriminating.** The evaluative methods must be capable of detecting differences in the performances of individual salespeople.

- **Useful.** The information provided by the performance evaluation must be valuable to sales managers in making various decisions.

As Ingram et al. (2004) emphasise, designing methods of salesperson performance evaluation that possess all these characteristics is a difficult task. The most common performance evaluation methods are: (1) a graphic rating/checklist, (2) ranking, (3) objective setting/MBO, and (4) the behaviourally anchored rating scale (BARS). Each evaluative method has certain strengths and weaknesses. No one method provides a perfect evaluation. Therefore, it is important to understand the strengths and weaknesses of each method so that several can be combined to produce the best evaluative procedure for a given sales organisation.

Graphic Rating/Checklist Methods
The graphic rating/checklist methods consist of approaches in which salespeople are evaluated by using some type of

performance evaluation form. The performance evaluation form contains the criteria to be used in the evaluation as well as some means to provide an assessment of how well each salesperson performed on each criterion. An example of part of such a form is presented in Table14.2.

This method is popular in many sales organisations. It is especially useful in evaluating salesperson behaviour and professional development criteria. As part of its assessment process, Eastman Chemical Company asks its customers to evaluate their satisfaction with the company by using a rating scale. As evident from Table 14.3, Eastman's salespeople are responsible for several behaviour-based performance factors. Rating methods have been developed to evaluate all the important salesperson performance dimensions. There are even employee-appraisal software programs, such as Performance Now!, available to assist in the review process. The program asks users to rate employees by goals, development plans, and competencies (Meade 1998).

Table 14.2 Graphic Rating/Checklist Example

1.	Asks customers for their ideas for promoting business						
	Almost Never	1	2	3	4	5	Almost Always NA
2.	Offers customers help in solving their problems						
	Almost Never	1	2	3	4	5	Almost Always NA
3.	Is constantly smiling when interacting with customers						
	Almost Never	1	2	3	4	5	Almost Always NA
4.	Admits when he/she doesn't know the answer, but promises to find out						
	Almost Never	1	2	3	4	5	Almost Always NA
5.	Generates new ways of tackling new or ongoing problems						
	Almost Never	1	2	3	4	5	Almost Always NA
6.	Returns customer's calls the same day						
	Almost Never	1	2	3	4	5	Almost Always NA
7.	Retains his or her composure in front of customers						
	Almost Never	1	2	3	4	5	Almost Always NA
8.	Delivers what he or she promises on time						
	Almost Never	1	2	3	4	5	Almost Always NA

Source: T. N. Ingram, R. W. LaForge, R. A. Avilla, C. H. Schwepker, Jr., and M. R. Williams, *Sales Management: Analysis and Decision Making* (Ohio: Thomson/South-Western, 2004), 279. Reprinted by permission of Thomson/ South-Western.

Ranking Methods

Otherwise similar to graphic rating/checklist methods, ranking methods rank all salespeople according to relative performance on each performance criterion rather than evaluating them against a set of performance criteria. Companies such as Ford, General Electric, and Microsoft use ranking methods. Many different approaches might be used to obtain the rankings. An example of a ranking approach in which salespeople are compared in pairs concerning relative communication skills is presented in Table 14.4.

According to Ingram et al. (2004), ranking methods provide a standardised approach to evaluation and thus force discrimination as to the performance of individual salespeople on each criterion. The process of ranking forces this discrimination in performance. Despite these advantages, ranking methods have many shortcomings, as indicated earlier. Of major concern are the constraints on their practicality and usefulness. Ranking all salespeople against each performance criterion can be a complex and cognitively difficult task. The ranking task can be simplified by using paired-comparisons approaches like the one presented in Table 14.4. However, the computations required to translate the paired comparisons into overall rankings can be extremely cumbersome.

Table 14.3 Eastman Chemical Company Customer Satisfaction Survey

Importance: Rate the importance of each statement (your buying criteria) by asking, "Would I place additional business with a supplier who improved performance in this category from average to outstanding?" **Performance**: Rate Eastman performance and your best "other supplier" on each criteria. *Product*	Importance: 5 – Definitely Would 4 – Probably Would 3 – Uncertain 2 – Probably Would Not 1 – Definitely Would Not NA – Not Applicable	Performance 5 – Outstanding 2 – Fair 4 – Good 1 – Poor 3 – Average NA – Not Applicable	
		Eastman	Best Other Supplier
1. Product Performance: Supplier provides a product that consistently meets your requirements and performance expectations.			
2. Product Mix: Supplier offers a range of products that meets your needs.			
3. Packaging: Supplier has the package type, size, and label to meet your needs.			
4. New Products: Supplier meets your needs through timely introduction of new products.			
5. Product Availability: Supplier meets volume commitments and is also fair and consistent during times of restricted supply.			
6. Product Stewardship: Supplier provides information about the transportation, storage, handling, use, recycling, disposal, and regulation of products and product packaging.			
Service			
7. Order Entry: Supplier has a user-friendly system to place orders that is flexible and responsive to routine order changes as well as urgent or special requests.			
8. Delivery: Supplier consistently delivers the right product on time and in satisfactory condition.			
9. Technical Service: Supplier provides timely technical support through training, information, problem-solving, and assistance in current and new end-use applications.			
10. Sharing Information: Supplier is a resource for product, market, industry, and company information that helps you better understand business issues.			
11. New Ideas: Supplier offers new ideas that add value to your business.			
Pricing/Business Practices			
12. Pricing Practices: Supplier is consistent with the marketplace in establishing pricing practices.			
13. Paperwork: Supplier provides clear and accurate paperwork and business documents that meet your needs.			
14. Commitment to Total Quality Management: Supplier exhibits strong commitment to total quality management in all aspects of business.			
15. Responsiveness: Supplier listens and responds to your business needs in a timely manner.			
Relationship			
16. Integrity: Supplier is credible, honest, and trustworthy.			
17. Dependability: Supplier follows through on agreements.			
18. Supplier Contact: Supplier is easy to contact and provides the right amount of interface with the appropriate personnel.			
19. Problem-Solving: Supplier provides empowered employees to solve your problems.			
Supplier Commitment			
20. Industry Commitment: Supplier exhibits a strong commitment to your industry.			
21. Regional Commitment: Supplier has the appropriate resources in place in your region to provide products and services needed.			
22. Customer Commitment: Supplier is strongly committed to helping your business be successful.			

Source: T. N. Ingram, R. W. LaForge, R. A. Avilla, C. H. Schwepker, Jr., and M. R. Williams, *Sales Management: Analysis and Decision Making* (Ohio: Thomson/South-Western, 2004), 280 - 281. Reprinted by permission of Thomson/ South-Western.

Table 14.4 Ranking Method Example

Performance Criterion: Communication Skills					
	Much Better	Slightly Better	Equal	Slightly Better	Much Better
Pat Mensah	X	------	--------	------	------- Ike Ansah
Tony Owusu ----- X -------- ------- ------- Pat Mensah					
Fiifi Banson ------ ------- X ------- -------- Pat Mensah					

Objective-Setting Methods

Management by objectives (MBO) is the most common and comprehensive goal-setting method. Applied to a sales force, the typical MBO approach, as suggested by Edwards et al. (1984), includes:

1. mutual setting of well-defined and measurable goals within a specified time period;
2. managing activities within the specified time period toward the accomplishment of the stated objectives; and
3. appraising performance against objectives.

As with all the performance evaluation methods, MBO and other goal-setting methods have certain strengths and weaknesses. Although complete reliance on this or any other goal-setting method is inadvisable, the incorporation of some goal-setting procedures is normally desirable. This is especially true for performance criteria related to quantitative behavioural, professional development, results, and profitability criteria. Absolute measures of these dimensions are often not very meaningful because of extreme differences in the territory situations of individual salespeople. The setting of objectives of quotas provides a means to control for territory differences through the establishment of performance benchmarks that incorporate these territory differences.

Behaviourally Anchored Rating Scales

The distinctiveness of behaviourally anchored rating scales (BARS) is due to its focus on trying to link salesperson behaviours with specific results. These behaviour-results linkages become the basis for salesperson performance evaluation in this method. The development of a BARS approach is an interactive process that actively incorporates members of the sales force. Salespeople are used to identify important performance results and the critical behaviours necessary to achieve those results. The critical behaviours are assigned numbers on a rating scale for each performance result. An example of one such BARS rating scale is presented in Figure 14.1 (Cocanougher and Ivancevich 1978).

Figure 14.1 BARS Scale

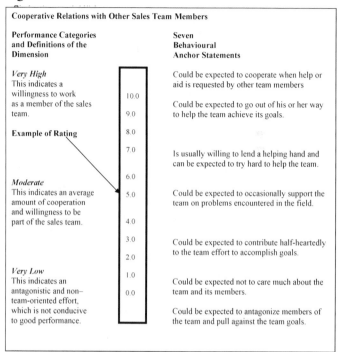

Cooperative Relations with Other Sales Team Members

Performance Categories and Definitions of the Dimension		Seven Behavioural Anchor Statements
Very High This indicates a willingness to work as a member of the sales team.	10.0 9.0	Could be expected to cooperate when help or aid is requested by other team members Could be expected to go out of his or her way to help the team achieve its goals.
Example of Rating	8.0 7.0	Is usually willing to lend a helping hand and can be expected to try hard to help the team.
Moderate This indicates an average amount of cooperation and willingness to be part of the sales team.	6.0 5.0 4.0	Could be expected to occasionally support the team on problems encountered in the field.
	3.0 2.0	Could be expected to contribute half-heartedly to the team effort to accomplish goals.
Very Low This indicates an antagonistic and non–team-oriented effort, which is not conducive to good performance.	1.0 0.0	Could be expected not to care much about the team and its members. Could be expected to antagonize members of the team and pull against the team goals.

Source: Cocanougher A. Benton and John M. Ivancevich, "BARS' Performance Rating for Sales Force Personnel." *Journal of Marketing* 42, American Marketing Association (July 1978): 91. Reprinted by permission of the American Marketing Association.

The performance result in this example is achieving cooperative relations with sales team members. Seven behaviours have been assigned numbers on a ten-point rating scale to reflect the link between engaging in the behaviour and achieving the result. This scale can then be used to evaluate individual salespeople. For instance, the example rating of 5 in the figure suggests that the salesperson occasionally supports the sales team on problems encountered in the field and thus achieves only a moderate amount of cooperation with sales team members.

Problems with Performance Evaluation Systems

Traditional performance evaluation systems usually suffer from several limitations. Some common problems with performance evaluation systems that rely on subjective rating forms, particularly those using the simple checklist type, as summarised by Johnston and Marshall (2006), include the following:

1. **the halo effect.** This occurs when sales managers tend to let one key factor influence their ratings on all other factors.

2. **the central tendency.** Some sales managers may be reluctant to take a stand, so they rate salespeople near the middle of the scale on all rating factors. Thus, little distinction is made between salespeople, and minimal information is provided for compensation or promotion decisions.

3. **a psychological resistance to negative evaluations.** A few sales managers suffer emotional distress when giving negative evaluations to salespeople, so they tend to avoid making negative evaluations.

4. **political concerns.** In order to look good themselves and prevent problems on their "watch," some sales managers will avoid giving any rating that is not acceptable to the individual salesperson.

5. **fear of reprisal.** Out of fear of reprisal for "discriminating" against employees, some sales managers are especially careful to avoid giving negative ratings to anyone who might take legal action (e.g., women, minorities, or older salespeople).

6. **varying evaluation standards.** Sales managers may have different evaluation standards. Some may have high evaluation standards and rate harshly, while others may be relatively lenient.

7. **an interpersonal bias.** The personal likes and

dislikes of the sales manager may influence his or her evaluations of salespeople. The chemistry between two people may not work, and resultant friction can lead to evaluation bias. Conversely, some salespeople can use personal influence techniques with the sales manager to bias their evaluations upward.

8. **questionable personality traits.** Although many rating forms include personality traits (such as enthusiasm, resourcefulness, or intelligence) as indicators of selling performance, there is little evidence to support this trait approach.

9. **organisation use.** Depending upon their internal purpose and use, performance ratings can be influenced. Sales managers often give higher ratings to salespeople when the evaluations are for compensation or promotion purposes, because they want to keep their people happy and see them do well in comparison to those in other organisational units. When appraisals are mainly for personal development of subordinates, however, sales managers tend to be more objective and to point out areas needing improvement.

10. **a recent performance bias.** Some sales managers are influenced too much by recent performance when evaluating individual performance; consequently, behaviour earlier in the rating period is neglected.

11. **no outcome focus.** Too many rating systems seem to have questionable validity and limited value for directing the growth and development of salespeople. They tend to rely on rating factors believed to be related to performance and fail to indicate how the salesperson might improve performance.

12. **an inadequate sampling of job activities.** Some sales managers either may not know about or may

not adequately observe all the activities in a given salesperson's assignment. Thus, the evaluation fails to include all important aspects of the job, or job tasks may be included that are not part of the current job.

Performance Evaluation Bias

From the foregoing, it should be clear that performance evaluation may be fraught with opportunities for biases and inaccuracies to creep into the process. One form of potential evaluator is the outcome bias. An outcome bias occurs when the outcome of a decision, rather than the appropriateness of the decision, influences an evaluator's ratings. This is when a sales manager allows the outcome of a decision or a series of decisions made by a salesperson to overly influence the performance ratings made by the manager. When sales managers rate the quality of a salesperson's decision, outcome information (e.g., salesperson did or did not make the sale) often influences their ratings across all criteria when the decision is perceived to have been inappropriate.

Avoiding Errors in Performance Evaluation

To guard against the distortions introduced in the performance evaluation system by problems such as those listed above, many companies provide extensive training and guidelines to sales managers on completing the forms and conducting the appraisal process. Some common instructions issued with such forms, as summarised by Johnston and Marshall (2006), include the following:

1. Read the definitions of each trait thoroughly and carefully before rating.
2. Guard against the common tendency to overrate.
3. Do not let personal likes or dislikes influence your ratings. Be as objective as possible.
4. Do not permit your evaluation of one factor to influence your evaluation of another.
5. Base your rating on the observed performance of the salesperson, not on potential abilities.

6. Never rate an employee on several instances of good or poor work, but rather on general success or failure over the whole period.

7. Have sound reasons for your ratings.

These suggestions can be helpful, particularly when the evaluator must provide the reasons for ratings. However, they do not resolve problems related to the selection of attributes for evaluation and how the resulting items are presented on the form. One approach directed at resolving this problem of traditional performance appraisal system is the BARS system, as shown in Figure 14.1. The BARS system measures key performance behaviours that the individual salesperson can control. Consideration of specific behaviours allows different sales managers to arrive at more consistent and objective evaluations, since the rating factors have similar interpretations.

Evaluating Team Performance

Sales organisations that use sales teams must also consider how to evaluate them. When designing the appraisal process for teams, sales managers must still consider the criteria on which members will be evaluated and the methods used to evaluate performance. In addition, it is important that sales managers establish a link between team performance and positive outcomes to promote individual and team efforts. The process is fostered by allowing team members to participate in developing team goals and objectives. Furthermore, members are more willing to participate when individual goals are linked to team goals. Individual and group assignments necessary for reaching goals should be prioritised to help the team better manage its time.

Ideally, the team as a whole should be evaluated, in addition to assessing individual member performance. Team performance can be measured by team members as well as by the sales manager. Figure 14.2 provides an example of a multidimensional approach team members can use to evaluate teammates' critical skills and behaviours. The measurement allows sales managers to develop a composite performance appraisal, merging each team member's viewpoint. The process helps strengthen teams, enhance morale, and contribute to a healthy working climate. In addition, the team and its members must be evaluated against predetermined performance criteria.

Steps for Measuring Team Performance

An outline of a process for measuring team performance, as summarised by Zigon (1997), is presented below.

1. Review the existing organisational measures. Make sure that the measures are known to the team and linked to the team's measures.

2. Define team measurement points. Select the best alternatives for identifying starting points for team measurement. Selecting the best alternative and using the team to identify the team's accomplishments provides the basis for all further measurement.

3. Identify individual team member accomplishments that support the team. Identify the results that each member must produce to support the team's results or work progress.

4. Weigh the accomplishments. The team should discuss and agree upon the relative importance of each accomplishment.

5. Develop team and individual performance measures. Identify the numeric and descriptive yardsticks that will be used to gauge how well results have been achieved.

6. Develop team and individual performance standards. Define how well the team and individuals have to perform to meet expectations.

7. Decide how to track performance. Identify how the team will collect the data for each performance standard and feed this data back to them.

Figure 14.2 Teamwork Effectiveness/Attitude Measurement (TEAM)

Source: T. N. Ingram, R. W. LaForge, R. A. Avilla, C. H. Schwepker, Jr., and M. R. Williams, *Sales Management: Analysis and Decision Making* (Ohio: Thomson/South-Western, 2004), 286. Reprinted by permission of Thomson/ South-Western.

Using Performance Information

It is worthy to note that using different methods to evaluate the behaviour, professional development, results, and profitability of salespeople provides extremely important performance information. According to Ingram et al. (2004), the critical sales management task is to use this information to improve the performance of individual salespeople, sales teams, and the overall operations of the sales organisation. Initially, it should be used to determine the absolute and relative performance of each salesperson. These determinations then provide the basis for reward disbursements, special recognition, promotions, and so forth.

The second major use of this performance information is to identify potential problems or areas in which salespeople need to improve for better performance in the future. If salespeople are evaluated against multiple criteria, as suggested in this chapter, useful diagnostic information will be available. The difficulty exists in isolating the specific causes of low performance areas. A framework for performing this analysis is given in Figure 14.3.

The first step in this analysis is to review the performance of each salesperson against each relevant criterion and then to summarise the results across all salespeople being supervised. The purpose of this step is to determine whether there are common areas of low performance. For example, the situation is different when most salespeople are not meeting their sales quotas than when only one or two salespeople are not meeting their sales quotas.

Figure 14.3 Framework for Using Performance Information

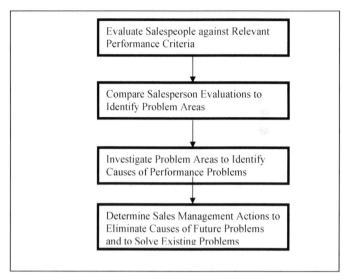

As the authors suggest, once the poor performance areas have been identified, the sales manager must work backward to try to identify the cause of the poor performance. Merely determining that most salespeople did not meet their sales quotas is not sufficient to improve future performance; the sales manager must try to uncover the reason for this poor performance. The basic approach is to try to answer the question, "What factors affect the achievement of this performance dimension?" For instance, in regard to achieving sales quotas, the key question is, "What factors determine whether salespeople achieve their sales quotas?" All the factors identified should be reviewed to isolate the cause of any poor performance. Several factors that might cause poor performance in different areas are presented in Table 14.5 (Allan 1994).

After identifying the potential causes of poor performance, the sales manager must determine the appropriate action to reduce or eliminate the cause of the problem so that performance will be improved in the future. Examples of potential management actions for specific problems are also presented in Table 14.5.

Table 14.5 Sample Problems, Causes, and Management Actions

Performance Problems	Potential Causes	Sales Management Actions
not meeting sales or other results quotas	sales or other results quotas incorrect; poor account coverage; too few sales calls	revise sales or other results quotas; revise effort allocation; redesign territories; develop motivational programmes; provide closer supervision; increase sales force size
not meeting behavioural quotas	behavioural quotas incorrect; too little effort; poor quality of effort	revise behaviour quotas; develop motivational programmes; increase sales force size, conduct training programmes; provide closer supervision
not meeting profitability quotas	profitability quotas incorrect; low gross margins; high selling expenses	revise profitability quotas; change compensation; devise incentive programmes; provide closer supervision; conduct training programmes
not meeting professional development quotas	professional development quotas incorrect; inadequate training	revise professional development quotas; conduct training programmes; provide closer supervision; develop motivational programmes; change hiring practices

Source: P. Allan, "Designing and Implementing an Effective Employee Appraisal System," *Review of Business* 16 (Winter 1994), 3-8.

Review Questions

1. Discuss who should evaluate salespeople and why.

2. What are performance criteria, and how should they be used?

3. What are the four major components of a sales plan? What component do you think would be most difficult to develop? Explain why?

4. Name the three stages in a performance evaluation monitoring system (PEMS), and describe the sales manager's role in each stage.

5. What type of performance appraisal techniques would you prefer your boss to use in evaluating you?

References

Allan, P. "Designing and Implementing an Effective Employee Appraisal System." *Review of Business* 16 (1994): 3–8.

American Marketing Association. *Marketing Definitions.* Chicago: American Marketing Association, 2008.

Anderson, R. E., J. F. Hair, Jr., and A. J. Bush. *Professional Sales Management.* New York: McGraw-Hill, 1992.

Anderson, E. and R. L. Olivier. "Perspectives on Behaviour-Based versus Outcome-Based Sales Force Control Systems." *Journal of Marketing* 51 (1987): 76–86.

Ansoff, H. I. *Corporate Strategy.* New York: McGraw-Hill, 1965.

Behling, O. and C. Scriesheim. *Organisational Behaviour: Theory, Research, and Application.* Boston: Allyn and Bacon, 1976.

Brewer, G. "Measuring Sales Effectiveness." *Sales and Marketing Management* 152, No. 10 (October 2000): 6–10.

Brown, S. P and R. A. Peterson. "The Effect of Effort on Sales Performance and Job Satisfaction." *Journal of Marketing* 58, No. 2 (April 1994): 70–80.

Burr, M. T. "Salespeople Get Caught in SEC's Governance Net." *Corporate Legal Times* 15, No. 164 (July 2005): 16–18.

Churchill, Jr., G. A., N. M. Ford, O. C. Walker, Jr., M. W. Johnston, and J. F. Tanner, Jr. *Sales Force Management, Sixth Edition.* Boston: Irwin, 2000.

Cocanougher, A. B. and J. M. Ivancevich. "BARS' Performance Rating for Sales Force Personnel." *Journal of Marketing* 42, No. 3 (July 1978): 87–95.

Collins, R. H. "JPSSM Introduces New Section." *Journal of Personal Selling & Sales Management* 14, No. 1 (May 1984): 56–57.

Cooper, R. and Kaplan, R. S. "Measure Costs Right: Make the Right Decisions." *Harvard Business Review* (September/October 1988): 96–103.

Cravens, D., T. Ingram, R. LaForge, and C. Younge. "Behaviour-Based and Outcome-Based Sales Force Control Systems." *Journal of Marketing* 57 (1993): 47–59.

Cravens, D. W. and R. W. LaForge. "Sales Force Deployment." In *Advances in Business Marketing,* edited by A. G. Woodside, 76. New York: JAI Press, 1990.

Darlrymple, D. J. and L. J. Parsons. *Marketing Management: Strategy and Cases.* New York: John Wiley & Sons Inc., 1980.

Dubinsky, A. J. and R. W. Hansen. "The Sales Force Management Audit." *California Management Review* 24, No. 2 (Winter 1981): 86–95.

Edwards, M. R., W. T. Cummings, and T. L. Schlacter. "The Paris-Peorie Solution: Innovations in Appraising Regional and International Sales Personnel." *Journal of Personal Selling & Sales Management* 4, No. 2 (November 1984): 27–38.

Etzel, M. J., B. J. Walker, and W. J. Station. *Marketing.* New York: Irwin/McGraw-Hill, 2004.

Fiedler, F. E. "The Trouble with Leadership is that It Doesn't Train Leaders." *Psychology Today* (February 1973): 23–30.

Fleishman, E. A. and J. G. Hunt (Eds). "Dimensions of Leadership Style." In *Current Developments in the Study of Leadership.* Carbondale, Illinois: Southern Illinois University Press, 1973.

Fleishman, E. A. "The Measurement of Leadership Attitudes in Industry." *Journal of Applied Psychology* (June 1953): 153–58.

Futrell, C. M. *Fundamentals of Selling: Customers for Life.* New York: Irwin/McGraw-Hill, 1999.

————. *Sales Management: Teamwork, Leadership, and Technology.* New York: The Dryden Press, 1998.

Hafer, J. C. *The Professional Selling Process.* New York: West Publishing Company, 1993.

Hauk, J. G. "Research in Personal Selling." In R. D. Still, E. W. Cundiff, and N. A. P. Govoni, *Sales Management: Decisions, Strategies and Cases, Fifth Edition*, 567–569. Englewood Cliff: Prentice-Hall International, 1988.

Ingram, T. N., R. W. LaForge, R. A. Avilla, C. H. Schwepker, Jr., and M. R. Williams. *Sales Management: Analysis and Decision Making.* Mason, Ohio: Thomsom/South-Western, 2004.

Johnson, M. W. and G. W. Marshall. *Sales Force Management, Eighth Edition.* Boston: McGraw-Hill/Irwin, 2006.

Kern, R. "IQ Tests for Salesmen Make a Comeback." *Sales and Marketing Management* (April 1988): 42–46.

Kerr, S. and J. M. Jermier. "Substitutes for Leadership: Their Meaning and Measurement." *Organisational Behaviour and Human Performance* (December 1978): 375–403.

Kotler, P. *Marketing Management: Analysis, Planning and Control.* Englewood Cliff: Prentice Hall, 1986.

Kreitner, R. and M. A. Sova. *Understanding Management: A Problem-Solving Process.* Boston: Houghton Mifflin, 1980.

Mang, C. C. and H. P. Sims, Jr. "Leading Workers to Lead Themselves: The External Leadership of Self-managing Teams." *Administrative Science Quarterly* (March 1987): 106–129.

Meade, J. "Automated Performance Appraisal for the LAN and the Net." *HR Magazine* 43 (October 1998): 42–52.

Narayanan, V. G. and B. G. Sarkar. "The Impact of Activity-Based Costing on Managerial Decisions at Instell Industries: A Field Study." *Journal of Economics & Management Strategy* 11 (2002): 257–288.

Naumann, E., S. M. Widmeier, and D. W. Jackson, Jr. "Examining the Relationship Between Work Attitude and Propensity to Leave Among Expatriate Salespeople." *Journal Personal Selling and Sales Management* 20 (2002): 227–242.

Nonis, S. A. and A. Erdem. "A Refinement of INDSALES to Measure Job Satisfaction of Sales Personnel in General Marketing Settings." *Journal of Marketing Management* 7 (1997): 34–46 .

Patty, C. R. *Managing Salespeople.* Reston: Reston Publishing Company, Inc., 1979.

Randall, E. J. and C. H. Randall. "Review of Salesperson Selection Techniques and Criteria: A Managerial Approach." *International Journal of Research in Marketing* 7 (1990): 81–95.

Perreault, W., W. French, and C. Harris, Jr. "Use of Multiple Discriminant Analysis to Improve the Salesman Selection Process." *Journal of Business* (January 1977): 208–224 .

Ruekert, R. W., A. C. Walker, and K. J. Roering. "The Organisation of Marketing Activities: A Contingency Theory of Structure and Performance." *Journal of Marketing* 49, No. 1 (Winter 1985): 13–25.

Sales and Marketing Management. "The Ten Biggest CRM Mistakes." In *Management of a Sales Force, Twelfth Edition,* edited by R. L. Spiro, G. A. Rich, and W. J. Stanton, 25–45. Boston: McGraw-Hill, 2008.

Schiff, J. S. "Evaluate the Sales Force as a Business." *Industrial Marketing Management* 12 (1983): 131–137.

Shapiro, B. P. and R. T. Moriarity. *National Account Management: Emerging Insights.* Cambridge, Massachusetts: Marketing Science Institute, 1982.

Smith, G. A, D. Ritter, and W. P. Tuggle. "Benchmarking: The Fundamental Questions." *Marketing Management* 2, No. 3 (1993): 43–48.

Solomon, P. J. "Strategic Planning for Marketers." *Business Horizons* (December 1978): 65–73.

Spiro, R. L., G. A. Rich, and W. J. Stanton. *Management of a Sales Force, Twelfth Edition.* Boston: McGraw-Hill, 2008.

Steinbrink, J. P. "Structuring the Sales Organisation." In *Sales Manager's Handbook*, edited by Britt, S. H., 90–95. Chicago: The Dartnell Corporation, 1989.

Stevensen, T., F. Barnes, and S. Stevensen. "Activity-Based Costing: An Emerging Tool for Industrial Marketing Decision Makers." *Journal of Business and Industrial Marketing* 8, No. 2 (1993): 40–52.

Still, R. D., E. W. Cundiff, and N. A. P. Govoni. *Sales Management: Decisions, Strategies and Cases, Fifth Edition.* Englewood Cliff: Prentice-Hall International, 1988.

Swift, C. O. and C. Campbell. "The Effect of Vertical Exchange Relationships on the Performance Attributions and Subsequent Actions of Sales Managers." *Journal of Personal Selling & Sales Management* 15, No. 4 (Fall 1995): 45–56.

Von Fleet, D. D. *Contemporary Management.* Boston: Houghton Mifflin Harcourt, 1991.

Weaver, R. A. "Set Goals to Tap Self-Motivation." *Business Marketing* (December 1985): 54 –66.

Weynes, P. *How to Perfect Your Selling Skills.* London: Kogan Page, 1990.

Widdap, F. R. "Why Performance Standards Don't Work." *Personnel* (March/April 1970): 15–27.

Wilson, M. T. *Managing a Sales Force, Second Edition.* Aldershot: Gower, 1983.

Wotruba, T. R. "The Transformation of Industrial Selling: Causes and Consequences." *Industrial Marketing Management* 25, No. 5 (September 1996): 327–338.

Zigon, J. "Team Performance Measurement." *Compensation and Benefits Review* 29 (1997): 38–47.